Golden Boy

Golden Boy

A BIOGRAPHY OF
WILF MANNION

Nick Varley

AURUM PRESS

First published in 1997 by Aurum Press Limited
25 Bedford Avenue, London WC1B 3AT

A catalogue record for this book is available from the British Library.

The author and publishers have made every effort to trace the owners
of copyright in material reproduced in these pages. If an application
is made in writing, we will ensure that any omissions are included
in later editions of this book.

ISBN   1 85410 524 8

1   3   5   7   9   10   8   6   4   2
1997 1999 2001 2000 1998

Printed in Great Britain
by Hartnolls Ltd, Bodmin

For Marianne

In memory of Tommy Lawton

· CONTENTS ·

· LIST OF ILLUSTRATIONS ·

The author and publishers would like to thank the following for their kind permission to reproduce the photographs in this book:

Alpha Ltd (page 2, BOTTOM); Bertie Mee (page 3, BOTTOM); Associated Press (page 4, BOTTOM); *Evening Gazette*, Teesside (page 6, TOP RIGHT); Hulton Getty (page 6, CENTRE and page 7, BOTTOM); PA News Photo Library (page 6, BOTTOM and page 7, TOP and CENTRE); Craig Easton (page 8, BOTTOM RIGHT). Other photographs: courtesy of Ken Dodds.

· FOREWORD ·

Wilf Mannion was a hero of mine.

When I was a fifteen year old, I signed schoolboy forms with Middlesbrough and, because I was an inside-forward like him, I looked up to Wilf and the other greats, like Len Shackleton. They were all my idols, and I wanted to be like them. Wilf to me was what Shearer is to the youngsters of today.

I left when I was seventeen and joined Fulham, but I'll never forget Wilf playing, even though I never played with him or even trained with him while I was at Boro.

He was one of the greatest – one of our national heroes. All the England team he played in were. What a side: Finney, Matthews and Lawton and, linking them, Wilf. He was a small man for an inside-forward, but packed with skill, very mobile getting around the park, with great ball control and a lovely first touch. He was a beautiful passer of the ball and a good header for his size. He could take the half chance and make it count, but he was also the brains of the team, the creative heart, the link between defence and attack. There was nothing he lacked. He was *the* number 10. Today I suppose you'd compare him to Beckham or Beardsley.

I was appalled at the financial – and personal – situation he was left in at the end of a glorious career. For such a great player to be left skint was a stain on the entire game. That's why, when I was England manager, I agreed to take a team up to Middlesbrough for his testimonial. I could only commit myself to one or two of those games – but Wilf's was one I wouldn't have dreamed of turning down.

Now I am absolutely delighted to welcome this biography of one of the greatest players I have ever seen. Perhaps some of the younger players and fans who have never heard of Wilf will realize from this book how brilliant he was.

It is a great pleasure and an honour to write this foreword and to be able to remember Wilf's career – and all the pleasure he gave to me and to others.

BOBBY ROBSON

· ACKNOWLEDGEMENTS ·

This book would have been impossible without the co-operation of many people, and the support of many others.

The author would like to thank Albert and Margaret Lanney for their hospitality, organisation and dedication, Ken Dodds for his enthusiasm and unrivalled collection of memorabilia, Bobby Robson, Tom Finney, Bertie Mee, Sir Walter Winterbottom, Sir Stanley Matthews, the late Tommy Lawton, the late Harold Shepherdson, Jimmy Hill, Ralph Birkett, Micky Fenton, Kenny Beagle, Dennis Docherty, Tom and Ivy Griffiths, the staff of the Green Howards Museum in Richmond, Richard Buck, George Hewling, Chris Blenkey, Stephen and Doris Chapman, Duncan Hall, Mike McCullagh, John Mapplebeck, David Barber, Sheila Murphy and Karen Ings at Aurum Press, Peter Montellier and the library staff at the *Evening Gazette*, Middlesbrough, Frank Butler, Ray Robertson, Graeme Ramsay and Carmel McCrowther, Andy Limb, Dave Allen at Middlesbrough FC, Kathryn Armstrong and Allan Boughey, Eric Paylor, Ian Cross, Pete Barron and Mike Amos of the *Northern Echo*, Sheila Middleton and finally, but absolutely vitally, Brian, Barbara and Adrian Varley.

· INTRODUCTION ·

J ust like every other England fan that morning, Kenny Beagle was sick as he laboured into work with the full implications of the Wembley night before slowly sinking in. Alf Ramsey's doomed effort to lead his team to the 1974 World Cup finals had finally died when a Polish goalkeeper, who had been labelled a clown by Brian Clough, made sure the visitors had the last laugh. Thirty-five times England tried to breach Jan Tomaszewski's goal; just once did he have to retrieve the ball from the net and even then only after the belated England equalizer, which was no consolation for a side which had to win.

With lead in his step, Kenny approached his 'office' – a Portakabin workmen's hut at one of Europe's largest chemical complexes, ICI near Middlesbrough – as choked as if he had swallowed a gulp of the noxious gases from the plant. He greeted his workmates with an appraisal of the team's shortcomings in language a good deal more colourful than the drab October day outside.

'Did you see it?' he spat out. 'What a load of absolute crap. I could have done better meself.'

The 'ayes' and 'I knows' which greeted him were joined by an elderly voice from the corner.

'I remember when I played for England at Wembley for the first time,' it offered.

Kenny looked over at the leather-faced, middle-aged teaboy, at least twenty-five years his senior, in washed-out overalls and thought to himself: 'Of course you did granddad. And I'm Charlie George.' Out loud he limited himself to muttering: 'Oh aye, that'll be right.'

As one, his workmates, colleagues only since Kenny arrived on the pipe-fitting crew a week earlier, jumped to the teaboy's defence. Not in an oh-don't-mind-him way, but in bloody hell, what-do-you-think-you're-doing horror.

1

'He did, you know,' they said. 'Don't you know who he is? He's Wilf Mannion.'

Almost a quarter of a century later, Kenny still remembers that day.

'I was staggered. Of course, once it was pointed out to me, I recognized him. And from then on I used to ask him questions about the old days all the time. Once I was asking about the quality of the pitches he played on and one of the other fellas just shouted: "Oh stop asking him daft questions, will yer? He could have played on a rice pudding." But I couldn't believe one of England's best footballers was making cups of tea in a shack. He had all those England caps and there he was making tea for me, a park player at best. It was staggering.'

Staggering perhaps, but not unique. Tommy Lawton, one of Wilf's colleagues in what some would say was the greatest-ever England forward line, was living in equally humble circumstances in Nottingham. When he suffered the shame of two court cases, one over unpaid rent of just £87, a stroll into the Trent seemed the only way out. Suicide appeared an attractive alternative to a life in which he left home every morning pretending to have a job. In reality he spent his days in the local library or wandering aimlessly around shopping arcades for hours on end. He lived the life of a hobo rather than a hero.

Both ex-England team-mates were stars in the golden era just after World War II. They earned good, but not fantastic, money and had few worries compared to those enduring hardship during rationing and rebuilding. In the long term, however, they were little better off than if they had never stepped on to a football pitch; victims whose short sporting careers prepared them for nothing more than a lifetime of subsequent disappointment. Some contemporaries – England wonder wingers Stanley Matthews and Tom Finney, for example – did not flounder; they were better prepared for life after football. Others were lucky never to have experienced such highs on the pitch that the contrast with later lows was so hard to bear.

Those post-war years saw a revolution in football and the creation of the modern game. Pre-match tactics, brought to the fore by Herbert Chapman at Huddersfield and Arsenal in the 1920s and thirties as he made the league championship his personal keepsake, became standard practice. Practice itself was subjected to a radical overhaul as managers began to change into tracksuits at training time and work with the players rather than watch them jog around the track, honing their fitness but nothing else. Pioneering ideas such as five-a-side games and blackboard-based briefings became commonplace.

Many players were staggered at being told what to do on the pitch – as if the manager knew better than them – but it was just one of the changes they would have to get used to. Foreign travel would be another, star status and ever-growing interest from the press and the nascent radio and television stations, a third. Partly because of the increased national and international coverage, players also began to realize they were worth more than the fixed wages the professional clubs – from the greatest to the smallest – paid them. Why should entertainers such as Tommy Trinder or Rex Harrison collect large pay packets when entertainers who drew even bigger crowds, but happened to be footballers, had their earnings capped by a maximum wage?

The players most affected by such considerations – those who had reached the peak of their profession and played for their countries – were witnessing developments in international football, as visits to and from overseas nations became more common. The England team was also getting its first-ever manager, Walter Winterbottom, albeit one whose professional playing career was short and undistinguished, and who, perversely, did not actually pick the team. The be-blazered FA officials and the butchers, bakers and candlestick makers who were club chairmen retained that task – as well as control over policy matters such as deciding if and when England would break the habit of a generation and compete in the World Cup.

Today all these changes, then so radical, are fading memories, unknown to a younger generation of fans who can't remember anything before Kevin Keegan's curly perm. They are being pushed even further into the background in the nineties as the game undergoes another revolution, regaining the mass popularity, and its position as the national sport, enjoyed in Wilf's heyday. Now all-seater stadiums are regularly sold out; players such as Alan Shearer and SuperRyan are supported via wall-to-wall media coverage; and the stars are paid tens of thousands of pounds a week by employers whose shares are traded in the City and whose turnovers are measured in the hundreds of millions. International footballers have the weekend off before playing for their countries and agents who ensure they won't be short of a bob or two if their post-retirement careers in the media or management don't quite come off. Forget making tea for pipe-fitters, the best players need never work again once their legs go.

Television has been both the driving force and the paymaster behind the recent transformation and trendifying of the game. The cash Sky in particular has pumped into football has led to refurbished stadia and transfer packages which attract the best players in the world. Hooliganism is practically extinct, at Premier League level at least. England has even staged the European Championship – unthinkable five years ago – and the nation was glued to the TV as Gareth Southgate's penalty miss ended the host nation's involvement in the tournament. Indeed, the quickest route to social leper status nowadays is not a pre-match ruck, but to say you don't support a team or ask, 'Gareth who?'

This TV-led rebirth is a far cry from Tom Finney's musings in his 1958 autobiography about the 'very tricky situation' of 'whether football should play ball with television'. He asked: 'Should we regard television as a monster, keeping it quite apart from football, lest it should do to the game what it has undoubtedly done to the music hall?' Perhaps Sky Variety could still be the music hall's answer.

But the fundamental concern which goes hand-in-hand with the televised revolution of football is obvious: as the game of today sweeps all before it, courtesy of rapid and rabid commercialization, that of yesteryear may be completely lost. There is a risk that the roots and history which set today's game in context may be submerged under the current surge of interest in which year zero is Italia '90, although with 1966, like some long-lost relative, allowed a place of honour. But how can any discussion of England's World Cup record skip over Brazil 1950 and the effect it had on England full-back Alf Ramsey? Or how can the rights and wrongs of the Bosman ruling be addressed without reference to earlier player-power battles such as the flight of England international Neil Franklin and others to Colombia?

That the present overshadows the past is no surprise. One big Premier League match in the late 1990s is better reported, particularly visually, than England's complete programme in the 1950 World Cup or entire seasons when Franklin was playing. The absence of TV means that stars such as Finney or Matthews are all too easily forgotten or overlooked. For no matter how much they are now praised in print, there will never be 'goals of the season' to replay, no slo-mo of the skills which captivated crowds far in excess of those that Premiership grounds of today can even hold; in short, no electronic skill spot.

In the last couple of years many of the stars of the 1940s and 1950s who feature in Wilf's story, such as Raich Carter, Franklin and Lawton, have died, their obituaries often the first time the general public have heard of them for decades. Having been failed several times over – by the rigid wage structure of the game, by the late, for them, advent of TV and the changes, financial and other, it would have brought – a glorious generation is fading away almost forgotten. Memories of the social conditions which created them, the battles they had to fight and the great games in which they played, are all slipping away too, often unremarked. All that lives on is the occasional event, such as the Matthews' Cup final or Hungary's visit to Wembley, which has taken a place in the nation's collective sporting consciousness.

Wilf Mannion's story encapsulates all of the above. Parts of it are unique – the particular trials and tribulations which punctuated his triumphs – but overall he was a typical, if extreme, example of that enslaved generation of footballers in which everyone from England skipper Billy Wright to Wigan's wing-half, whoever he may have been, was tied to a club and could not leave unless that club said so. For such enforced loyalty the rewards were the fixed wage covering all, taking no account of individual skill or the ability of certain players to raise a team, lift their colleagues' games or win trophies, never mind put an extra 10,000 paying spectators through the turnstiles.

Wilf was one of those who could attract those crowds. Born as World War I was moving to its conclusion, his career peaked immediately after World War II. That conflict took almost seven years from his career, years when he could have tripled the number of England caps he actually won from twenty-six to about seventy. Within a year of his debut, aged eighteen, for his home-town club, Middlesbrough, in 1937, England called him up as a reserve to a team which included Stanley Matthews as its right-winger. Just over a decade later the pair were members of the England team which recorded an incredible 4–0 away win over World Cup holders Italy in what was only Wilf's thirteenth England game. But two decades later, as a national debate was beginning to rage over whether Matthews, aged forty-three, should be asked to reconsider his recent international retirement in order to play in the World Cup in Sweden, Wilf was in unofficial internal exile, playing non-league football.

After the war his relationship with Boro, the club which nurtured him, had degenerated into acrimony when he requested a transfer and the directors refused, as they were within their rights to do, and ordered him to stay. In 1948 he went on a one-man strike for half the year to try to force Boro to let him go but, despite questions in Parliament and a groundswell of public sympathy, he was eventually forced to return to resume, reluctantly, his one-club career. He only played for another club when he made a comeback with Hull a few months after retiring in 1954, after 368 games and 110 goals for Boro. A single season of seeing the name Mannion on Hull's teamsheet was strange enough for fans in Teesside and beyond, but was as nothing to what followed.

In the weeks between leaving Boro and joining Hull Wilf had been busy working with a Sunday newspaper, determined to expose football's dirty linen. The stories were explosive: the £3000 'bung' offered to sign for Aston Villa while on strike, an offer five times the size of Villa's from Juventus and another from Real Madrid, an attack on the England selectors and even criticism of manager Winterbottom. At the end of the season Wilf was banned from football. It was the start of the downward slope which culminated in the job as a teaboy as well as stints in the dole office, illness and premature reports of his death.

Today in Middlesbrough, once jokingly renamed Mannionbrough in honour of its greatest-ever player, Wilf is rehabilitated. He watches games at the Riverside Stadium as fans' excitement outstrips anything known since the town's forefathers discovered ironstone in the nearby hills. The brand-new stadium has replaced the ninety-two-year-old Ayresome Park ground where the trophy cleaner could have been put on a job share with Hartlepool and Darlington and still only worked one morning a month, including travel.

Any of the handful of curious fans who turned up for Boro's first fixture 120 years ago would be open-mouthed at what they would see now. Players from the amateur side whose birth they witnessed earn small fortunes as pros; the club's home, then an out-of-use archery ground in the corner of a municipal park, is a £16 million super stadium which seats as many fans as the town of their day had residents; and football is as important to the town as the steel foundries and lifeblood heavy industry of those late nineteenth-century years.

On the pitch, the arrival of Brazilian wonder waif Juninho, one of the world's top players, weaving £4.75 million-worth of magic, confirmed English football's transformation and Boro's. He is slight but skilful, boyish but adept at making the men look like monkeys. He is almost a clone of Wilf Mannion.

In fact Nat Lofthouse, labelled the Lion of Vienna after a supreme centre-forward's display for England against Austria in 1952, once saw another Brazilian whose skills brought back memories of his former international team-mate. He told readers of the *Daily Mirror*: 'When I watched Pelé playing I thought of Wilf.' What's more, he added: 'Great though Pelé is, I am proud to think I played with as great a player – perhaps even greater.'

But where Juninho is given time to commute halfway round the world for internationals, Wilf was once stopped from playing for his country because the Boro manager refused to release him. He just had to accept it and get on with his club career. Whereas Juninho jets off to games, Wilf was once famously forced to sit on his suitcase in a third-class railway carriage on his way back from a match played in front of 134,000 people. And while Juninho was reported to earn £13,000 a week, Wilf earned less in his entire career. He was forced to get by on £8 per week, or a tenner if Boro won. In today's money that is between £290 and £350 – not nothing, but not a fortune either.

The footballing pair from oceans, and generations, apart lived within a few miles of each other, Juninho in a detached home on an exclusive out-of-town development, Wilf in a small council bungalow more modest than the homes of thousands of the generation he captivated. You cannot imagine such humble anonymity afflicting the boy from Brazil or any of his Boro colleagues, or even many of today's lower-division journeymen.

As long ago as 1956 Ian Wooldridge, the *Daily Mail*'s acclaimed sports columnist, wrote: 'I feel the full story of Wilf Mannion needs telling. And needs telling sympathetically.' It is actually more of a fable than a straightforward story. At the end of it perhaps you will never look at Gazza in his designer pink suit worth thousands of pounds, or read of any of his colleagues or successors signing contracts which pay more in a week than many people earn in a year and think, 'That's wrong.' What is wrong is that Wilf Mannion – a player whose boots Gazza is unfit to lace, according to one contemporary – and others like him never had those riches. Because television had not colonized sport, such enormous sums of money were not swilling around the game, but the huge crowds generated more than enough revenue to allow football's stars a fortune, however small. Certainly, Wilf and his contemporaries may have squandered them, but did they not at least deserve the chance to?

· ONE ·

A dazzling discovery

On a small concrete schoolyard in the heart of industrial Teesside, a flyweight footballer was showing his elders and biggers, but not betters, how to play the game. His blond hair marked him out in a scene dominated by browns and greys; his tiny frame, weaving between bodies almost twice his size, drew the eyes of those watching, and playing, all the more; but it was his skill which really made Wilf Mannion, aged seven, stand out from his fellow players, aged thirteen and fourteen, in the lunchtime kickabout.

Standing on the sidelines at St Peter's School, South Bank, and getting ever more excited, was a distinguished looking young man wearing wire-rimmed glasses. Sports master Joe McCullagh was in his element in South Bank, on the outskirts of Middlesbrough, where football was a passion more than a pastime. He was a useful full-back for one of the many small teams in the area. He also managed the school sides with devotion and determination. Now he was looking upon a player he knew could grace any XI, not just at school but at professional and international levels too: a gem.

In a carbon copy of his reaction to the discovery of other budding stars, he turned on his heels and strode inside the school building, heading for the office of headmaster Andrew Skillen. Excited even by his own standards, Mr McCullagh burst in and told of his latest find from the new intake in the first year, Standard One.

'Will you come and see?' he begged.

Mr Skillen later recalled: 'I said, "Joe, we've had this before. I haven't the time to keep coming out." He said, "The Standard Seven [final year] boys are letting him play with them!" I said, "Joe, I'm coming."' It was not a wasted journey. 'It was really marvellous to see this little boy's control over the ball.'

The two teachers were lucky enough to get the first glimpse of a talent which would take the name of the town which nurtured it around the world. But they could have discovered Wilf earlier still if they had ever had any spare time to watch the games staged in the streets and on wasteground around the school. For he lived on Napier Street, just further along the road from St Peter's, and could always be found playing out, kicking a ball, a tin or whatever came to hand, or foot.

He was one of five brothers and five sisters born – Wilf in May 1918 – in the terraced house to an Irish immigrant couple who were among the many who arrived in Teesside around the turn of the century in search of work. His father, Thomas, a County Mayo man, worked at the Bolckow Vaughan blast furnace, just one of the monolithic steel and shipyard sites which had replaced the riverside fields of only a few decades before. From a community of only twenty-five residents in 1801, Middle Borough had become, a century on, a thriving industrial town of 100,000.

In the heart of the industrial sprawl, South Bank, or Slaggy Island, was made up of row upon row of homes running from the banks of the river Tees, broken up only by corner shops and pubs. Above them all rose vessels in the shipyards and the towering metal of the steel plants; around them, the din of the manufacturing process was joined by the rumble of trains scuttling back and forth. At night the blast furnaces made the sky glow amber long before orange street lights were invented. Even in daylight the flames and white-hot sparks offered industrial illumination as they cut through the clouds of steam and smoke.

From the nearby Eston Nab you could look down to see how the Tees formed the natural backbone to the town's toil. You could also see the odd patch of open ground – the wasteground, literally, where the flotsam and jetsam of the industrial process was deposited. It was on these filthy slagheaps, outposts of the urban landscape, that the children played. Among their other games, they played football. Puddling from the steel-works, settled and solidified, could be used as a pitch, albeit a filthy one. Unlike grass, it did not waterlog, so the budding footballers could play come rain or shine.

'We played all the ruddy time – morning, noon and night,' Wilf remembers. 'You might see the police inspector coming in the distance and that might make you stop but not much else did. We'd play with anything: cans, rag balls, we'd even get a pig's bladder from the butchers and if you could control that, you were a ruddy genius. And we'd play on anything, the puddling most, though, because it was playable all year round. It was bumpy, but that didn't bother us. We even played against the black people off the boats in their bare feet.

'One favourite was goalie-goalie, you know, one-on-one. Shamrock

9

Stores off-licence, where all the beer used to come in, that would be a goal and we'd put something down for the other. I remember one Saturday I was playing with a lad, Snotty Jack we used to call him – he was always running with two candles, you know. A lad called Robert Rule, a goodie-goodie type, was walking by and he'd been running errands for his mum and had two pies on a plate to take home. I chipped the rag ball and knocked the pies clean off the plate for a bit of mischief. He was terrified of going home to his mother.'

By the time Wilf was causing mischief and so impressing Joe McCullagh, the puddling pitches' roll call of former pupils was already a who's who of talent, much of it gracing league grounds and some even international stages. Perhaps the best-known graduates were the Carr brothers, a sort of footballing version of today's acting McGann clan but rather less good-looking. Four of them had played for Middlesbrough, three in the same team at one point. A fifth brother could have joined but preferred to continue playing for South Bank, which was then a top amateur side.

Jackie Carr's skills took him furthest afield as an England international, despite being so slight that he had to have his kit taken in with safety pins. He had been rejected by Sunderland as a youth because of his size, but nonetheless he went on to play with his brothers Harry and Willie in the South Bank side which lost in the final of the FA Amateur Cup in 1910. Later that year he signed as a professional with Middlesbrough FC, football offering him an escape from a life of slaving in heavy industry, as it had scores of others on Teesside and in other industrial heartlands.

Locally there was no shortage of outlets for the talented to showcase their skills. In South Bank, five top-level amateur clubs, with grounds situated within a few hundred yards of one another, drew players from a population of just 30,000. South Bank, of the Teesside League, were the best with St Peter's, East End, St Mary's and Princess Street vying for supremacy below them. Then there was South Bank Rovers, the Corinthians and Millbank Street Celtic and dozens of smaller works teams and other ad hoc sides.

In contrast, by the time Jackie Carr's nineteen-year, one-club career was coming to an end and Wilf, the heir apparent who lived a street away from the Carr family home, was emerging, jobs were becoming, for the first time, harder to find. The traditional employers were struggling; steelworks were closing; even Bolckow Vaughan, the firm which built the first furnace in town, was shutting plants.

When there had been work it had been back-breaking, manual tasks repeated over and over again during shifts which regularly lasted from 6 a.m. to 10 p.m. Thomas Mannion did the 'long turn' shift every three weeks. Wilf used to trek down the Black Path to deliver his father's dinner, carried in a pudding basin. But demanding work was better than the alternative: no work and men left loitering on the streets with nothing to do but discuss their prospects for an odd shift and sign on. Teesside still made two million tons of steel each year, a third of national output, but it was not nearly enough to provide jobs for everybody. One in three were soon out of work.

Mr McCullagh's eye for talent was true. Winky, as Wilf was nick-named because of his acute shyness, was a fantastic prospect. On the puddling and streets he continued to play football and other games which gave him agility and an elastic body-swerve – leavo (a type of British Bulldog), kicky-tin and the one-touch football of tip-tap – with his playmates unable to get any closer to catching him than many a defender would, even at the very highest level, in years to come. He was also being built up. Mr McCullagh knew his charge was in danger of being too small to realize his full potential, and set about improving his fitness with long walks up and down the Nab and in the nearby countryside.

Despite the age, and size, gap between first and final year pupils, Wilf's school debut came almost immediately and he stood out – not initially for eclipsing any other player but because he looked like a cross between the Milky Bar Kid and an extra from Oliver Twist. His blond mop topped off a tiny frame less than four feet tall and barely troubling the scales beyond six stone. His kit hung off him and when his shirt came out of his shorts, it looked like a mini-dress. A less likely looking matchwinner could not be imagined. One rival school's coach even said to Mr McCullagh: 'What have you brought that bugger along for?' He soon found out.

From inside-forward, a position now consigned to coaching's history but essentially a role equivalent to the one Peter Beardsley has played with such success for Newcastle in recent seasons, Wilf inspired St Peter's. Prompting attacks by feeding his fellow forwards – two wingers, another inside-forward and the centre-forward – or by driving on himself, he created or scored the goals which meant success and silverware arriving at the school. In 1930, the end-of-season photograph featured three trophies with the catalyst for their arrival sitting among them, an angel-faced Wilf, on the floor at the feet of the parish priest, Canon McMullan, looking barely capable of holding the large shield next to him.

Some of the local senior teams heard of the boy wonder and got in touch. The senior St Peter's side even gave him the honour of being the mascot before a Cup final. Just before his tenth birthday he led the team's players out at Ayresome Park as they prepared to play the Boro reserves in the final of the Shipowner's Cup. He was so small he had to have a shirt specially made for him and, although he had no say in the destination of the Cup, he got experience of big match atmosphere.

Of course, Wilf was not the only promising player at school. Alongside him in the school team was defender Dave 'Mick' Murphy. The pair shared both an academic and a footballing education; topics covered in the latter included some of the darker aspects of the game. One lesson came one Saturday when they both travelled with the school team to Lingdale in rural Cleveland to play in the final of the regional Cup sponsored and named after Lord Starmer. The opponents were another South Bank side, Princess Street, and hundreds from the community made the short trip to watch the game. With many local fans also turning out, the attendance was over a thousand, and this for a game involving schoolboys.

All was well except that the guest referee was Jackie Carr, an ex-Princess Street pupil. When Titchy Cooper, one of the Princess forwards, pushed forward, Murphy was too quick for him and stole the ball away.

'He took it off him quite easy,' Wilf says, 'and made a fool of him. But from out of the blue Jackie Carr gives them a penalty. We all said, "What for?" but it was no use. They scored and we got beat 1–0. You should have heard the language our fans were calling him.'

Wilf trudged off – only to get lesson number two of the day. Lord Starmer himself greeted him, congratulated him on his performance and handed over ten bob with the words, 'Well done.' It was a scene repeated later in his schoolboy career when Danny Welsh, a JP who, in the habit of the great and the good of the day, sponsored another Cup, gave him ten bob after another final. And after yet another big game, one of the councillors in South Bank gave the dynamic youngster a pair of boots, his first-ever new pair.

His success for his school led to honours at district and county level. But the biggest game in his schoolboy career came in his final year at St Peter's and was his biggest disappointment. Aged thirteen, but only 4ft 2in tall, he travelled to Durham for a North versus the Midlands trial for England boys – a game in which his chances of making it as a pro would become clear. There were selectors watching and he was playing against the best the country's scouts could offer. On Wilf's side was Johnny Spuhler, later to be a Boro team-mate, while Jimmy Hagan, subsequently an inside-forward at Sheffield United and an England rival, captained the side.

Even in this esteemed company, Wilf shone. Mr McCullagh, who had taken his protégé to the game, watched happily from the sidelines. Yet he still had to break bad news at the final whistle.

'You were marvellous, but I'm sorry to say that they won't pick you because you're too small and they're afraid you might get hurt.'

And that appeared to be that.

It was not an unusual story, then or now: a promising lad fails to make the grade because he is too small. Others were lost perhaps because they had the wrong attitude or not enough skill. Part of the reason was simple.

'There was that much talent about it was unbelievable,' as Wilf himself says, 'and it was hard to pick the right people. There was some who never made it to the top who were fantastic players but they never got picked.'

He left school at fourteen and began the sort of jobs he expected to fill for life, or at least until unemployment or illness took over. First he was an apprentice welder at Smith's Dock, but not for long.

'I only worked there for a short period and left not long after I got my first pay of six bob and four pence. I thought I'm not having that, and played up to me mum, complaining the atmosphere was playing hell with my eyes. It was a lie, but it got me out.'

A job in the rolling mill, handling red-hot steel as it passed through the production process, proved more enjoyable though equally demanding. Wilf, crucially, had kept one important link with the docks: playing for the works football team. From Monday to Friday he grafted, but on Saturday he still had his football.

This was no ordinary works side. For a start Wilf's wingman on his preferred left flank was Bobby Turnbull, another South Bank lad and former Boro, Leeds and Bradford winger who had played with Jackie Carr for England, but who was on his way back down through the league structure to a job in the docks. Other team-mates included some of the brighter young prospects from the puddling pitches and elsewhere on Teesside. Many of them had a point to prove; and all of them, having tasted the toil of shipyard shifts, knew football could offer a better future.

Wilf's second chance to escape came early in his first season with the dockers. It was their toughest match to date as they faced the league leaders, St Peter's. At the centre of its defence was Micky Ruddy, a member of another Teesside football family. One of his brothers, Paddy, was a professional at Derby, while another, Martin, was a leading non-league player. Martin preferred it that way as he made more money as an amateur, with a job provided by his club, than if he went professional. So when a fourteen-going-on-twelve-year-old danced past Micky after selling him an outrageous dummy, his pride was dented; and if there is one thing a veteran defender hates, it is being shown up by an opponent who doesn't even look like he has the strength to blow the ball up.

Wilf remembers: 'I went up to him the first time, sold him a dummy and he almost ended up running down the Normanby Road. He came after me and said, "You do that again and I'll break both your legs." I just smiled and said, "You can almost hear the rhinos coming, Micky." Then Bobby Turnbull ran up to him and said, "You should be bloody ashamed of yerself – he's only a boy and the way you're talking to him." And Micky said to him, "If you don't keep out of it, I'll do you too." But, of course, Micky didn't get near me for the rest of the afternoon.'

It was still not enough for the dockers, who were crushed 5–0. But there was one winner on their side. Wilf signed for the victors in a move which, although he could not know it at the time, would seal the shape of the rest of his life. For the depression which was ripping through Middlesbrough's industry was also affecting the football club. Limited resources meant record-breaking transfers which Boro had been able to afford before – they were the first club to break the £1000 barrier for a player – were as impossible as paid study leave at the iron mills. So the Boro board took the far-sighted decision to find their own talent from the boys who played on the puddling and other local pitches. As part of what would now be called a youth policy, two local amateur sides were 'sponsored', for £50 and £15 respectively, by Boro. One of them was Wilf's new club.

Although innovative, the potential of the idea was already clear from the case of Stockton-born striker Micky Fenton. A couple of years earlier, Fenton had been signed from East End and he had already made a scoring debut in the Boro first team. Equally significantly, he highlighted exactly why it was so important to develop links with young local players. Wolves, among a pack of other clubs, had heard of abundant talent gracing the South Bank sides and swept in to offer Fenton a trial. Fortunately for Boro, the bustling young prospect lasted a day of his four-week stay (because he did not meet the physical specifications demanded by the Midlands club) and headed back to Teesside to sign for his local side, Boro, whose success was in marked contrast to that at Molineux.

As a club, Boro had hardly enjoyed the most auspicious of starts. On a February afternoon in 1877, thirteen curious souls had braved a winter's day to watch the first game. Ninety minutes later and the support was already dwindling after one spectator died. Generations of Boro fans might ask if the death was an omen for an undistinguished future. Another of the early spectators was so unimpressed by the first-game fare that, feeling the cold, he started up a baked potato stall to keep warm. One contemporary commentator reported the fans' reaction: 'They shook their heads and thought it poor goods compared to rugby.'

The youth policy held out the possibility of finally making a long overdue difference to all that. So it was that a director, Bob Rand, was sent on a scouting mission in March 1936 to watch a young lad who was getting a game in St Peter's senior side. Other league clubs were known to be interested in Wilf, but Boro's links with St Peter's gave them an advantage. Rand, however, was not overly impressed. He reported back: 'Mannion (seventeen and a half, 5ft 4in, 9st 11lb) is a clever little player, but very small.' He recorded the fact that Wolves were also thinking of offering Wilf terms. But time was on the Boro board's side. They had a couple of months to consider their next move because the player was refusing to sign for anybody until after another milestone in his fledgling career.

The North Riding Junior Cup final brought Wilf face-to-face with a future England great, Harold 'Shep' Shepherdson, who thirty years later would be Alf Ramsey's right-hand man as England won the World Cup. A big defender with opponents East End, his job in the final was to nullify the threat posed by Wilf, and at the final whistle he was pleased with himself as the scoreline read: East End 5, St Peter's 1. Shep was looking forward to getting his hard-won winners' medal; what he also received was his come-uppance. He may have got the better of his man – or, more correctly, boy – but he had not counted on his vanquished opponent's auntie. His ecstasy was interrupted by the sort of whooshing noise most frequently heard as golfers send a club slicing through the air on its way to smacking a ball 300 yards. Then came contact. Katie Duffy put as much into her attack as Shep had into his first tackle on her strip of a nephew, Wilf.

Just weeks before his death in 1995, at the age of seventy-six, Shep's face lit up as he recalled events nearly six decades before.

'First time there was a challenge I whacked him, accidentally on purpose if you know what I mean. We knew full well that the only player we had to stop was Wilf. After that my team went on to win and Wilf was very quiet. I was pleased my team won but as I went up to get my medal I got hit on the back of my head by this big umbrella and the woman with it was calling me an animal. It certainly took the sheen off the day.'

Wilf still winces at the memory of the match.

'It was all over in the first few minutes. Shep finished me. It was clean but yet it was dirty, if you know what I mean. They kicked off and the ball come to Shep just on the halfway line and just right for him to clip it, you know, and I couldn't get out the way. I was about two yards away and he thumped this ball and it hit me in the privates. Good gosh, I didn't know what day it was. That was me, I was finished.'

But his professional career was only just about to start.

Ask Wilf how great a player he was and you will get a simple but surprising answer: 'I had a brother who was brilliant – far better than I was.' Far from basking in glory, he refuses to claim he was even the best player in his family, let alone Middlesbrough or, at his best, England.

Tommy Mannion, a docker, was also shy and lazy, however.

'He didn't really want to know,' Wilf says. 'He played for the South Bank teams but he was never really bothered about turning pro or anything. He could have beaten the legs off me but he couldn't be bothered to change for a game. He always demanded to play with his long trousers tucked into his socks.'

Furthermore, Tommy was deeply suspicious of professional football in general and Middlesbrough in particular. By the time Boro came knocking, despite the result of that Cup final, at the door in Napier Street to sign his brother, twelve years his junior, he had already seen the club in action off the pitch. He was a regular at a pub where the landlord was one George Carr, ex-Boro centre-half and brother of Jackie. There he had heard how Jackie, then Boro's greatest ever servant, was treated after nearly two decades of giving his all for the club.

Wilf tells the story:

'He was a brilliant inside guy, Jackie Carr, and he'd given Middlesbrough nineteen years. But they were playing away once and it was first time he'd met the new manager, Peter McWilliam. He was one of Jackie's friends from playing together years before. When he met him on the rail station he wished him the best of luck. "Peter, I hope everything goes great for yer." McWilliam said, "Not so much of the Peter from now on. You address me as Mr McWilliam.'" Carr bristled at the order.

Hauled before the directors, he was ordered to apologise for the scene. It was supposed to teach him, and other players, a lesson; instead it taught Tommy Mannion one. No matter how loyal a player had been, he was treated little better than a slave. In return for a life away from industrial toil he had to accept conditions of employment as bad as the most menial worker. He signed his life away and accepted his place at the very bottom of the club for as long as he was needed and no longer. And any player, no matter how big a star he was, who thought differently was either foolish, or looking for trouble, or both.

So when three directors from Boro came knocking at the Mannion family home they were met with a frosty reception from Tommy. With Wilf three years below voting age – in those days, twenty-one – and so having no say in his future, Tommy tried to warn his parents away from Boro. He pointed out that Spurs, who wanted to send their son to a farm to fatten him up, and the mighty Arsenal were both after him. Celtic, via St Peter's church priest Canon McMullan, providing a useful pastoral function for the Glasgow club, were keen too.

The Boro directors had an answer: 'Would you really want wee Wilf going away? If he signs with us, we'll look after him and he'll be near you.'

'Tommy didn't want anything to do with them,' Wilf says, 'but my mother and father knew no better. The directors put the fear of God into them. They said, "If he's away, you've got no control over him and he'll be staying with landladies. You don't know how he'll be looked after or what he'll get up to." Tommy was saying, "Take no notice," but my parents took no notice of him. I don't blame them – they didn't know any better, they had no education or anything. And there was the £10 signing-on fee. That was a fortune for them. Tommy said to me afterwards, "You've signed your own death warrant." He wanted me to go south but my old man and my mother just said no.'

And so, eventually, the decision was made. On the surface it was a clear one. Wilf, after his parents signed a contract for him, swapped life in the steel mills for the less exerting career of a footballer and exchanged 18 bob for £3 10s a week, with a £2 bonus for playing in a first-team win. But he remained a chattel. Only his owners and market value had changed. Not that Wilf minded; he was away from the mills.

'It was a good way out. If you didn't make it you'd be in the docks or

17

the steelworks for your life. That's where I would have gone if I hadn't made it. Just like Tommy and me old man.'

The *North-East Press* carried a brief piece on 18 September 1936:

> Middlesbrough last night brought their list of professionals to thirty-one by signing Wilfred Mannion, the young inside-right, of South Bank St Peter's. Mannion, who belongs to a well-known South Bank family, is on the stocky side [sic] and is already well-known for his ball control. Other clubs were much interested in the lad.

Sadly, one man was not around to witness the signing or advise on it. Joe McCullagh had contracted pneumonia and died before the talent he had spotted graced the wider public stage. His influence was to be missed. No one could begin to imagine how much.

· TWO ·

'Where on earth did you dig this little chap up?'

Like many young professionals, some of the new players shared a ride to the ground. Wilf, Paddy Nash and Mick Murphy, as well as others of the South Bank contingent, would meet in the morning ready for a day's work, though carrying no outward sign of what that work was. Their kit was kept at Ayresome Park, their boots and training pumps likewise, and they travelled in smart new suits. That was just as well as the South Bank to Middlesbrough bus was crowded enough without a bunch of foot-ballers lumping big bags of belongings with them.

'We used to get the United bus every day – sixpence I think the fare was,' Wilf says. 'There'd be Mick and Paddy and others too. Hughie Turner was one. But no one would ever bother us, even after we were playing in the first team. No one asked for your autograph or anything – they just let you alone. You were just going to work and doing a job, like them.'

There were plenty of familiar faces at work. Shep, who had joined Boro as an amateur two years earlier and had now signed as a pro-fessional, for one. Two others from East End included one George Hardwick. He was another whose talent had led him to play with older boys when he was a junior pupil at his school. The difference was that he was an assured defender and from a remote mining community out on the Cleveland coast. For his away fixtures for his village team, Hardwick had his own personal driver – an older team-mate who perched him on the crossbar of his bike and cycled to the games. At one of them, a small, rotund and elegantly dressed gentleman watched from the sidelines. At full-time, George Allison, Herbert Chapman's predecessor at Arsenal and a native of Cleveland who was home for a weekend, was introduced to Hardwick, a future England captain, only to say: 'Little lad, you have a lot of skill and tremendous strength but I think you are too big in the backside ever to make the grade as a footballer.'

The boyish features of the likes of Hardwick, just sixteen and still on amateur forms, and Wilf stood out at Ayresome among such seasoned professionals as club captain and centre-half Bob Baxter. Keystone of the defence, he set the tone for the side. A sunken-eyed former miner, his black, parted and slicked-down hair and square jaw made him look like he would be more at home with Al Capone's 1930s Mob than Ayresome's equivalent. Discovered on a Scottish scouting mission by manager Peter McWilliam, he had given up a life in the pits – and supplementing his income by running dance bands – to move to Ayresome. Four years on from his debut, he was one of the longest-serving players and one so adaptable that he played in nine different outfield positions for the first team. The only criticism ever levelled at him, and then only by the bravest of colleagues, was over his alarming tendency to try to dribble past forwards in his own box.

One man who could often be heard screaming at his skipper's antics was goalkeeper Dave Cumming, the most expensive goalkeeper ever to have been transferred from Scotland to England. Generally he wore a wide grin – Baxter's penalty-area efforts were one of the few things which wiped it off – but once provoked it was best to stand back. In one game, Arsenal's Les Compton delivered a sly kick in the middle of a goalmouth mêlée following a corner. Cumming brushed himself down and strode towards the 6ft 4in centre-half, let fly with a haymaking right-hander and savoured his revenge as Compton toppled over. Then he calmly stripped off his roll-necked jersey, handed it to a colleague and walked off the pitch without giving the referee the pleasure of sending him off.

Among the other regulars was left-back Bobby Stuart, whose most eccentric moment more than matched Cumming. He refused to captain the reserve team in one game and then lay down near a goal after the team ran out. Unsurprisingly, he was transfer listed. On the pitch he linked on the left flank with another Scot, Billy Forrest, who was such firm friends with Baxter that they courted and married sisters. Another chum, and a regular visitor to Teesside, was another Scottish exile who had played for Manchester City but who had recently been transferred to Liverpool – Matt Busby. Forrest would have struggled to make it as a footballer in later years, particularly alongside some of those Busby oversaw as Manchester United manager, for he appeared to have a pathological inability to look straight at the camera for team or other photos.

Such pictorial correctness did not appear to bother the centre- and inside-forwards. Legendary number nine George Camsell, generally sporting a threatening, tight-lipped frown which hinted at his uncompromising approach, led the line. Two-footed, skilful and a serial scorer, he was as hard as the next man. When the next man was Benny Yorston, that meant granite-like. A Scottish international inside-right, he was just 5ft 5in tall and bald as a coot, but what he lacked in hair he made up for in hair-raising tackles. He was renowned for enjoying a good Friday night out before running off any ill effects on Saturdays. Then at inside-left there was Fenton, who boasted a blistering turn of speed and Hotshot Hamish shot. Other skills, like the pursed-lipped scowl, he did not have to learn from Camsell, merely to perfect. Neil Ruddock would not have flattened the upturned white collars on any of these red shirts.

In contrast, outside them was flame-haired winger Ralph Birkett, one of two recent purchases patrolling the touchlines. The other, Tom Cochrane, was fresh in from Leeds, but Birkett had an even more impressive soccer CV – he had come from Arsenal, where he had helped secure Chapman's final league championship. His path to Highbury, via non-league Dartmouth United and Torquay United, had culminated in Chapman himself appearing at his father's pub to sign the twenty-one-year-old for £2000. But just days into 1934 Chapman died after contracting a cold while watching a game, leaving a legacy only rivalled by George Graham's recent reign. The difference? Months before he died, Chapman put a defender on the transfer list for conceding a penalty – a deed considered so alien to the club's tradition that the culprit's departure was deemed the only option.

The death of the man who signed him hastened Birkett's departure from Arsenal after just nineteen appearances. He left behind Highbury's famous marble floors and imposing architecture – a stadium fit to host the best team in the land. It even boasted floodlights, an idea Chapman had imported from the Continent, but which the FA would not allow to be used in competitive matches in case other clubs might also want the new-fangled lighting contraptions and have overstretched themselves financially to buy them. That was an unlikely scenario at Ayresome, Birkett's new footballing home.

As he surveyed the ground, which could generously be described as homely, he wondered what he had let himself in for. True, there was a grand main stand which ran the length of the pitch and which contained the players' dressing-rooms. The playing surface was good too, but one of the two ends was little more than a mound of earth and punctuated with as many sleepers as a railway station. Opposite the teams as they ran on to the pitch was a fifty-foot stand which had been rebuilt, plank and nail, after being dismantled and transported from the previous ground. A decaying relic of the club's Victorian foundation, it was still the best they could afford at their new home. Ralph, now eighty-five, remembers his first sight of his new club well.

'After I arrived I thought, "What have you done?" Arsenal were the top team then and Middlesbrough were among the bottom, if not the bottom. At Arsenal the crowds were 30,000; at Middlesbrough they were half that. But the kind of football the team had been playing hardly gave the spectators a lot to get excited about.'

Indeed the sum total of Boro's glory stretched to twice winning the Amateur Cup in the 1890s. Most of the headlines the club made came from off-the-pitch activities generally as praiseworthy as those at Graham's Arsenal.

First there was the outcry which greeted the signing of Alf Common in 1905, not because of his Freddie Mercury moustache, but because the record fee broke the £1000 barrier. In those days buying your way out of trouble was just not the done thing and relegation-threatened Boro, second from bottom and two years without an away win, as well as sellers Sunderland, were pilloried. Even Boro fans seemed to disapprove, with attendances as much as halving to 6000 in the home games after his arrival. Soon after a national fee limit was set. One paper was moved to comment:

> As a matter of commerce, ten young recruits at £100 apiece might have paid better and as a matter of sport the Second Division would be more honourable than retention of place by purchase.

Then there was the sterling example set by chairman Lieutenant-Colonel Gibson Poole, the man who bought Common. After another transfer swoop the following season, for the acclaimed England international Steve Bloomer, rumours began to circulate that a number of other clubs had helped Boro, struggling again, with their purchases because they all wanted to see Bury go down. Both league and FA inquiries uncovered book-keeping irregularities including the chairman keeping gate receipts and owing the club money. In the manner of these things down the ages, it was settled quietly and all but forgotten until four years later when allegations were made that Boro and Newcastle fixed a match to give the Geordies, preparing for a Cup final, an easy ride. The allegations were not proved, but hardly helped Boro's tarnished image.

The goals-for-votes scandal cemented Boro's reputation for rogue finances. By 1910, the Lieutenant-Colonel was trying to move from football into politics by standing as a Conservative in the General Election. With the Liberals favourites to win, he needed all the help he could get – for example, his team beating Sunderland two days before polling. Some of the Boro players had spoken during the campaign on behalf of their chairman, while the Liberals were forecasting, rather disloyally, a Wearside win.

On matchday, manager Andy Walker decided to do his bit and approached the Sunderland captain with an offer of £10 for him plus £2 for each of his players as long as there was a home victory. The skipper told his trainer, who told the Sunderland chairman, who told the FA and, although Boro won the game 1–0 through entirely fair means, the club was in dire trouble. Weeks earlier it had been fined £100 and Walker banned for a month after he made an illegal approach to a Scottish player. It had been their final chance and the new offence meant Poole, who lost the election, and Walker were banned for life. The remaining directors were warned that if there was any more rule-breaking Boro would be banned from the Football League.

What playing successes there were tended to be individual ones. Goalkeeper Reginald Garnet Williamson, mysteriously better known to everyone as Tim, became an England international despite the poor name of the club. But he then proceeded to drop the ball in his own net on his debut – at Ayresome, in the days before fans in the north had to trek to London to watch the national side. Jackie Carr and others wore the England jersey too, while Camsell made a short-lived, record-breaking name for himself by hammering in fifty-nine goals, including nine hat-tricks, in thirty-seven games in the 1926–27 season. Everton's Dixie Dean broke this new league scoring record by one the following season. The record would still be Camsell's but for a missed penalty: the ribbing he received for the blunder meant he refused to take any more spot kicks that season, and there were at least four. The burly centre-forward also played for England, scoring a staggering eighteen goals in nine games before being dropped.

Even Boro's most famous match at that point, against Oldham, was noteworthy for what? A pulsating game? Memorable goals? No, a Keanesque episode of tempers, tantrums and lonely walks to the dressing-room. The difference on this occasion was that it was the referee who trooped off in a huff. The trouble began when Oldham went 1–0 down and refused to restart the game properly. Three times they just kicked the ball off the centre spot; three times the referee ordered them to start again. Later a relentless torrent of verbal abuse from Jackie Carr provoked an Oldham player into kicking him. The Latic offender was sent off but wouldn't go; his team-mates failed to convince him, so the referee went instead and the game was abandoned.

Throughout these episodes of high drama and low farce, Boro's league form had more ups and downs than a lift: relegated from the first division in 1924; promoted in 1927; relegated again in 1928; and promoted again in 1929.

Birkett was bought in spring 1935, for almost three times as much as Arsenal paid for him, to try to save Boro's division one status again. He scored twice on his home debut in a 3–1 win against Spurs. Then he got on the scoresheet on two of the other five occasions Boro netted in the remainder of the season. Unfortunately, a return visit to Highbury was not among them. Boro were stuffed 8–0 in front of 45,000.

'It was looking very dicey,' he says. 'But we avoided the drop.' Just. Come the last day of the season, the club preserved its top-flight status by one point from a home draw against Chelsea. It seemed unlikely that a golden era was about to begin.

Deep in the bowels of Ayresome Park was the engine room of the club. Below the seats where the directors and other better-off fans sat in the grand North Stand were the rather less sumptuous surroundings of the players' dressing-rooms. In one corner of the home dressing-room was an anonymous noticeboard the like of which could be seen in any sports or social club. This particular one, however, had just given Wilf the biggest thrill of his life.

Beneath the well-known names of Camsell and Birkett was a new one – Mannion. Just three months into his professional career, Wilf saw his name next to some of the best players of the day. He was only selected as reserve for the match at Bolton and, barring injuries before the game, he was unlikely to play. But it was a start, and a winning one. Boro won 3–1 to record their biggest away win – albeit only their second – of the season thanks to a Camsell hat-trick.

Wilf didn't play but nevertheless made his debut in the national press. *The Littlewoods Sports Log*, a guide which accompanied the pools, reported Boro's joy at finding a new lucky charm.

He is a young lad named Mannion – a promising inside-forward they picked up from a local team. Mannion has never played for the first team, but he was thrilled to the extreme the other week when he glanced at the teamsheet and read 'Reserve: Mannion'. It was the first time the honour had fallen on him. It was an away match, too, and Mannion, both on the train and in the hotel, was rather nervous and shy. The other players –

they all knew the ropes – were ready to cheer him up and set the lad at ease, and he soon settled down to what to him were strange surroundings. And that day the Borough scored their finest away win of the season. It broke the cherished home record of a famous club. Mannion was rewarded not only with a £2 bonus to supplement his small wage, but on the way back to the north east he was labelled as the Borough mascot. And you can take it that if ever Middlesbrough players are asked who they would like to travel as reserve they will answer in unison 'Mannion.' For all we know the lad may shortly be playing in the Borough side. A boy must be good to be chosen as a reserve for a first division side.

Preparation for that debut moved ahead apace. Trainer Charlie Cole had delegated Billy Forrest to act as Wilf's personal fitness instructor, a job that basically involved taking his charge for long walks.

'We used to do quite a few miles, around town and into the countryside,' Wilf says. 'Then we'd get back and start on the running. Honest, by the end you could hardly walk.'

The running included shuttle sprints and laps of the track around Ayresome – and lots of both. Cole, a carpenter by trade, had been a top local athletics coach and he valued fitness above all else. The result was that the only real question players faced in training was would it be ten, twenty or thirty times around the cinder track. One player, recently transferred to Teesside, once even shouted out to the unyielding trainer: 'What are we training for Charlie, the ruddy Grand National?'

The players saw little more of a ball than Red Rum's predecessors. Cole, a club stalwart who joined in 1912 and stayed for more than thirty-five years, subscribed to the popular school of thought that said if the players were kept away from the ball in training, they would be hungry for it come matchday. The alternative analogy – that their ball skills would die of malnutrition – was not countenanced. What ball-work there was tended to be games of head tennis played on the concrete yard backing on to one of the stands, or five-a-sides. There was no set-piece practice or discussions on formation or tactics.

'When we got on the park, that's when we decided how to play,' says Wilf. 'You didn't have systems – everyone could play and just wanted to. Baxter would be dribbling the ball around in his own box, with Cumming calling him all the names under the sun, and that's how the game was played.'

Wilf's first taste of it at a professional level was in the reserves, the 'stiffs', who played at home on Saturdays when the first team were away and went travelling when Ayresome was hosting a first-division game.

25

One Saturday Carlisle were the opponents, away, and Wilf was in the team. The Cumbrian programme editor made a mistake – listing the teenaged inside-forward as 'W. Mamiam' – which would not be repeated as his fame spread. For it was clear to reserve-team watchers that Mamiam was passing through, even though there was fierce competition for first-team places in a squad which had every position covered three or four times. Such was the strength in depth that Boro sold four second- and third-choice players to Brentford between 1932 and 1934 and they helped the side to win successive promotions from division three and two. Two of the quartet even played for England.

Ken Dodds, then a fourteen year old starting off in the world of work, was one of the fans who followed the reserves. Boro-mad and none the worse for it, he was often to be found outside Ayresome's main entrance asking players for their autographs. On matchdays his targets would be visitors such as Stoke's Stanley Matthews and Sunderland's Raich Carter and during the close-season he would target cricketers instead. But it was the Boro players who were his first love to the extent that he travelled to Carlisle to see the reserves, and realized there would not be too many opportunities to see the emerging star playing for them.

'I'd seen Wilf play for St Peter's,' Ken, now seventy-five, recalls, 'so I knew he was a good player. For a small man he was packed with skill and even then, when he was playing for the reserves, I knew you didn't want to miss a game he played in. It was only a matter of time before he moved up. I remember saying to my mate, "I think this chap's going to play a bit of football." It was obvious how good he was.'

His playing style was becoming well known, dispelling any worries about his size as he danced through defences, arms outstretched and palms facing the floor, all for balance. With his tongue sticking out through pursed lips and a smile never too far from his face, he seemed like a boy trying hard in a man's world. But his appearance disguised a football mind way beyond his years. His passing was impeccable whether over five yards or fifty; his running was as educated as any of the greats; and his shooting was lethal from close range or the edge of the area.

When the inevitable call-up came, the news spread courtesy of a tobacconists opposite Ayresome. The shop, next door to an ice-cream parlour and café called Rea's – run by the family of present-day rock star Chris – where the players could often be spotted after training, offered a unique take on the teamsheet pinned in the dressing-room. In its window a display football pitch was decorated with figures of the players selected for Boro's forthcoming fixture, so the public could get an early taste of the team news. In January 1937 there was a new blond-haired figure on the 'park'.

Many of the regulars, the backbone of the team, were in place for the match against Portsmouth on 2 January, but several were missing as the club suffered a heavy injury list. Camsell and Yorston were out, as were cheery-faced right half-back Billy Brown and his defensive partner Jack Martin. Instead there were some unfamiliar names: Higham at inside-left for only his sixteenth game, Ross at right-back for his twelfth and Parkin at right-half for his fourth. The total novice at inside-right was Wilf Mannion, eighteen, earning a debut just two months after his call-up as a reserve and five months into his professional career. He had shown in the reserve team that he had deadly feet and a quick footballing brain, but he also seemed to have an even temperament. He was not going to be phased by playing against one of the better sides in the first division, in front of 25,000 people, even if it was for his home-town team, with people he knew watching.

'To be honest, I can't really remember it now,' Wilf says. 'But then I was never one to get nervous or to worry about a game, however big. It was just a game of football and I'd been playing them for long enough. I always took games in my stride like that – even at Wembley and abroad. Some players you couldn't talk to before a game but I was never like that. I was asleep. I only woke up on the pitch. Once I walked on there, it was easy.'

He was asked to partner Birkett on the right wing. Most of the side had played against Leeds at Elland Road the day before, New Year's Day – playing on consecutive days was not unusual then – in a lacklustre display which also no doubt hastened Wilf's call-up. Pompey, on the other hand, had rested. So in the circumstances a 2–2 draw was not a bad result for Boro. It was a point dropped at home, perhaps, but more realistically a point gained in the midst of an injury crisis. The youngsters came through well enough.

'Wilf played well, not outstandingly, but well,' Ralph Birkett recalls. 'And you could see he had it all: control, skill, ability – and temperament. Off the pitch he was such a nice little lad too. He was so shy, but he had the most infectious laugh I've ever heard.'

The following Monday's *North-Eastern Evening Gazette* made a small prophetic announcement on its front page in a report on England's cricketers' fortunes on the Ashes tour in Australia, of all things. Correspondent C. B. Fry, outraged at the emergence of something called tactics, signed off tersely: 'Australia hold a conspicuous lead and it has been a good day for football.' Boro fans did not need telling; they had the evidence of their own eyes and, if that was not good enough, they had *Gazette* football writer Eddie Rose to help them. His match report was headlined: 'The New Football Star'. He was not referring to Wilf at this early stage, but to Micky Fenton, scorer of both Boro goals. Rose had spotted potential fulfilled in the bustling centre-forward's performance. Fresh from a run of ten goals in seven games – and playing 'grand football' to boot, according to the reporter – he was now good enough to challenge George Camsell for the centre-forward's position when the legend recovered from his injury. Alternatively, the youngster could continue playing at inside-right, a rapier to Camsell's burgeoning target-man role, where he had also proved his worth. The report even suggested the young player could do for Boro what Carter had done for Sunderland as he skippered them to the championship, from inside-forward, the previous season: provide a vital second thrust to the attack.

About the man who actually did go on to replace Carter as the country's greatest inside-forward, Rose was less effusive. In fact, as always, it was Wilf's physique which drew the first comments.

> A lightly built lad, looking almost pathetically boyish against these hefty Portsmouth fellows, he did quite nicely, showing exceedingly clever footwork in flashes, the ability to drop back and help a harassed defence and a cool head. He lacks a little speed at the moment and is apt to be nonplussed by the faster and more crafty first division opposition. Mannion appears to have more than 'a chance' of making good later on. This outing will have done him good.

Other observers were equally impressed. The *North-Eastern Weekly News*'s football man, writing – as was common then – under a pen name, T-o'-T, said:

> For size he has his limitations, though his figure is compact, and he can grow a little yet. But he has craft. He gets quick control; he goes up well to a ball, and he passes accurately and with discrimination ... He is a natural footballer and can go far.

The prescient *Gazette* reporter spotted the way forward. Fenton, he said, was skilful and adaptable enough to play centre- or inside-forward. He, and other emerging stars, were comfortable swapping positions as play developed rather than sticking to rigid areas.

> Splendid from every point of view except that of the opposition. That is the way to beat the stopper centre-half and the way to score goals. If that can be perfected – and there are others on the books who could play it too – Middlesbrough will have an attack second to none in the country.

A severe test of such optimism came within weeks when Arsenal visited Ayresome amid unprecedented scenes. To add to the excitement of having the team which had won three titles out of the last four visiting, the home side were pushing Highbury's finest for the championship – Boro's first challenge since before the Great War. In November 1911 Boro had topped the table, with Newcastle second and Sunderland third, but finished the season seventh. Two seasons later the club achieved its best-ever final position of third. Twenty-three years on, hopes were high again.

For the Gunners' visit, Boro's morale was high from a 3–1 win the previous day, Good Friday, over Birmingham in front of 25,000 fans. But Arsenal were the Manchester United of the 1930s. If you watched only one game a season, it was the Gunners' match. The eleven-year-old ground attendance record was smashed as 44,773 people, crammed in to see if the mixture of promising local lads and mature stars could maintain the title challenge.

Wilf was not in the team, having given way to Fenton after just one match when Camsell returned from injury, but he was among those watching the remarkable scenes which boded well for Boro's future. A couple of minutes into the match, supporters had overflowed from the terraces to sit on the pitch-side track, while one fan, who was one of many sitting on the roofs of the stands, slipped and nearly fell to the ground before regaining his footing. By the start of the second half the supporters encircling the playing area were standing up, prompting others still on the terraces and in the stands to shin thirty feet up metal supports to get a better view.

The view was of Boro players losing for much of the game. Despite holding the upper hand, they had gone behind after a mix-up between Cumming and one of his defenders allowed Ray Bowden to fire into an empty net. Quite what the goalie's reaction was is not recorded. Camsell had also picked up an injury and, with no substitutes allowed, was exiled to the wing and asked to do what he could. On the opposite touchline, Cochrane was also hobbling. But Camsell persevered, Fenton was fine and that was all it took for an equalizer two minutes from time.

Camsell crossed and Fenton flung himself at the ball, beating the Arsenal keeper and unleashing pandemonium. From every direction the fans who had been hugging the touchlines ran towards the scorer. Eddie Rose reported:

They all wanted to congratulate Fenton and the player bolted, apparently in sheer terror. Camsell was on the verge of collapse under the shoal of congratulations he received for his share.

Order was somehow restored for the remaining minutes to be played out and then the scenes were repeated all over again as even more fans ran on to the field at the final whistle to chair Fenton and Camsell among others from the pitch.

Boro's unbeaten home record was preserved and they had achieved a creditable draw with the mighty Gunners, but it was the beginning of the end for the Teesside title dream for that season. Only one of their final six games ended in victory and four were lost, leading to a final position in 1936–37 of seventh. In one of those matches, away to Preston, preparing for an FA Cup semi-final the following week, Wilf got his second game, but it proved 'rather too much for him', according to Rose. T-o'-T added:

> There have been many advocates of young Mannion for early inclusion in the senior side. The player certainly has skill but the occasion appeared completely to overawe him. It is a big leap from North-Eastern League levels to football against FA Cup semi-finalists – too big.

The forwards generally came in for flak from Rose for 'a most unsatisfactory display'. Fenton was too selfish, while Birkett and Higham were patchy. The reporter at least found hope in the performance of the defence:

> Given the proper set of conditions, the Middlesbrough club now have a defence that is liable to hold up the opposition and, if not win a match off its own bat, certainly save one from being lost.

For eighty-nine minutes against Preston the back three were impassable; in the other sixty seconds Preston plundered two goals to secure a leisurely victory before their big match the next week with West Bromwich Albion.

But the Boro faithful clung to a new underlying sense of potential. Next season would be theirs, they predicted confidently – and with some justification, as ambitious manager Wilf Gillow, who had replaced Peter McWilliam in 1934, was assembling a blend of not only talent and workrate, but youth and experience too. Gillow's managerial spurs had been earned at Grimsby, whom he took into division one for the first time in twenty-six years, only to resign when his side returned from whence it came. When he took over at Boro two years later, it looked like he might suffer another relegation with his new club. The threat was banished, however, and from then on every season under his leadership finished with an improved league position.

Gillow's skill lay in spotting good players and getting them to play above themselves. During his tenure at Ayresome he managed Baxter, Birkett and Cumming to international debuts; blended older players with the up-and-coming, and the imports with the local lads, into a forceful unit; and engendered a healthy team spirit where the men looked after the boys – a spirit which reflected the general air of well-being at the club. Birkett's capture had been the first step, proving the board were backing Gillow and were not prepared to endure another relegation. The double signing of Cochrane and Cumming, in October 1936, had taken it a stage further, putting down a marker that there were ambitions beyond mere survival. Meanwhile the first crop of local talent from the youth policy was flowering nicely.

Off the park, events were adding to the momentum. The directors' ambitions for a first-class club did not stop at the pitch; they wanted it to have a suitably impressive home and ordered the first large-scale improvements to Ayresome Park since it was built in 1903. The ancient and embarrassing stand salvaged for a second lease of life finally met its long overdue date with demolition and was replaced by a stand even grander than the grandstand. The new South Stand stretched 250ft along almost the entire length of one touchline and accommodated some of the 9000 fans it held in the most modern surroundings imaginable: seats.

The remaining terraces along the touchline were also improved, with concrete steps replacing the ashes and railway sleepers. The West End terracing was covered with a roof for the first time and the main North Stand was re-roofed. Then new staircases were built for both ends. The whole stadium was repainted and even the billiards room was given a new concrete floor. The directors clearly thought a clean home was a happy home; and increasingly, so it was.

Christmas came slightly late for Boro fans in 1937. In those pre-war days, football made no concession to Christmas holidays so, on the day everyone else was celebrating, a Saturday, the Boro faithful were forced to endure a 5–3 defeat at Leeds. It was just the latest in a line of disappointments which had seen early season hope recede quicker than Benny Yorston's hairline and left their league form reading: P20 W7 D4 L9. Not disastrous, but not title-winning either.

Two days later, though, Leeds made the return trip to Ayresome and suddenly Santa's red-and-white outfit seemed to be significant. For not only were the visitors beaten 2–0, and in front of 35,000, the biggest crowd of the season, but they were outclassed by a lad who was fantastically talented and, at not yet twenty, could offer Boro years of service. It was only Wilf's third first-team appearance, but from then on he was a regular.

He and Nash were promoted to the first team after Higham and Cumming were made scapegoats for the defeat at Leeds. Reserve-team watchers had been clamouring for Wilf's elevation after dazzling displays which suggested he was ready for another first-team chance. Now he linked up with Jackie Milne, a newly bought winger who had been showing only flashes of the form which prompted his purchase, and it looked like they had been playing together all their lives.

New *Gazette* football correspondent Captain Jack heralded the Christmas miracle with a piece headlined: 'Mannion's Promise As A Second Jackie Carr'. He wrote:

> He showed ideas of construction, the distinct possibility of establishing a partnership with the newcomer Jack Milne; he shot strongly and he scored as neat a goal as you could ever wish to see. And he stood the pace well, never being perturbed by the robust opposition such as is served out by Jack Milburn and others in the Leeds United team.

Come the final whistle Boro secretary Herbert Glasper, a club man for forty years, solemnly took the Captain to a team photo from 1912–13 hanging in the Ayresome boardroom.

'Do you know,' he said, pointing to a young Carr, 'I think Mannion shows every promise of becoming a second Carr. They say, perhaps, that this lad Mannion is not a big one ... but the great Jackie was comparatively small. During my long experience here I have never seen a young player who suggests Carr possibilities as Mannion does and, of course, I have seen quite a lot of him in the reserve side.'

The new Jackie Carr? There could not be higher praise – or possibly a greater burden, or, no doubt according to Tommy Mannion, a worse omen.

Nash, too, had a good game, making some outstanding saves, including one of Milburn's usually unstoppable free-kicks. Fenton scored the other Boro goal from the penalty spot, while the young Teesside contingent was boosted to four by Hardwick making his fourth consecutive appearance since his dramatic debut. In the first minute of that debut match, Hardwick, the youngest full-back in the first division, had managed to prod the ball into his own net with his first kick in the first team. Things could only get better and against Leeds he was beginning to be noted for the assured defensive play he specialized in rather than a stupid own goal.

Captain Jack concluded his Leeds report:

This victory, bringing two much-wanted points, and revenge for the tantalizing defeat at Leeds, revived drooping spirits among officials and supporters and enables the club to look forward with confidence to the visit of Sunderland on Saturday.

Those three words 'visit of Sunderland' were enough to bring Boro fans back down to earth. Sunderland were not just bitter rivals and league champions eighteen months earlier, but they were the reigning FA Cup holders too.

Relentless drizzle did its best to dampen expectations, but with 5000 Wearsiders making the short hop down the coast to Teesside, only a storm of biblical proportions could have diluted the excitement. The groundstaff had laid ten and a half tons of straw on the pitch to make sure it was clear of frost. At 5 a.m. they were up to clear away the festive giant manger scene. Home fans prayed for a miracle similar to the one in the stable: a repeat of the result in Sunderland's championship year – 6–0 to Boro and Carter sent off for kicking, as well as his wingman Davies. Sunderland's supporters knew things couldn't be as bad again.

As the turnstiles clicked, the excitement was higher still in the board-room. The directors' ambitions were being repaid by another record attendance. Pressmen, usually kept blissfully unaware of the amount of filthy lucre made on matchdays, were summoned to be told the crowd was 45,858 and the receipts £3,509. On-pitch matters were also 'giving tremendous satisfaction', Captain Jack concluded in his report on a 2–1 home win. Boro went 1–0 down after eleven minutes, only for Wilf to equalize early in the second half. Five minutes later Birkett provided the winning goal, a mazy run ending with a cross as he reached the by-line and ran out of play. As he tried to avoid a crash landing in the crowd, the crowd erupted. Milne had met the centre and buried the ball in the back of the net.

Captain Jack singled the South Bank trio out for praise:

They've evidently got the required temperament. It was unquestionably a big test. Mannion was again a success and scored a good goal – a feat he accomplished in the Leeds match. Good going indeed! I think Sunderland folk, officials, players and supporters got a surprise when the boy began to trouble – and penetrate – their defence. If the boy maintains the form he has shown in the Leeds and Sunderland games, he's bound to become a regular member of the side.

He did, developing his partnership with Milne. The partnership, however, failed to produce a goal at Stoke, where the home team got three, or against Portsmouth at Ayresome. At least Pompey also failed to score. Perhaps the festive period had been just another false dawn, some thought. In fact it signalled the start of Boro's most concentrated assault on the league championship ever.

Benny Yorston beat Jackie Charlton by more than thirty years. Inside the Scot's locker in the changing room there was a list – sometimes short, sometimes long but rarely empty – headed 'To Be Got'. Decades before Charlton started his little black book in which he recorded the names of opponents who had crossed him so he could settle his scores, Yorston had the Bald Avenger act down to a fine art. After a match, any offending opponents' names would be added to the list in preparation for retribution in the return fixture. And, being the generous sort, Yorston did not just look after himself: any crimes perpetrated on his team-mates would also be recorded ready for reprisals.

He was no McVinnie, however, and his bare head covered a shrewd footballing brain. Years of experience meant he knew what he was doing on the park and what he wanted his team-mates to do. He also knew a star in the making when he saw one. And so Wilf had a guardian angel. If a defender was giving him a hard time, Yorston would tell him: 'You go on the wing lad. I'll look after you.' He protected his fellow inside-forward, shielding him but also encouraging him and pushing him on; master and pupil.

In one game against Brentford, defender Joe James was giving Wilf such a bruising that Yorston stepped in. He pushed his protégé out to the wing and began the battle. A few minutes later he gained possession and looked for the youngster. He threaded a defence-splitting pass through to him but into the area where James was covering. Natural instinct took over. Wilf ran onto the perfectly weighted ball and, without thinking of the challenge which would have hit him if he failed, he skipped past the defender. He learnt the lesson: skill can always beat force.

Yorston was responsible for honing a distinctive part of Wilf's all-round game: his heading ability. A small, skilful midfield player is expected to pass with precision, control with ease and shoot with venom. But leap to head exceptionally? Not often, but Wilf could. He had always been a good header for his height. Yorston took it further, showing him how to time his jump so that he almost hovered at the apex of his flight, waiting for the ball. And so it came to be that many a defender with height, but little skill, would be beaten in the air by a relative midget. Skill could beat size too.

The odd-looking couple's first game together came after Boro recovered from the post-New Year hangover by winning 1–0 at Chelsea, scorer Mannion, and beating Charlton 3–1 at Ayresome. At Preston, where he scored both goals in a 2–0 win, and Grimsby, Yorston gave backbone to the side again and his fierce self-belief sent a confidence more infectious than the flu through his team-mates. Once again a flicker of hope danced in fans' hearts, although a glance at the fixture list swiftly administered a healthy dose of reality. It was all very well beating the middling teams and putting together a run which marked a mini-revival, but there was a five-game sequence looming that would give a truer test of Boro's abilities.

Derby were first up. Theoretically a tricky warm-up to the real meat of the forthcoming fixtures, they were sent home on the wrong end of a 4–2 scoreline – a result which took Boro to eighth and rising. The first major test came courtesy of Manchester City, reigning champions and packed with internationals. Only one City player was not capped, and that was Frank Swift, soon to be England's undisputed number one goalkeeper. Every player was a quality player, the pick of them being Peter 'the Great' Docherty, the only challenger for Carter's mantle of the best inside-forward in the country. He began working as a bus conductor in his native Ireland before being snapped up, aged sixteen, by Blackpool and then sold for a record fee to City.

But despite their quality players, City were struggling. Even though they were among the highest scorers in the League and only eight points behind Boro, they were third from bottom. Luck was failing them, as it did again within ten seconds of kick-off when they tried to play the ball out of defence, were caught in possession and punished by a Cochrane goal. Five more – three for Cochrane and two for Fenton – followed with just a solitary reply. It was embarrassingly easy.

The next opponents would be no such walkovers. Leaders Arsenal were due at Ayresome for a match which would again be crucial in deciding the destination of the league title. The omens were good: Boro had now won their last six league games and had only lost once in ten league matches since Christmas; they had also already beaten Arsenal earlier in the season at Highbury; and there was the encouraging draw of the year before.

People were queuing by midday. An hour before kick-off all the seats were full. At 3 p.m., as the referee blew for kick-off, 46,747 were in, or hanging off parts of, Ayresome – a new ground record, the third in twelve months. The crowd exploded with celebrations just after the half-hour when Wilf linked up with Forrest to provide Fenton with the type of opening he thrived on. Three minutes later he repeated the act, this time from a Yorston pass. Bastin managed to pull one back for Arsenal with fifteen minutes to go marking the start of a frantic finale.

But Boro held on and went to third in the table, just two points behind Arsenal with a game in hand. Captain Jack, who was told by a Gunners director that the better side won, described the win as 'a triumph for the Boro's skilful team work, fast, exhilarating and suggesting great possibilities of the first league championship coming to Ayresome Park.' He picked out Baxter, Fenton, Yorston and Cochrane as the stars. Of Wilf he wrote: 'It was a big ordeal for Mannion against those big Arsenal chaps, and sometimes he was overshadowed, but he was always a grand little trier.' Little did he know the best was being saved for the biggest game: Wolves, joint top with two games in hand, at Molineux.

First there was a tricky visit to Everton, who had new scoring sensation Tommy Lawton in their line-up. The 2–2 draw dropped Boro to fourth as Preston leapfrogged them, increasing the need to get a result at Wolves. Rival managers were on hand at Molineux to pick up hints on either teams' weaknesses and watch another instalment in the denouement of the title race. Jimmy Seed of Charlton, George Jobey of Derby, and Frank Womack of Leicester, took up their places. Ninety minutes later they were united in praise of one team and one player from it.

Wilf scored the only goal in the 1–0 win after Milne cut a cross back for him, but his contribution included so much more. Creating chances, covering for colleagues and even helping to marshal the forces after Stuart sprained his ankle and was forced to just hobble up and down the touchline. Another novice, Shep, also drew good reviews for his performance in the defence in only his fourth first-team outing. But it was Wilf who stole the show. Jobey eulogized the 'ideal football' he had witnessed, while Captain Jack's report was headlined: 'Jimmy Seed says "Mannion is a marvel"'. 'The boy I liked was Mannion,' he was quoted as saying. 'In fact, I'd put it like this: Mannion is a marvel. I've never seen a boy take the ball away from experienced players in such tantalising fashion as this one.'

The tribute to top them all, though, came as Wilf walked from the pitch. Wolves' Bryn Jones, then the most expensive footballer ever transferred, trotted up to him, patted him on the back and demanded of the

Boro bench: 'Where on earth did you dig this little chap up? He's a wonder.'

High above them in the main stand, in the full flush of the victory which lifted Boro level on points with Preston and Wolves and only one behind Arsenal, chairman Bill Kelly gave Captain Jack an interview.

'I'm more than delighted,' he said. 'We've got over a stiff hurdle and our standard of play encourages me to think that we have a distinct chance of winning the Championship. I am delighted with the spirit of the team. You can see that they mean business.'

Within three weeks, the receivers were in, metaphorically. The old blues lament of 'If I didn't have bad luck, I'd have no luck at all' was once more applying to the reds. At 0–0 in the next game, at home to Brentford, Wilf hit the bar, Milne hit the post and Fenton had a goal-bound free-kick deflected away by a hand, unseen by the referee. The visitors scored and held on for the win.

A 1–0 win at Leicester suggested Brentford was a blip. Then came Easter week and Boro were crucified, not to rise again. The day before Palm Sunday they lost at home to Huddersfield. Camsell and others missed gilt-edged chances to wrap the game up but, at 0–0 in the last minute, at least a point looked safe. Then the visitors scored. Similarly, a 1–0 lead against Liverpool on Good Friday was surrendered after a late defensive mistake. At Blackpool the next day Boro had a 2–0 half-time lead, having had a third disallowed, then conceded four goals in the last half-hour. At Liverpool on Easter Monday, a single goal saw the Mersey-siders home. All that remained was for Wolves, to beat Boro at Ayresome the following Saturday, and record their first win there for thirty years, and that was Ayresome's league challenge dead.

Boro finished fifth, missing fourth place on goal average. They won the final game of the season at Ayresome, condemning visitors West Brom-wich Albion to relegation. The only really happy man at the ground was the Grimsby chairman who had seen his side saved from the drop by West Brom's defeat. The crowd of just 13,000 indicated the disappointment of the championship dream dying.

In the nine games played after beating Wolves, Boro won just twice. On the plus side, Fenton had won his first England cap in a game against Scotland, but then his club form dipped so badly that he was dropped. Cumming had been among his opponents in that international, making his Scottish debut, and with Baxter only missing the match because of an injury, Boro were getting the recognition their stylish play deserved; but still not in the form of trophies.

If it wasn't to be the league, what about the FA Cup? As Wilf won a regular place in the first team, the annual campaign was looming. It was a chance to start afresh, with a team much improved from the early season stutters. Forget that inconsistent league form, here was a club ready for Cup glory – players who could beat anybody on their day; a manager whose shrewd leadership promised to outwit any opponent; and fans who were desperate to see some silverware crown the majestic performances they had been witnessing, albeit sporadically, at Ayresome.

Most importantly, the luck of the draw seemed to be on their side. The first opponents were Stockport, comfortably dispatched by a brace of goals from Micky Fenton at Ayresome the Saturday after the Sunderland match. An away tie at Nottingham Forest a fortnight later proved no more difficult with Wilf, Camsell and Milne scoring the three goals which beat Forest's one. Then the draw was made for the fifth round: third division north York City away, one of those awkward away games against unfancied opponents who had nothing to lose and everything to gain. But at this stage Boro had only lost once in their previous six games in the top flight. They were a team packed with internationals; and, although fans couldn't foresee it, the back-to-back victories against Derby, Manchester City and Arsenal were only a couple of weeks away.

Great expectations of a place in the quarter-finals with Wembley on the distant horizon, as well as the short distance to the heart of Yorkshire, meant a red-and-white exodus on matchday from what was then the North Riding. Outside the Middlesbrough town-centre infirmary named after the county, Dennis Docherty, eighteen, and his mates gathered. Together they formed Walker Celtic, named after a local butchers, a side drawn from the streets around the hospital. On the morning of 12 February 1938, marshalled by the former army sergeant who managed them, the lads were supporting rather than playing. At 10.30 a.m. the bus arrived to take them to York's Bootham Crescent. Dennis, now seventy-seven, remembers it well.

'We were convinced Boro were going to win – not just at York but the Cup too. We got to the ground well before the kick-off and joined the queue to get in. It was a big match for them, too, and there were thousands waiting outside.'

From Teesside, the Saturday shift workers had dashed from work to the station or their alternative transport rendezvous. Festooned in red-and-white scarves, rosettes and two-toned cloth caps, they followed the team's southerly journey. A couple of hours beforehand the players had been whisked through the parcels office at Middlesbrough's elegant Victorian railway station to avoid the adulation which Captain Jack rightly noted 'in such circumstances is sometimes embarrassing'.

What was even more embarrassing was the result: York 1 Middlesbrough 0. In his *Gazette* report on Monday the Captain avoided mentioning the romance of the Cup, even though it was St Valentine's Day. Instead the headline was: 'York – It Was Almost Unbelievable'. As he wrote, the players longed to be shepherded through the parcels office on their return too, but their shame had no such hiding place. They were 'deeply conscious of the profound disappointment created on Teesside by their totally unexpected defeat.' The Captain added: 'Make no mistake about this: the Borough players themselves feel this defeat intensely ... I do not think I have ever travelled home with a more depressed team.'

An excuse lay in the gale-force wind which battered the Bootham pitch. It was so strong a Milne corner was almost blown into the net at 0–0. York's luck was such that their best wind-assisted effort went in.

'Spooner, their winger, sent in a high ball across our area which I thought was a centre,' Dennis Docherty recalls. 'Dave Cumming strayed off his line a bit to start to come for it, the ball curled as if a gust of wind got it and in it went.'

Captain Jack said of the wind: 'The Borough were so uncomfortable in it; so erratic. They blundered, stumbled, sliced, hesitated, failed in doing anything like their usual in the way of constructive work.' But he wasn't making excuses. For all their skill, Boro lacked what today would be called competitiveness. Then he described it as 'that something ... shall we say adaptability, or strength, or team power, or vigour ... or shall we say "the man and ball" habit which is not absent in Cup ties.' York had plenty of it – as Fenton's bruised shins attested. He was blocked trying to get a shot in and, as he hobbled away, Boro's Cup dream went lame too. In front of 23,000, so crammed into the ground that spectators were packed along the touchline and the ball kept bouncing back off them when it went out of play, Boro were shamed. At the final whistle it was the York players who were chaired from the pitch.

Captain Jack described the exit as a blow which was 'the worst ever inflicted upon the club. This, yes humiliating, Cup exit came at a time when the club, striking a new era, had captured the public interest in such a way as to suggest that a record season was to be experienced.' It was not to be. More than fifty years on, it still rankles. For Ralph Birkett, Micky Fenton and Wilf, it remains the worst day of their careers. For Dennis Docherty and other Boro fans like him, it is still an appalling, deeply embedded memory. Boro would have won ninety-nine times out of a hundred, just like Newcastle would ordinarily beat Hereford and Arsenal would beat Wrexham.

Ralph remembers: 'I still think we would have won the Cup that year but for that result. We all thought we would win it, even more so when we were drawn against York. We were in the top three or four in division one and they were third division north. It ended up being one of the worst games I played in. There was the hundred-miles-an-hour wind which was blowing you all over the pitch. York had one shot on goal and in it went. We couldn't play football to get back – we had been brought down to their standard as soon as we walked on the field.'

Wilf adds: 'We thought we were going all the way to Wembley. We had the players. Their manager said beforehand, "I wouldn't give tuppence for our chances ordinarily, but on a day like today it's different," and he was right. The second half was one-way traffic but the ball just wouldn't go in. When the final whistle went it broke our hearts. It was the most disappointing game of my whole career.'

And what of Dennis Docherty? The young men of Walker Celtic headed off to a local pub to drown their sorrows, but Dennis was too young and instead arranged to meet them later. He went to the cinema, still wearing his Boro scarf. Up came the organist singing a song about York's win, then a newsreel came on recounting the giant killing.

'Everyone could see I was a Boro fan and they started laughing. I was just sitting there crying my eyes out,' he says. 'I'll always remember that day.'

One man was noticeably absent from the unfolding drama of the season. Thomas Mannion's visits to Ayresome were as rare as a Dave Cumming goal. Only once did he make it to the ground to see for himself his son's prodigious talents, and that was because the directors provided him with tickets and sent someone to collect him. It wasn't that he was snubbing Wilf's new-found celebrity, just that he had no interest in football. He wasn't a player; he had never pulled on the shirt of a Sunday league team, let alone a professional side. Unlike many footballers now and then, the ambitions of the father were not being realized by the son.

'He just wasn't interested,' Wilf says. 'He'd keep away. The only time he went was when the directors took him – that would have been the only time he was in Ayresome Park, because the directors called him and asked. He didn't want to watch me. He didn't go locally to watch any teams or play at all.'

Tommy was there though. Not in seats courtesy of the directors, the very men he warned the family against, but on the terraces with his mates. He watched his brother bring midfield flair and a new dimension to Boro's attacking efforts – thrusts which nudged Boro ever nearer the elusive title. But Tommy remained unhappy. Wilf's play was never good enough; or, more accurately, it was never selfish enough.

'He never liked the way I played. He'd never give me anything, you know. Never say I was good or played well. He says I was a clown. I knew what he was on about because I was making the bullets for others when I could have done it for myself. "Play for yourself," he used to say. He didn't believe in the way I was coming deep and running all over the ruddy place. He'd say, "Forget those other bloody idiots." He never liked any of the others, he was very hard – all because of Jackie Carr and what he said they did to him.' For Tommy, at Boro you only looked out for number one – and that didn't mean Dave Cumming.

Other critics were less harsh. Bryn Jones's gesture and the praise of the managers after the Wolves game had been noted. There was speculation about an international call-up, which was not surprising given that the England selectors had already noticed him – in November 1937, after just two first-team games, Wilf was named as a reserve for an England v Wales match. It was a remarkable honour, albeit one which meant little more than the selectors putting down a marker, for, in the era of no substitutions, reserves were called upon only in the rare event of a pre-match injury to another player. It was also a geographically inspired tribute, as the game was being played at Ayresome to mark the modernization of the ground. But, with Stanley Matthews and Bryn Jones playing, Wilf was beginning to move in international circles.

The press, too, quickly latched on to the emerging star. After one game, a Liverpool player, one Matt Busby, coined the name 'Wonder Boy' which started to stick with the journalists.

'Matt started it all with Wonder Boy,' Wilf says. 'He was walking off on the opposite side of the ground he was that dizzy at the end and I says to him, "You're going the wrong way, Matt. Come on this way." I gave him a run around.' Gradually, no doubt thanks to the blond hair standing out like marble in a coalmine, that mutated into Golden Boy and a legend was born. Not that Wilf ever cared.

'It was all a press thing really,' he says. 'It never bothered me. I just went out and played. That was it.'

The accolades were all a long way from the uncertain Boro debut against Portsmouth. In less than a season Wilf had gone from an amateur playing non-league football to the fringes of the England team. In the *Gazette* report of his league debut, Eddie Rose had written: 'If only the club's long run of misfortune will end ... the outlook will be bright indeed.' Sadly, the outlook was not very bright, and it was getting bleaker.

· THREE ·

From towser to trooper

Training was coming to a close. The players were looking forward to completing another day's circuits of the pitch and heading back to the dressing-room for a soak in the bath. Charlie Cole was winding up the session when the besuited figure of Wilf Gillow came into view and watched the closing stages. As the players continued exercising on the cinder track, he walked among them until he came to Wilf and took him to one side.

'You've been picked for England,' he said matter of factly. Wilf's face had no time to register any emotion before Gillow continued: 'They're going to South Africa for a three-week tour. You're not. I've already written to the FA telling them you've got to have complete rest from a ball.'

A pause suggested Wilf should say something.

'Thanks very much Mr Gillow.' The manager gave a slight nod.

'Right, back to work then,' he said, and off he went.

Wilf recalls: 'You had to address them as Mr this or Mr that or you'd be up in front of the board – remember Jackie Carr. Their word was final and that was that. You had no shout at all. I just had to say thank you but I was thinking why didn't they at least re-imburse me the money I would have been getting from it.'

A neutral might see the club's view that a rest would do him some good. After all he was only twenty and, in 1938–39, had only just finished his first full league season, a highly dramatic one at that. But he had never had a break from a ball, and certainly never sought one. Micky Fenton was selected for that same summer tour in 1939, and was being allowed to go. He was only four years older and not very much more experienced. He would be getting the chance to travel to a far-off country, and earn the international rate of £10 per match.

There wasn't much point thinking about it. There was nothing anyone could do if the manager said no. But why did he? International call-ups for players were often more trouble to the clubs than they were worth. Yes, there was the kudos of seeing an England side with one of your players in it, but almost all the internationals were played on Saturdays, so the clubs lost their best players for their own games. The chances were that Smith or Jones would come back with an inflated sense of his own importance, wanting this, that and the other, which generally translated as the same treatment, financial and otherwise, legitimate or otherwise, that his new international colleagues told him they received. Apart from all that, other clubs might realize how good the player was and decide to try to buy him, with all the disruptive transfer talk that would bring.

Of course, the board retained the right to sell players if it so decided. Ralph Birkett had discovered that at the start of the 1938–39 season as he became a victim of Boro's new-found desire for success. The strength of the squad meant he was not getting regular games, and the reserves' North-Eastern League matches were not the place to impress the England selectors and resurrect his own international career. He may have been second only to George Camsell in Boro's scoring list two years earlier, but by 1938 he was no more than a reserve – an important squad member for a club challenging for honours and in need of strength in depth, but a reserve nonetheless.

In July, Wilf Gillow accepted a £6000 bid for Birkett from Newcastle. After 101 appearances and thirty-six goals, the winger reluctantly left Boro and dropped down a division.

'Those times at Middlesbrough were my happiest,' he remembers. 'The club was friendly, there were great players and the manager was good to play for. Wilf's [Gillow] philosophy was to go out every game and enjoy ourselves. There was none of the ranting and raving that there is today when teams lose.'

But Gillow was no dippy romantic. Birkett was sold so that Boro could buy. The fans may have been concerned at the departure of their England winger, but the arrival of Duncan McKenzie from Brentford soothed them before the start of the new season. For eighteen months there had been plenty of competition for the numbers seven to eleven shirts, and enough for the defence, too, but where Boro needed strengthening was between the two. Right-half McKenzie, another Scot and a maestro at bringing a sense of unhurried calm to the midfield battleground, was just what was required.

Yet still something didn't click. Consistency was the problem. Up until the middle of November, Boro won five games by scoring three or more goals; but they also lost four conceding three or more. They veered from beating the mighty Wolves one week, to being hammered 4–0 by Everton the next and then beating Huddersfield 4–1 after that. It was clear that on their day they could beat anyone; but on an off-day they could lose to anyone. If any fan needed to ask how that could be, they obviously weren't real Boro supporters. Even so the diehards hoped that every win would signal the start of belated title form.

That form seemed to come on 10 December when the tangerine-shirted stars of Blackpool were the visitors. Little did they know the rout which awaited them, orchestrated by the twenty-year-old Golden Boy. Wilf scored four and made several more as Boro won 9–2, with the luckiest 17,166 people on Teesside watching at Ayresome. At seven the crowd was cheering 'one-two-three-four-five-six-seven' which was swiftly upgraded to eight and then nine before Jackie Milne missed an easy chance to take it to ten. Blackpool's manager Joe Smith said: 'Who could have resisted this Borough team today? I don't know of a team that could have escaped a towsing.'

Wilf was towser-in-chief in his best game so far as forager, schemer and scorer. Captain Jack reported:

> Standing out in this Borough victory, whirlwind-like, and leaving us almost breathless, was 'four goals' Wilfred Mannion. More than once I have expressed the wish that Mannion would shoot harder and more frequently, a hope entertained too, by his most ardent admirers. The boy has proved his value – and class – in the 'open'. It was emphasized in unmistakable fashion in this game. And he proved he can shoot. He shared in the movements which led to most of the goal scoring, especially in the first half. The lad gave a positively dazzling exhibition. And I also want to say that I know that bouquets, even a big one like this, will not disturb his equilibrium.

The Captain even made Blackpool's goalkeeper, Wallace, his team's man of the match for keeping the score down.

No doubt to Tommy Mannion's disgust, it wasn't a total one-man show. Milne, too, starred on the right wing; McKenzie's value was underlined as he anchored the midfield and provided the passes others developed into attacks and goals; and Fenton played what the Captain called 'an improved game, and with three goals into the bargain, gave considerable satisfaction.' That counted as a good review. Such were the *Gazette*'s man in the stand's expectations of the Boro centre-forward that Camsell had once received the tribute 'scored four but did little else'.

The win almost kick-started Boro's season. They lost only once in their next six league games, but then they lost three and drew one of the next four. Once again they spluttered back to life with three straight wins, followed by a 6–1 defeat at Wolves. It took another rout to underline that the title dream wasn't dead for another season. A 4–4 draw with Everton and a single-goal victory over Huddersfield gave no indications of the result to come against FA Cup finalists Portsmouth, with everyone in their team playing for a place at Wembley, just over a month away. It was hard to believe Pompey were the team with a looming Wembley date. Boro could have even surpassed the trouncing of Blackpool. Instead they had to settle for 8–2, including another Mannion hat-trick and with George Camsell, deputizing for the injured Fenton, grabbing a couple. The Captain wrote:

> The Teessiders were in dazzling form, especially in attack. Outstanding features were a brilliant display by Mannion, a most spirited exhibition by Yorston, both in attack and defence, a sparkling performance by Milne and a most useful game by Camsell.

It was 1–1 after six minutes but then 'came the Borough in hurricane style. The Portsmouth defence was out-positioned and out-manoeuvred.' Wilf's first was another example of his deadly shooting; his second, his coolness in a one-on-one with the keeper after being put through; and his third, his latest trick – arriving late and unmarked to net from close range. The Captain concluded:

> Portsmouth's defence could seldom hold the bewilderingly clever Borough forwards. The Borough gave a grand all-round exhibition, magnificent team work, and I think that any team in the League would have had a bad time against them on this form.

Five weeks later Portsmouth won the Cup. By then Boro had gone on to win at Arsenal and had beaten Brentford and Leicester at home. They stayed in touch with the title race, but then they lost to Leicester. Blackpool, so comprehensively beaten before, turned the tables to record a 4–0 win. When the final whistle of the final match blew to end a 1–1 draw with Aston Villa, Boro were fourth. Again Gillow had taken them higher than before, to the loftiest league position the club had occupied for twenty-five years.

Fenton, top scorer with thirty-four goals in just thirty-three games, had blossomed into the complete centre-forward his early promise had hinted at. Wilf, showing outstanding form and consistency, was second with fourteen goals. The more senior players showed no signs of being outshone by the young duo's rise, and the fans were flocking to see their side. A new record crowd – 51,080 – had watched Boro's Cup clash with Sunderland, which ended in a 2–0 disappointment for the Teessiders, but showed the support was there. No doubt about it, 1939–40 would be the year.

In a way, Boro fans were right, but it was nothing to do with football. There were more important things to worry about that season and for the next six after that.

It kicked off as normal, despite the fact that as long ago as the victories over Arsenal and Wolves in the climax of the 1937–38 season, war was looming. On the day of the former, Nazi Germany annexed Austria; the papers which carried news of the latter also reported on air-raid preparations and a 70 per cent increase in the numbers joining the army. But while the rising tensions throughout Europe may have dominated the front pages of the newspapers, on the back pages sporting life appeared to be carrying on almost unaffected, for a while at least.

In Middlesbrough, August 1939 was a month of optimism as fans hoped the relentless upward drive of Gillow's reign might even see the team rise the three positions needed to secure the long-sought-after top spot. But pre-season training was a rather listless affair, with everyone well aware that there might not be any matches to train for. Some players had already joined the Territorial Army or other services in response to an FA circular in April reminding clubs they ought to set a patriotic example. The whole Brentford squad responded by joining the War Police as one, while Liverpool, including their manager, opted for the TA.

Games were played though, Boro's first two ending in defeat. On Saturday 2 September they won their first point – although they stayed bottom of the table – in a 2–2 draw with Stoke City in front of 12,298 at Ayresome. Micky Fenton scored both goals. They were his last in division one for more than seven years. The Sunday papers which carried those first tables also forecast a declaration of conflict, stemming from the German invasion of Poland and the first mass evacuation of children to the countryside. Barely had the gloomy headlines been fully digested than they proved accurate when Chamberlain made his historical broadcast to the nation.

Hitler, whose regime had been reluctantly recognized by English footballers just a year earlier when they were ordered by the FA to give a Nazi salute before a match against Germany, brought all sport to an immediate halt. A ban on crowds assembling in public places, as the country braced itself for aerial attacks, put paid to everything from soccer to steeplechasing.

The Boro players were left to rue what might have been. Micky Fenton, then approaching twenty-six and his prime, now says: 'We were just coming to our peak as a team, but we never had the chance to reach it. There were so many good players – the team was packed with them. We finished fifth and fourth in consecutive seasons and I don't think there's any doubt that we would have won the championship the following season but for the outbreak of the war.' Fenton himself would probably have cemented his place in Boro history by going on to surpass Camsell as the club's record goal scorer. Instead the powder blue of the RAF beckoned.

Wilf, too, believes silverware was on its way to Ayresome. It was a point of view with which everyone on Teesside agreed and still does to this day.

'We had a good mix and strength in depth,' he says. 'Every position was covered three or four times. If you were off your game, someone else would be breathing down your neck for a place. We would have won something. That was the best team we had all the time I was there. People like McKenzie and Milne and Baxter, they were all internationals. It was almost a team of internationals.'

The ban on sport was in marked contrast to the reaction when World War I erupted. Then first-class cricket continued unhindered to the conclusion of the 1914 season. Football went even further and completed a full league season as well as staging an FA Cup final. But able-bodied, fit young men enjoying themselves on the playing fields, and being paid for it, while others died on the killing fields of Europe understandably proved to be universally unpopular.

Eventually a footballers' battalion was formed in response to public calls for soccer stars to do their bit. In 1915 it saw action in France, with Frank Buckley – later to become one of the most innovative and controversial league managers ever – soon gaining the rank of major, which made him stand out among his post-war rival Mr managers. Football and rugby also regularly played a direct part in the battles of 1914–18: troops on the charge were more than once seen hacking a ball towards the enemy lines in play which gave new meaning to leading the attack.

Among the professional footballers of the next generation left wondering what the future held for them in 1939 was Tommy Lawton, the legendary Dixie Dean's replacement at Everton, who as a teenager, had achieved all that had been asked of him. Top scorer in the first division in the last two seasons, he had made his England debut, aged nineteen, living up to his own boast. When he was transferred to Everton, Joe Mercer met him with the comment: 'Aye, son, you're a big 'un.'

'Aye,' Tommy replied, 'and a good 'un.'

Now his football, learnt in games with the unemployed at the pit-heads organized partly for fun, often for money so the winning team could pocket the pooled subs and enjoy a night out, appeared to be irrelevant. The skills developed under the eye of Burnley's Welsh international Roy Bennin, who ensured accurate shooting in his protégé by rolling balls to him and ordering him to hit a designated letter in the pitch-side advertisement reading Burnley Beer is Best, would be of no use in the forces, he thought. In his book *Football is my Business* he wrote:

> Then came the war and, with it, the end of my career or so I felt. Surely there couldn't be room for a professional footballer in a world gone crazy? I, of course, being a young, fit man of approaching twenty would go into the services. Meanwhile, in the leisure time I had left I wound up my personal affairs, cursed Hitler and all his rats and occasionally sat down to think of what had been and what might have been.

With a heavy heart, he set off on a thirteen-hour journey from the north west to Aldershot where he had been told to report for duty. He and many other sportsmen were surprised when they arrived at such bases and began playing football again. Within a month of the declaration of war the total ban on sports was deemed unnecessarily cautious as the initial dire scenarios of war being waged in Britain eased. The Government also realized the value to morale of the diversion to the war which sport could offer. Obviously there was no question of the peacetime leagues restarting. Using petrol for coach trips to carry footballers from Portsmouth to Newcastle, for example, might be seen as unnecessary given the circumstances. Instead, eight regional leagues were established, with crowds limited, for safety reasons, to an all-ticket absolute maximum of 8000 – or 15,000 for grounds usually holding 60,000.

The professionals' contracts had been cancelled – although their registrations were kept ready for post-war football – almost as soon as the war broke out, putting them out of a job but freeing them to join up. They were told they could play for the side nearest to their camp, providing the match didn't interfere with their soldiering. They were even paid thirty shillings per match. The result was that familiar faces appeared in unfamiliar strips – Matt Busby played for Boro, Stanley Matthews for Rangers and Lawton for Morton (while on his honeymoon, one of the 'personal affairs' he had to wind up). Perhaps the luckiest team was Aldershot which, by virtue of the mammoth military camp in town, soon had more internationals in its ranks than at any time before or since.

Other teams often had to make do with guests of a lower calibre, lower-division men or amateurs, who in peacetime would have only been at grounds such as Ayresome as spectators. In one wartime season, Notts County managed to call on 132 different players. A not unusual scene occurred on Christmas morning 1940, when Brighton headed for a game at Norwich with only five players, hoping to make up the numbers on the way. Eventually a couple of Norwich reserves and soldiers from the crowd completed the side, but Brighton still lost 18–0. Bonanza scorelines – another came when Leslie Compton of Arsenal scored ten in a 15–2 win against Clapton Orient – certainly gave the crowds value for money. Freak results became the norm – Everton beaten by Crewe, Chester and Wrexham – and indicated a variable standard of play, which meant that many spectators stayed away from the matches, leaving the 8000 limit looking optimistic. Whatever Bill Shankly said later, football was less important than the matters of life and death occupying the nation's minds.

Home international fixtures, friendlies between service teams and even the FA Cup, which survived in a truncated form, all provided further opportunities for players and fans alike to enjoy ninety minutes away from the war when they could. The bulk of the gate money went to war charities or towards helping with the cost of the conflict in some way. But some were still not convinced of the value of the matches or of other sports fixtures staged on an ad-hoc basis. Sir Stafford Cripps, the leader of the House of Commons, voiced their concern and called for the elimination of unnecessary spending with the soundbite: 'Our motto can neither be "Business as Usual" nor "Pleasure as Usual"'. A press campaign prompted by the concern of Baptist, Methodist and Quaker religious leaders of the time attacked fans of all sports for wasting fuel, taking time off work and then going on benders after fixtures.

But with Winston Churchill making an appearance at games, sport was safe. At one wartime international between England and Scotland, Attlee, Bevin and five other Cabinet ministers were seen among the large crowd of 75,000. The only indication of the war was a Spitfire which passed overhead and the plea to the crowd to throw their tickets and programmes in special wastebins provided so the paper could be re-used. With the blessing of the highest in the land and with modest modifications, it was a case of the games must go on.

For Lawton, posted to a footballing battalion which formed part of the physical training (PT) corps, that meant that within a week of joining up he was playing football for the British Army, alongside Mercer once more and Busby, against France. In what was the last big football match before Dunkirk, 35,000 troops watched the same stars they had seen before the war. Lined up against them were nine men who had been serving in the frontline only three days before.

Such fixtures, at home and abroad, gave the troops a boost, but also became part of a propaganda war between the enemies. Goebbels had exploited the hiatus when football was stopped because of the threat of German bombers, and wanted to have the British running scared again. Just by stepping on to the pitch, therefore, the players were helping the war effort; not that everyone appreciated that. In the wake of Dunkirk the soccer stars and other athletes drafted into the PT corps were sarcastically branded PT commandos and, later, D-Day dodgers. Lawton refuted such tags in his book:

> I was one of the fortunates who, by reason of my retention in this country on Army service, was able to get in my weekly game throughout the period of hostilities. And incidentally there was periodical hostility from people who thought it wrong that fit, able-bodied young fellows like myself should be playing football in England while their husbands, sons and sweethearts were fighting in the sun-baked deserts of Libya and the Middle East, were flying out over Europe or were dying in the dangerous seas. I am not going to defend myself, I have done nothing to defend myself against. The War Moguls ordered that I stayed in England to do my war job. Football was incidental, but in its way it too played a part. I appeared in hundreds of charity matches for England, the Army, combined services and unit sides. Let me make it clear. I didn't ask to stay in England.

Shortly before his death in 1996 he added: 'You fought as well you know. Not very often, but you fought. And anyway we did our jobs – we entertained the troops and kept morale up and that's what we were asked to do. We thought we did a good job because the lads seemed happy. And that's what people wanted.'

Ivy Griffiths can still remember the night, more than fifty-five years ago, when she could have become public enemy number one on Teesside. At a dance in the picturesque North Yorkshire market town of Richmond, one of the soldiers from the nearby Green Howards regimental training base decided to have a dance with her, without clearing it with her first. So she thumped him. The small, fair-haired lad fell back and tumbled down some nearby stairs. Then he got up, dusted himself down and accepted that no meant no. Wilf was unhurt. Ivy, now seventy-five, says: 'I just thank goodness he didn't injure his legs. But he deserved to be hit.'

It was his second lucky escape of the year. Some months earlier, he had had to use his fitness to the full to endure a forced march retreating through northern France. In Middlesbrough he was reported missing in action, but in fact he had managed to join the million men in the thousands of small craft evacuating from Dunkirk. On the weekend he arrived back safely in Britain, the first wartime FA Cup final was being staged. A year earlier such games would have been his life, but things had changed.

Wilf was conscripted in January 1940, aged twenty-one. In the early months of the war he had played in the regional leagues for Boro in such games as an 8–1 win over Darlington, in front of 1000 just before Christmas. His call-up to the seventh battalion of the Howards, and his dispatch to Bridlington for training, meant missing a couple of games as he square bashed with fellow recruits more used to watching him from the terraces of Ayresome Park. But by March he was playing for Boro again, including an 8–0 defeat by Darlington in front of 5500.

Former apprentice joiner Richard Buck, only eighteen at the time, was already a soldier at Bridlington when Wilf arrived. Now seventy-five, he remembers the young footballer.

'Wilf came to us from Middlesbrough for his basic training, with the intake of his age. He was a hero to many of them and to many of us – remember we were only eighteen or nineteen. He was a bit older and the lads all looked up to him. There he was doing his bit for the war with them.'

Fellow ex-Lance Corporal George Hewling, also at the depot at the time, now seventy-six, adds: 'He was privileged in that they used to let him off at weekends regularly so that he could play football. But no one resented that. We treated him the just same. If he had played his cards right, he could have had a very good war at home but he wasn't that type of fellow. He was there with everyone else.'

He had already had the chance to secure his 'very good war at home' courtesy of Sergeant Major 'Squeaker' Bennett – the man Harold Shepherdson MBE credited as the key to his seventeen-year career as trainer with England teams, including the 1966 World Cup winning one. Bennett was the officer who steered Shep into the physical training corps and a job at a convalescence depot where he learnt to treat injuries far worse than groin strains and pulled muscles. He also learnt the art of motivation, to ease his charges' memories of warfare and gee them up for a return to the front if necessary. They were skills he put to good use in his subsequent peacetime football career. Wilf had the chance to acquire them too.

The sergeant had summoned the pair of them and told them they were being transferred to a PT unit. Shep wasn't overly keen, but he realized that here was the chance to learn a specialism. Wilf said no, he wanted 'to stay with the lads'. Shep remembered the occasion.

'I said to him, "Don't be a daft so and so." If he had taken that chance perhaps his whole life would have been different, but he wasn't interested. To be honest, I didn't realize how much it would change my life. When I look back on it now, it was the best thing that could have happened to me. There I was going into the Army as a young man with no skills other than football. I got the opportunity to develop in a different area. Six-and-a-half years later I came out with training in something I'd never even have considered otherwise, and a new direction. I benefitted more than anyone else I knew from the army training.'

'It wasn't for me,' Wilf says. 'It was all right for Harold because he had the brains, but not for me. I didn't want to join the physical training corps. I just wasn't interested. I was happy just being a normal soldier.'

So while Shep was stationed at the Bedford Convalescence Depot, playing for Northampton Town, Wilf carried on training for war and playing football, but he soon saw more dramatic action. In March he and his colleagues were dispatched to France, even though they were not fully trained. They were sent to build a makeshift landing strip to be used to bring men in for a push forward. The Germans had other ideas and within three months the only moving the Howards and all other British troops was doing was towards Dunkirk, double quick march.

'We weren't there long,' Wilf says. 'Then we had to have our running pumps on to get back home. There was a forced march – you could drop out if you wanted to, but you really didn't want to – for two or three days to get to the escape route at Dunkirk.'

As the organized chaos of the evacuation hit full pelt, there were those back on Teesside who had Wilf killed off. The *Gazette* reported the rumours, but on Saturday, 8 June 1940 it carried the good – and accurate – news under a headline: 'Wilf Mannion Fit and Well':

All Teesside soccer fans, and the sporting fraternity generally, will be pleased to hear that Wilfred Mannion, the Middlesbrough FC 'star' is fit and well. It will be recalled that some time ago there was a most persistent and disturbing rumour concerning the safety of the South Bank boy, who had been serving with the BEF in France. The rumour was soon proved to be without foundation and it now transpires that Mannion has returned from France to this country and is expected home on leave this week-end.

Along with about 700 men, including Lance Corporals Buck and Hewling, Wilf had managed to get aboard a supply ship, the SS *Neptune*, and return home. He spent some time back on leave before being called to the Howards regimental headquarters in Richmond, Yorkshire. There men from the dales of the North Riding and the industrial towns of Teesside came to serve in the region's regiment. On the hillside overlooking the River Swale, new recruits learnt the history of the regiment and its traditions; the skills they would need in action; and the camaraderie which would be as important, all in tranquil settings far removed from Dunkirk or the horrors that awaited them.

For Wilf, football again took precedence. From December onwards he played almost weekly for Boro, often alongside Matt Busby, in the League, War Cup and West Riding Cup. More importantly, the England selectors remembered him. In February 1941 he made his first appearance in his country's strip, albeit in an unofficial international for which no caps were awarded, and with the three lions absent from England's shirts. The 3–2 defeat against Scotland at Newcastle was his first game in a decade of international football.

The match was also significant for the foundations it laid. Among Wilf's team-mates were Jacky Milne, but more importantly, they also included for the first time Tommy Lawton and goalkeeper Frank Swift.

The Lancastrian pair, who had travelled to Aldershot to join the Army together, were playing with and against each other in the war games and developing a double act which would criss-cross Europe with England. With his ready grin and joker's nature, not to mention the telegrams which arrived before every game saying: 'Stick in, Love, Mother', Swift was the genial host of the dressing-room. Scores of other young players would later tell how he eased their entry with a friendly smile, a firm handshake and a cheery: 'Come and meet the lads.'

Swift made his name in his teens when, in May 1934, just four months after his first-team debut, he played for Manchester City in the FA Cup final. At the end, the photographers behind his goal who had been counting the minutes for him cheered the lad – and then watched him collapse as he succumbed to the nerves that had been so bad before kick-off that he was only prevented from being sick with a shot of whisky offered by a medicinally minded team-mate. His colleagues brought him around and a minute later he followed them to the Royal Box to be congratulated by the King.

'How are you feeling now, my boy?' the King asked.

'Fine sir,' big Frank replied.

'That's good,' came the response. 'You played very well. Here's your medal and good luck.'

Swift didn't need any luck. He was a dedicated professional, always working to improve his game and that of his colleagues. He could often be found trying to work out how a shot had beaten him. He was also the first keeper to use his clearances to launch attacks rather than just to get rid of the ball. His kicks and revolutionary throws regularly paved the way to a Manchester City or England score. All he really needed to overcome were those nerves. In one of his early games with non-league Fleetwood, he was so scared of a voice from the crowd that kept calling him that he edged further and further from the goalline. At the end of the match the coach driver, who just wanted a chat while the ball was at the other end, said: 'What's wrong with thee, lad? Are you deaf?'

Wilf's link-up with Lawton and Swift was successful enough, despite the defeat, to warrant a second appearance in the next international, also against Scotland but this time at Hampden Park, in May. He partnered Stanley Matthews. A 3–1 win helped ensure that Wilf retained his place for the next two games, also both against Scotland, in October 1941 and January 1942, when Denis Compton was also among the England players. At the same time he was appearing in familiar colours back at base – the green and white of the Green Howards matching that of St Peter's. Playing alongside him were some equally familiar faces: Tom Blenkinsopp of Sunderland, and Jimmy McCabe, another of Boro's South Bank contingent, as well as three league players from lesser sides. Also playing was Sgt Tom Griffiths, by then husband of Ivy.

Tom Griffiths had joined the Army in 1932 and rose through the ranks to earn his three stripes just before the war. By the summer of 1939 his fixed seven-year stint was coming to an end. He was told he would soon be heading to the service's vocational centre in Jarrow, Tyne and Wear, for advice and training to ease his exit from the Army. But when the day came and he went to sign off, he was told in no uncertain terms that he was going nowhere.

'There was this Scottish Major and he said, "You better sign on again, I think."' Tom, eighty-two, says, 'I just laughed, but he didn't. So I signed on for more. I could have gone home I suppose but the red caps would have come and got me.'

A little over a year later staying on might have seemed worth it. He wed Ivy not long after her Frank Bruno effort. He also ended up sitting on a bench not only with two proud officers and in front of some gleaming silverware, but sharing it with Wilf Mannion and the other league stars, each of them with XIX on their breasts instead of any club badge. The 19th unit of the first battalion the Green Howards lost only one game in the season of inter-service matches, bagging three trophies in the process. It was the most silverware Wilf ever got his hands on.

Within weeks of playing against Scotland in January 1942 he had also made his last appearance in Britain for four-and-a-half years. The lad born and raised in South Bank was to make his furthest excursion overseas – to South Africa and then on. It would be a voyage as perilous as it was long, and its conclusion – Wilf's salvation through football – the only remotely predictable aspect of it.

It began routinely enough. He may have missed out on the pre-war England tour to the Cape, but in spring 1942 there was no one from Middlesbrough watching over him, telling him he couldn't make the same journey; and no one ordering that he had complete rest from a ball when it was the one thing he never wanted a break from.

Even so, he got one for two-and-a-half months aboard the troop ship *Sumaria* as another 3000 tommies joined him for a round-the-world cruise courtesy of His Majesty's Government. The itinerary took in Bombay, Calcutta, Cape Town and Freetown, in Sierra Leone, zig-zagging all the way to avoid U-boats. Fellow traveller Chris Blenkey, then nineteen, now seventy-seven, says: 'They called us Thomas Cook tours because of all the travelling we did. We went to Persia, Iran and on to Rome afterwards – and we didn't even know where we were going most of the time.'

Back on Teesside, Captain Jack was doing his bit for the war, keeping tabs on Wilf's wanderings and reporting them back to concerned Boro fans. One of his worldwide network of informants sent in a clipping from the *Rand Daily Mail*:

One of Britain's greatest present-day soccer forwards in the person of Wilfred Mannion, Middlesbrough and England inside-right, is in Cape Town. He turned out for the Peninsular Club at Hartleyvale in the first-division competition ... A clever dribbler with a genius for making openings rather than a goalscorer, Mannion was largely responsible for the Middlesbrough centre-forward Micky Fenton, who toured South Africa with the FA team in 1938, topping the English first-division goalscorers list in 1939. Though short of practice, Mannion revealed his class. He is a very fast dribbler with brilliant ball control and footwork but the outstanding feature of his play is his immaculate passing of the ball and unerring eye for a gap in the opposing defence.

The Captain's report prompted another correspondent with connections in South Africa to send in another tribute. The piece, 'The World Goes By' by Alan Nash, captured something of Wilf the man, rather than just the footballer:

War has allowed South Africa to obtain a glimpse of many outstanding British sportsmen who otherwise would probably never have visited the Union. In Cape Town, local soccer followers have been privileged to see a few top-notch British professionals in action at Hartleyvale, men whose value in transfer fees is assessed in thousands of pounds. At Hartleyvale last Saturday, for instance, we had the pleasure of watching twenty-three-year-old Wilfred Mannion, of Middlesbrough, who is regarded as the best inside-right in England and has been capped in four international matches against Scotland. Those fans who drifted over to the B ground to watch Mannion were delighted by the brilliant footwork and distribution of the fair-haired, diminutive English international, whose inspiration was largely responsible for Peninsula scoring their first win of the season against Maitland. Private Mannion, to whom I was introduced by a few Tommies, is remarkably modest as professionals go. Crack soccer pros are popularly supposed to be hard-bitten [types] after the limelight. Not so Wilf Mannion. His keenness and modesty are shown by the fact he turned out for Tamboers Kloof, a second division team, last Saturday and it was only when Kloof's game was scratched that he decided to turn out for a first division team, Peninsula.

Nash also noted £8000 wouldn't buy Private Mannion from Middlesbrough. Perhaps it would be nearer the £14,000 offered for his 'pal' Scottish international and fellow soldier Tommy Walker, with whom he was pictured in the paper; or even more. In the coming months, however, transfers, team-talks or anything else to do with football would be the last thing on Wilf's mind.

· FOUR ·
A much-needed mentor

The troops were gathered in a country lane, the calm of the early morning sky above contrasting with the sounds of battle filling the air. The push into Italy was underway. Men of the Green Howards had moved from Persia and Damascus to help take Sicily. After a year in the regiment's own words 'wandering the Middle East in search of a war', the First Battalion had found one and fought its way from the island on to mainland Italy.

Awaiting their orders for the next drive, the soldiers spotted a runner coming back from the front. There was whispering and a few nudges, not only because it was time to move off but because the messenger was Wilf. A special correspondent in the *Yorkshire Post* reported:

> A blond, sunburned runner came up the road. 'That's Wilf Mannion, the England and Middlesbrough footballer,' someone said in a reverent whisper. Mannion had come back with orders for the next company of infantry to move forward. The company set off down the road.

Wilf had arrived in Italy in July 1943 when the Howards were among thousands of troops transported from Egypt via the Suez canal to fight Mussolini's men. Nor was he the only famous sportsman there; Lieutenant Norman Yardley, the Yorkshire and England cricketer, was also on hand, while the commander of B company was a Captain Verity, better known as another White Rose and England cricketer, Hedley Verity, a veteran of the Bodyline Ashes series. On the day Wilf made his debut for Middlesbrough, Verity was in Australia playing in another Ashes series. In Italy, Wilf was the runner in the cricketer's company.

Verity was an officer and a gentleman, but a cricketer and a gentleman first. His path into the Army began when he approached the Howards' Lieutenant Colonel Arnold Shaw in the pre-war pavilion at Headingley to ask about enlisting. Unable to join the Territorial Army because of cricketing commitments, he instead read the volumes of military books Shaw gave him. When war broke out, Shaw recruited him and he was given a commission – and later the new ball in the cricket matches which were staged wherever the Howards set up camp. For Shaw saw to it that a portable cricket pitch was carried everywhere, as well as concrete mix to flatten the area around a wicket, so that any piece of flat ground that could be found, from desert to jungle clearings, was turned into a cricket strip.

On the eve of the invasion of Sicily it was no different, with Verity taking 6 for 37 – not as good as his 7 for 9 in six overs in his last peacetime game for Yorkshire, figures which meant he finished the season heading the averages; nor some of his performances ten years earlier, which also resulted in him topping the averages in his first county season. But they would have to serve as a suitable memorial to his talent: Hedley Verity was one of many who were to lose their lives in the campaign in Italy.

In the early hours of 10 July, the battalion landed on the eastern side of Sicily, in sight of Mount Etna. It advanced fifty miles inland in ten days, to the outskirts of the town of Catania, where it met modest Italian and stronger German resistance. The enemy held the high ground and were well dug in, with machine-gun posts built into the rising railway embankment every twenty yards and crack troops from the Hermann Göring Division in place.

The Allied plan was for an artillery barrage to clear the way for the foot soldiers to pierce the German defences, but crucially – and fatally – there was not time for any proper ground reconnaissance before the night attack. At 12.45 a.m. the big guns started to pound the German lines and the British troops moved up under the cover, Verity's B company backing A on the right flank. Progress was good until a couple of hundred yards from the railway line, when unexpected deep ditches held up the troops – but not the artillery bombardment, which continued moving forward. The result was that when the infantry eventually advanced, their cover was well ahead of them; the Germans had re-emerged from their shelters, were manning their machine guns again and mowing down the Howards.

In the confusion B company outflanked A, became the leading company and endured the brunt of the enemy fire. To make matters worse, German mortar fire had set nearby cornfields on fire and the British were silhouetted, sitting ducks. At about 4 a.m. Verity was hit in the chest by machine-gun fire. His batman, Private Tom Rennoldson, used field dressings to try to stem the flow of blood. Then he saw Wilf just yards away.

'Get back to company headquarters for the stretcher bearers,' he shouted. 'The Captain is badly hurt.' But the group were too isolated for help to reach them quickly.

Rennoldson later told the *Yorkshire Evening Press*: 'Some of our fellows smothered the fire in the corn and there we stayed. When the Captain asked for water I raised him to give him it, and each time the Germans saw the movement, they let us have it. Worst of all that night was their mortar fire.'

His efforts were in vain. Before the medics or reinforcements could get to the front, dawn came and with it a Nazi advance. Rennoldson was ordered to leave Verity at the scene but within fifteen minutes convinced an English-speaking German officer to help him retrieve the Captain – on an ammunitions carrier padded with corn sheaves. He stayed with Verity while he underwent emergency surgery, but was moved away with the other uninjured prisoners of war. He never saw Verity again.

He used to joke with the cricketer: 'I can't understand how anyone who bowls as slow as you can get anyone out.' Verity would laugh as he replied: 'Some day I'll show you,' but he never had the chance. He never recovered from his injuries and died behind German lines as a PoW. The news reached England four years to the day since he last played for Yorkshire.

Such deaths were not the only losses endured by the men of the Howards. Arms and legs were blown off and shrapnel wounds were common. Then there were the mental scars. Like many old soldiers, Wilf remembers little of those years, perhaps by choice.

'I remember we lost half the company that day,' he recalled over forty years later, on one of the rare occasions he spoke of the war. 'We were pinned down all day by the enemy. Hedley was caught in the crossfire and hit in the chest. He was a wonderful man and I was his company runner for a number of years. We served together all over the place.'

Today Wilf remembers nothing of the further battles through Sicily; nor of the immediate invasion of mainland Italy which followed, the trying conditions, with food shuttled to the front via mule and arriving cold, hours after it was prepared; nor the bloody battles around Anzio, as the push for Rome began in scenes reminiscent of the trench warfare of World War I. Such were the losses, in the minefields and from repeated attack and German counterattack, that the battalion was eventually withdrawn so it could be reorganized and reinforced. Two officers and seventy-eight men were killed in one day's abortive attack. Four officers and seventy-one men were injured.

When Rome fell, the Thomas Cook troops were told they would be setting sail once more. They left from Naples and headed for Alexandria, via Malta, then on to Cairo, this time for some much-needed rest –

especially in Wilf's case. For perhaps the real reason he remembers little of the war in Italy is that he was in no fit state to.

When he arrived in the Middle East, Wilf was in an appalling condition, exhausted and almost out on his feet, a shadow of the easy-going lad of 1939. Even so, one man recognized him immediately. Bertie Mee, later to manage Arsenal to the double, had been a Derby County reserve before the war. Now seventy-eight, he says: 'I'd never played against Wilf but I'd watched him play on a number of occasions. I'd seen him playing against Derby along with Micky Fenton and Dave Cumming in 1938–39 and I was a great admirer of his.'

When war came, Mee had joined the medical corps and was posted to a hospital where he trained and guested for Southampton at the weekends. By 1944 he was in charge of physiotherapy at a convalescence camp in Palestine, doing much the same work as Shep was doing back in England.

'They came to us from all over the Middle East for two things: treatment for specific injuries, but also general rehabilitation for people who were absolutely done. There were between 1000 and 2000 men, some of them in a very bad state. Others were just resting before heading back to the fronts.' Physio and fitness were prime ingredients of the regime as well as rest and recuperation. Wilf needed all four – and more.

'He'd had such a rough time that medically he was downgraded, withdrawn from active service and sent to our convalescence depot,' Bertie says. 'He had gone from an A1 to a B2 – the lowest grade still considered rehabilitable. But when you're in the line and someone gets killed next to you, I can understand you losing it.'

Wilf was suffering from jaundice, then malaria struck and he was found collapsed under a palm tree. He recovered, only to suffer ten relapses. Even before the illnesses, he appeared to have lost all interest in football. But Mee, who was in charge of arranging games throughout Palestine, was determined to do something to bring the sparkle back to the Golden Boy. He drew up an exercise programme and also kept a much-needed eye on him. Wilf remained a hero to many of the troops at the camp, and there were plenty who were quite prepared to take him out, buy him a drink and generally show him a good time. Bertie took on the father figure role which Joe McCullagh had first shouldered twenty years earlier.

'I took him out training and made him work. He was a lovely lad, but easily led, and a great player,' he says. 'I just wanted him doing something to get him back again. We built him up and got him playing football with the depot team. There was basketball, cricket and hockey too – anything to get him fit. I used to take him out riding as well, in the early morning at 7 a.m. with a fellow called Harry Blackshaw [a jockey who had ridden for the King before the war]. I wouldn't tolerate any excuses of any kind. I built him up and he improved a good deal. The mere fact that he played any football ever again gave me all the satisfaction I wanted.'

Slowly, Wilf's health was restored, his strength renewed and his stamina rebuilt. His skill was simply dusted down. There were hiccups as his status still meant he was treated to nights out. Mee intervened.

'Inevitably he was a hero and people led him astray, but I held enough sway to have them posted elsewhere. Basically I got him taken on to the staff of the depot and then got him taken on by the Military Police. It meant I could use him as a footballer and, more importantly, keep an eye on him.'

When in one game Wilf went past one defender, glided past a second and then nutmegged goalkeeper Ted Sagar, an England international and Everton's number one for more than a decade before the war, Mee knew his protégé was back to his best. He went on to play for the Army and mixed services teams, in particular one called the Corinthians who also featured former professionals from Liverpool, Sheffield Wednesday and Spurs. They ensured Corinthians were one of the better sides in the area, although not the best in the local league. That honour went to a team which featured no former pros and played under the name Middlesbrough.

Back on Teesside, Captain Jack renewed his reports of sightings of the wandering star, courtesy of correspondence from servicemen to their families. A Flying Officer Alan Oates wrote to tell his father that Wilf scored two and set up another two in an Army v RAF fixture in Palestine. He added: 'The name was on everyone's lips and the general opinion was that he will "walk" into the England team.' A Corporal William Dermont wrote to his parents that he had seen Wilf play in a match between Corinthians and a team called the Spearheads at Maccabi Stadium, Tel Aviv, Palestine, in front of 8000 fans:

I have just had a royal day watching Wilf Mannion play. I've boosted him up to the lads here about him being the best inside-forward playing football. So the other day I was put to the test – or at least Wilf was. And, oh boy, he came through with flying colours, being the best player on the field. Well, all the lads agreed that he was in a class by himself. He was not just a schemer – he scored a beautiful goal.

The Captain's own contacts also sent in reports. A Sergeant Eddie Cullnean sent an airgraph to say:

> I have just had a real red letter day for I had the pleasure of seeing two Borough players figure in a match – none other than Wilf Mannion and McCabe. Mannion was bang on form. His football was great and he delighted the crowd. Wilf also scored a wonderful goal after eluding at least five opponents. McCabe had a nice steady game and pleased the crowd with his grand, clean kicking. I had a short talk with both the players. They seemed to be happy enough but, like me, will be more than pleased when we return to the Borough.

An anonymous former member of Redcar Rugby Club sent in a cutting from Howard Cobbin in the *Egyptian Mail*, who wrote:

> I might mention that I have received letters from Palestine referring to the brilliant play of Wilf Mannion, the Middlesbrough inside-right. One of them is from Lt. H. G. Lowther, chairman of the Football Sub-committee of the Palestine and Transjordan Army Sports Boards and he says: 'Mannion's ball control is uncanny even on sandy grounds and his passes, placed to an inch, slit the defences wide open time after time. There has recently been much discussion regarding the composition of future England teams. Never once has Mannion's name been mentioned in this connection and it would seem that this player, who was at one time one of the most discussed forwards in England football, has been allowed to slip into obscurity. Critics in this part of the world are all of the opinion that Mannion will walk into the England team on his return home. It will certainly take an exceptionally good one to keep him out.'

Another correspondent impressed by the form of the reborn Golden Boy was John Blair, later of the *Glasgow Evening News* but then writing for an Army newspaper. He too predicted international honours come peace-time:

> There is a Middlesbrough player, Wilf Mannion, out here playing on occasion for services sides, who will startle England and the world when he comes back to professional football after the war. He is the greatest international player I've ever seen; mark my words well.

Another Tommy, or more accurately Tom, who needed no telling of Wilf's form was a tank driver/mechanic from Preston. Tom Finney had come a long way from his home town to Tel Aviv and Jerusalem, from overcast Lancashire autumn days to blazing skies above the desert and from the grass of North End's Deepdale to the dirt pitches of Palestine.

Finney, then twenty-two, had been all over since he joined up and left behind a double life as part-time footballer, part-time plumber. He signed for Preston as a seventeen year old in January 1940 and became a regular in the regional leagues, although he had to wait until after the war for his proper league debut. He visited Wembley just after turning eighteen in the wartime version of the Cup when the winners of the Northern League played their southern counterparts, Arsenal. Finney, barely known in Lancashire, let alone London, played against England internationals such as Eddie Hapgood, Cliff Bastin and the Compton brothers, and helped his side win the replay 2–1.

In 1942 he signed up. Now seventy-five, Tom says: 'I did six months training in England. I happened to be in the Royal Armed Corps, which was the tanks. I went down for my training – you didn't get any option what you wanted to go in. It was just a matter of "You're here and we'll decide what you're going to do". I did about three months at Tidworth, then got moved to Catterick to do my final training, driving and whatever. I joined in April and soon I was on the boats to go abroad. We didn't know where we were going of course. We knew it was somewhere hot because we had the topees and all the gear for a hot country and landed up just outside Cairo. Just near the pyramids. We were under canvas there for three or four months.'

He kept up his football too, eventually winning a place with the most famous of the service sides, the Wanderers. It was the England team of service football, made up of the best the forces had in the Middle East. The Wanderers toured the region playing against other service teams as well as local sides, and to be picked for it was an honour.

'Bertie Mee played for it,' Tom says, 'Micky Fenton, Harry Clifton and Don Kelly from Newcastle, a lad called Telfer from Scotland; Falkirk I think he was with. It was virtually a professional side which was going around entertaining the troops. You went away for two or three months or something like that. You were reckoned to be doing a good job of work like the entertainers from Ensa. We were playing in front of quite big crowds, the games were that popular. There were regiments coming in from all over the show.'

When the Wanderers toured Palestine and Syria, Finney enjoyed his first meeting with Wilf, a player he later described as 'a ballerina in tiny boots, he glided across even the muckiest of pitches, hands spread out at right angles to his body, leaving would-be tacklers with empty space and anguished expressions'. The clash between Wilf's Corinthians and Finney's Wanderers was a tight one, settled by a single goal. Wilf set up his side's first in the 2–1 win, but any disappointment the Preston plumber may have felt would have been quashed if he knew the glory which lay ahead for the Mannion–Finney partnership.

The war games kept the troops happy, and the players too. It meant they were allowed to go off on tours and away from duties, although obviously not at critical times.

'It took us away from the routine duties to a life of relative luxury,' says Bertie Mee, 'and gave the troops something to enjoy as well. Whilst the players were with the unit they were not treated any differently at all. But when they went on a trip, life was slightly different. It was only when there was a match on that you were treated a little bit special. On a day-to-day basis you had your duties and that was that.'

By Christmas 1945, Mee was even more cheery, partly because of the season but mostly because on Boxing Day he was to be demobbed. A back injury meant his football playing career back in England was over, not that he thinks it was going anywhere.

'I couldn't compare myself to Tom Finney, Micky Fenton or Wilf. I made up the numbers, if you like. I gave that up and concentrated on coaching.' Much to the eventual pleasure of Gunners fans.

Wilf stayed on in the Middle East for a few more months. When he finally pulled on the red of Middlesbrough again, he played his way towards England caps and the greatest football of his life; and played as if he knew how close he'd come to losing his life, with every game from now on a bonus to be exploited to the full.

In ones and twos they returned. Unfamiliar names like Heweston and Harnby made way for more recognized ones such as Cumming and Shepherdson. By the beginning of the season – the first since the end of the war – other pre-conflict favourites were back at Boro too. Full-backs Stuart and Laking were reunited, as were winger Cliff Chadwick and Micky Fenton in the forward line. But there was no Yorston, who had retired; no Forrest, who'd also hung up his boots; and no Baxter, who returned to mining in Scotland when the war broke out and stayed in his homeland to play for Hearts when it ended.

Then there were other more poignant absences such as wing-half 'Mick' Murphy, Wilf's former St Peter's sparring partner. He had continued to play for Boro during the early years of the war, including one occasion when he arrived at the train station with seconds to spare after missing his bus from Redcar and borrowed a passerby's bike to ride to

Middlesbrough. When he was posted overseas he kept in touch with Captain Jack, sending several letters to him including 'one, coming from Italy, [in which] he mentioned, rather naively, that he understood Wilf Mannion was not far away – "just a hill or two" beyond where he was situated'. Months after looking for a friend to remind him of home, he died a long way away from it, in the Middle East.

George Camsell was still around, on the coaching staff now, though, and working for a new manager. Quietly spoken Wilf Gillow, who had remained Boro boss on a part-time basis during the war, died in 1944 when complications set in after an operation. He was replaced by a man with football in his veins. David Jack's father Bob played for Bolton Wanderers and later became manager of Plymouth Argyle, where Jack junior began his playing career. In 1920 he was transferred to his father's other old club and wrote himself into the history books in 1923 when he scored the first-ever Cup final goal at Wembley. In fact, he scored both Bolton's goals in a 2–0 win over West Ham, but his thunder was still stolen. This was the famous White Horse Cup final where a huge crowd of more than 200,000 spilled on to the pitch and had to be inched back to the touchline by police, including one officer on a white horse.

Jack's playing career took him back to Wembley in 1926 with Bolton, before a move to Arsenal for a record fee of £10,340 in 1928. Further Cup finals in 1930 and 1932 and three league championship medals meant there was no disputing his achievements as a player. As a manager, however, he was more of an unknown quantity. He spent six years at Southend before the war, but was in charge of Sunderland's greyhound stadium when he was called to Ayresome Park.

To make his opening spell even more fraught, the player everyone was expecting so much of on his return was still absent in Palestine where he stayed until March 1946, more than four years since he last played for his home-town team. Much had changed in that time, from global events to the parochial comings and goings at Ayresome. Wilf had changed too. His happy-go-lucky attitude had been dented by what he had seen and done in Europe and the Middle East. Before the war he had been a footballer, nothing more and nothing less. After it he was also a war veteran with a new outlook on life and a revised opinion of his own position in it.

He had spent years fighting for his country's future, yet his own was uncertain. He knew how much his soccer skills meant to supporters, but he knew they were of little use to him in the long-term; he couldn't play forever, however much he wanted to. The war gave him a taste of life without football, the type of life which lay ahead when his playing days were over. With no skills or trade, he had nothing to mark him out for anything but labouring or some other unskilled job. What's more, he began to realize there was not much he could do about it as long as he stayed in football. Middlesbrough and Ayresome Park may have been little more than distant memories for much of the war, but as soon as he came back to Britain there was only one team for which he could play. Middlesbrough had not paid him a retainer but they had held on to his registration and so had the first and only claim on him. Even if he had refused to re-sign for Boro, he would not have been able to play for anyone else as the club held his 'licence to play'. Against this soccer serfdom, even the Army seemed to be a haven of freedom.

His return, when it finally came, could not have come sooner for Boro. As Wilf trained to regain full fitness, Liverpool visited Ayresome and ran out 5–2 winners. It was that unexpected result which prompted his return in the number eight, inside-right's, shirt for the next game, against Bury. Wilf didn't score in the 3–0 win but he was the catalyst for the goals. Captain Jack declared himself pleased with the win and

> . . . some highly satisfactory features. Outstanding of these was the display by Wilf Mannion, back in the team again after over four years service in the Middle East. His forward line generalship, for which we have so often yearned was quickly in evidence, coupled with cool, adroit play and picture passes that played a significant part in the side's superiority.

Best of all, Wilf told the Captain after the match that better was to come. He would more than live up to the promise.

Meanwhile, as Bury were dispatched, George Hardwick, the new leader of the pack at Ayresome was elsewhere. The dashing figure, looking not unlike Clark Gable, had led the welcome committee when Wilf first reported back for training. Hardwick had gained a moustache, which completed his film-star looks, when he joined the RAF and was told that no one would obey his orders unless he looked like an officer. Now his commands were on a different stage – an international football pitch. While Boro beat Bury, Hardwick was man-of-the-match in an England trial at Wembley. Displaying the best form of his career, he was acclaimed as the best left-back in the country.

Two Teesside boys would soon be in the England team; the old gang were all back at Ayresome. When Wilf returned, gorgeous George had given him a firm handshake to say hello as the smiling faces of Shep, Micky Fenton and Jimmy McCabe, his former Green Howards colleague, looked on. It seemed as if everything was dandy but, as in every other walk of life, it would never be the same as it was before the war.

It appeared that David Jack's FA Cup pedigree was rubbing off on his new charges. With barely fifteen minutes to go, Boro were heading for a semi-final place for the first time. Second division Burnley were 1–0 down and on the ropes. The 53,025 crowd was convinced they were watching Boro on their way to a debut appearance in the final four. In 1947, the success which had eluded the pre-war teams appeared to be looming in the first proper post-war FA Cup. The 5000 fans, mostly from Burnley, locked out when the gates were shut before kick-off were probably glad to be absent when a Geoff Walker goal sparked noisy home celebrations just before half-time and even happier when a second roar engulfed Ayresome Park just after the break.

Micky Fenton had turned and begun to make his way back to the halfway line as his team-mates congratulated him on the goal which gave Boro a 2–0 lead. His thirty-yard free-kick had rifled into the net. The referee followed the jubilant stars after pointing the way back to the centre circle. Only then did the Burnley players notice the linesman and point out his raised flag to the referee. It had gone up as Walker made a dummy run over the ball and winger Johnny Spuhler moved forward. A brief discussion between the officials followed and the goal was disallowed. Despite Boro protests, Spuhler was given offside, even though he was standing nearer the touchline than the goal and the ball had flown into the net straight from Fenton's boot.

Within a couple of minutes Burnley were level. From the free-kick they went to the other end for practically their first attack of the second half, and scored. Nine minutes later the final whistle went. All around the ground Boro fans could not believe what had happened; neither could the players. 'When I scored with the free-kick, Spuhler wasn't offside at all,' Micky Fenton says. 'He couldn't have been.'

For the replay three days later, hopes were still high. After all, Jack's record in the Cup was second to none and the previous season, 1945–46 – when each tie was played over two legs up to and including the quarter-final – he took the team a good way down the road to Wembley. In round three Leeds had been dispatched 11–6 on aggregate; a replay in round four ended in a 1–0 win over Blackpool. It had taken Jack's old club Bolton to stop Boro's Cup run at round five with a 2–1 aggregate victory. Bolton went on to the infamous semi-final clash with Stoke City at which thirty-three people died when a gate was opened, allowing too many people into part of the ground.

But that Boro Cup run was before Wilf returned and the best possible first team was available. Moreover, Boro were used to progressing at the second bite of the cherry. Before Burnley, both Queens Park Rangers and Nottingham Forest were beaten in replays. An almost unheard of Mannion own goal gave Forest a draw in round five, but Wilf made up for his error by scoring a hat-trick in the replay. Captain Jack, for one, was confident before the return trip to Turf Moor:

> Personally I still have the confidence in the visiting side's ability to rise to the occasion – and get through. The lessons of Saturday's game will have been absorbed and the strengths and weaknesses of the Burnley side duly noted.

It was misplaced optimism. The real lesson which should have been learned was nothing to do with the opponents but the referee. This time he gave a goal which should have been disallowed – for Burnley, the winner, in extra time. Boro were furious. Captain Jack reported:

> The Borough's cherished hopes of reaching the FA Cup semi-final stage were shattered at Turf Moor by a Burnley goal that was, in the solid opinion of the visiting players, a gross injustice to them.

The whole team, most unusually in those days, engulfed referee Ellis to protest against another poor decision. Again he consulted with a linesman, but this time he was unswayed. The goal had come in the first minute of extra time after the ninety minutes ended in a goalless stalemate on an ice rink of a pitch. It sprang from full-back Dickie Robinson being harshly adjudged to have fouled Burnley's left-winger Peter Kippax just outside the area. Kippax took the free-kick himself but got no height on the cross. The danger appeared to be gone when Dave Cumming bravely came for the ball at ground level. But as he collected it, he got a kick in the face and dropped the ball. In the goalline scramble which followed Harrison, practically sitting on Cumming, squared the ball to Morris, courtesy of a hand not a foot, who fired past Hardwick on the line. Boro smiles at the cheek of the effort turned to fury when the players realized the goal was going to stand. The jokes with the Burnley players became protests to Mr Ellis, but to no avail.

Fenton came close to equalizing with just a couple of minutes to go, but it was not to be – not that year, nor the next, nor any of the following twenty-two, in which Boro never managed to get as far in the Cup again. In the dressing-room after the defeat, Cumming said: 'A Burnley forward's boot seemed to come right over the ball – and that was all I knew for minutes.'

'The Burnley player just flicked it across the goal with his hand,' Micky says now. 'Everyone saw it except the referee who let the goal stand.

David Jack said afterwards he didn't wish the referee any harm, but he hoped he would break his leg.'

'I still remember the name of that referee now,' Wilf adds. 'An Irish fella, he was. He was terrible. They punched the ball in the back of the net. Everyone in the ground saw it. We were beat through this ruddy referee.'

Until 1997, the controversial defeat in extra time in 1947 was the nearest Boro came to an FA Cup semi-final. But for the referee they would have had a chance of a place in the final, which Burnley achieved. Perhaps they would even have contributed to a better game than the dreary one fought out between the red rose side and Charlton, who won 1–0 in extra time.

Instead Boro won just one of their remaining thirteen league games. The early promise of wins at Aston Villa, Liverpool and Wolves, not to mention a 5–0 victory at Blackpool, faded to nothing. Once again it was a case of so near but so far.

Soon after, Shep left Boro although not for long. He joined Southend United, but within months suffered a Gazza-style knee injury which ended his career. He got in touch with Boro trainer Charlie Cole and offered his assistance, putting into practice at the club the health and fitness expertise he'd learned during the war. Eventually, this led him to link up with another pioneering disciple of modern methods, England's first manager Walter Winterbottom.

From assistant trainer at Boro, Shep became part of the England set-up in a decade. He helped prepare teams for the World Cup finals of 1958 in Sweden, and 1962 in Chile. When Winterbottom was replaced by Alf Ramsey, Shep feared he would be axed too, but the new boss saw what the trainer offered – perhaps most of all an affable nature at odds with Ramsey's dour reputation. Shep's light touch and easy humour relaxed the whole camp.

At the same time he remained at Boro. The England job was only part-time, and he was settled in his home town.

'There were offers to manage clubs, big clubs, but I never wanted to leave Middlesbrough,' Shep said. 'I spent most of my life here, my family were settled here and I was happy. I don't look back and regret it.'

He was an integral part of Boro for more than fifty years. He was there for the highs – gearing up to win the league title pre-war and topping division one in the seventies – but also for what was almost the end, when the receivers padlocked the gates to Ayresome in 1986 and Middlesbrough FC went into receivership. He started out as a lad with puppy fat signed as a trainee, and ended up being caretaker manager four times and finally chief executive.

Plenty of happy, and not so happy, days were in store when he returned to Ayresome from Southend, with the best and worst centred on his old adversary from the North Riding Cup more than ten years before. But that was to come. As Shep's career was taking a new direction, Wilf's was also moving on, taking his talents to a wider stage and still earning the bouquets with cultured ease.

· FIVE ·

'The best inside-forward game seen for many a long day'

Unsurprisingly, given that the first full international for seven years was about to be staged, the atmosphere at Windsor Park, Belfast, was overpowering. Fans, starved of such fixtures for so long, were desperate to see the match between Northern Ireland and England. Some were too young to have ever seen a proper international, while even those who had were excited by the prospect of sport allowing them to escape the post-war austerity for an afternoon.

When the England team arrived at the ground they found it in a state of chaos. Police, posted at each turnstile to try to ease the expected bumper crowd through, were being overwhelmed. Telephones had been installed inside and outside the ground to help the police control the flow of people, but with only thirty officers on duty, it was proving tricky.

The game, in September 1946, had been made all-ticket – one of the first to be so – but as 58,000 struggled to get in, the ground was just too small. The crowd began to spill over from the sideline terraces on to the cinder track circling the pitch. Boys who had been at the front of the terraces but now found their views blocked, raced over the pitch to get a place behind the goals. Before anyone could say White Horse Cup final, the chances of the showpiece fixture kicking off at all, let alone on time, were being smothered by a mass of over-excited fans.

Scottish referee Willie Webb visited the dressing-rooms and ordered the players to stay where they were. In the England dressing-room there were nine players about to make their full debut; only Raich Carter and Lawton had won caps before the war. Some of those pulling on the white shirts – with the three lions on them again after an absence of seven years – may have been nervous, disturbed by the commotion outside, but not Wilf. For him, selected at inside-left, it was just another game; in fact one which should be easier than most.

'This is the easy weekend,' he said to one of his team-mates. 'We're with the good players.'

Among those good players were right-winger Tom Finney, assured Stoke City centre-half Neil Franklin, George Hardwick, captain on his debut, Frank Swift and an unassuming right-half from Wolves by the name of Billy Wright. The next time Wright played for England in Northern Ireland he became the youngest ever captain of his country and went on to notch up another eighty-nine appearances as skipper.

Wright had more reason than most of his team to cherish pulling on an England shirt. Eight years earlier, as a fourteen year old on the ground-staff at Molineux, his career almost came to a premature end. He was cleaning the stands and preparing the kit for the first team one day when he was summoned to see the manager, Major Buckley.

'I'm afraid you haven't grown up enough, sonny, to become a professional footballer,' Wright was told. 'So I'm sending you home.'

The youngster cried his eyes out as he stripped off his club issue kit and got ready to go back to his home town of Ironbridge, probably to join his father working in an iron foundry. Then he was called back to the office and told that the Major, known for his eccentricities, had changed his mind. Wright won a reprieve because he was a 'nice lad'.

In Belfast his pale face, with dark, deep-set eyes, topped by unruly, high-rise blond hair, could well flush with pride. Any tension Wright or any of the other newcomers felt when the team first gathered, with its attendant press pack, at the Slieve Donard Hotel overlooking both the Irish sea and the Mourne mountains, was quickly dispelled by the antics of Lawton and Swift. One day, as some of the players chatted in small groups on the lawn in front of the hotel and manager Walter Winterbottom mixed with the reporters, raised voices shattered the tranquillity. Everyone turned to face the source of the commotion and there, in full view of Fleet Street's finest, Swift, 6ft 2in and nearly 14 stone, and Lawton, just an inch shorter and a little lighter too, were squaring up. A punch was thrown and the pair fell to the ground locked in combat. They rolled and grappled as Winterbottom and his other players looked on mortified. Just as they prepared to step in, the noise from the brawling pair stopped them in their tracks. Swift and Lawton were giggling, then roaring with laughter as they realized their mock feud had duped the boss and many others. It became a regular routine during their England trips together, but its debut provoked more than a few haughty sniffs among the press. How on earth would they have the energy to play properly? And what if they'd been injured?

With Willie Webb's return from clearing the pitch, they were about to get the chance to make the reporters eat their words. Webb had walked on to the pitch as an announcement was made that if it was not cleared in three minutes the game would be called off. He began walking around the perimeter of the pitch and, with a Dickie Bird-style mixture of authority and humour, edged the crowd back on to the terraces. The pre-match entertainment band accompanied him, physically and musically with a no-nonsense 'Abide With Me'. After a fifteen-minute delay, international football was ready to kick-off again.

Hardwick lost the toss, but it was the only English set-back of the day. Within two minutes Carter put the visitors 1–0 up. Wilf got a second from a Lawton cross; then, before half-time, his own second, following up a crashing Lawton drive which came back off the wood-work. Finney added a fourth after the break before Wilf completed his hat-trick. Northern Ireland pulled one back but then Lawton and left-winger Bobby Langton, of Blackburn Rovers, got one each. A second home goal with two minutes to go was nothing more than a very slim consolation in a 7–2 defeat.

For Wilf it was a dream return, his debut in a recognized international.

'We run 'em to death. I walked off the field with Peter Docherty and he says, "Wilf, it was a wonderful game to watch." Imagine – Peter Docherty saying that!'

The press couldn't decide on the best story – Mannion and his three goals, or Finney and his blistering debut which threw a big question mark over the international future of Stanley Matthews, missing from the game due to a late knee injury. Carter and Lawton, the old hands, also received plenty of praise.

The glory, however, was tempered by pretty much universal agreement that the opponents were awful. John Robertson, of the *Sunday Dispatch*, wrote: 'England were made to look superlative by the poverty of the Irish defence.' Henry Rose in the *Daily Express* added: 'As an international, it was a farce in two acts. Never before have I seen a national team so lacking in speed and skill as Ireland.' But Charles Buchan, the former Arsenal player credited with inventing the stopper defence and suggesting it to Herbert Chapman, gave praise where it was due in the *News Chronicle*. Under the headline: 'Mannion was the star at Belfast', he wrote:

Even allowing for the glaring weaknesses in the Irish side, England gave a remarkable display of skilled footwork, clever distribution and balanced team work. Mannion fitted in perfectly with Carter and Lawton and took his chances with the ease of a master.

Both Wilf and his colleagues had the chance for a reprise just two days later. The party moved south of the border for the first-ever game against the Republic of Ireland, and if Belfast had been a triumph for the flashing-blade attack, this was to be one of equal proportions for the defence. Swift and Franklin shared the man-of-the-match claims as they held their mostly amateur opponents – who included both Docherty and Gorman, of Brentford, from the game in Belfast – at bay. Wave after attacking wave was repelled.

The 32,000 crowd loudly egged their men on as, according to Buchan, they attacked England in 'rugby-like rushes'. Once the bar came to the visitors' aid. Then, with only nine minutes left, Langton, in midfield, collected a pass in his solar plexus. Before doubling up, he freed Wilf into space on the left wing. Wilf advanced and shot, only for the keeper to save. But the rebound fell to him and he hit it back into the box. Eventually Finney emerged from a goalmouth scramble to fire home. Billy Wright wrote that there was not a single cheer: 'One could have heard the proverbial pin drop.'

Back on Teesside, Thomas Mannion was a little more vocal. Wilf remembers the match was tough, but so was his dad's reaction to England beating his home country, with his own son a key part of the English team.

'What a ruddy battle the game was,' Wilf says. 'We got it harder from playing them than that team in Belfast. We just scraped home, but when I got back my father called me all the names under the sun, what with me making the goal for Finney to score. He was listening to it on the radio. I got the ball in the last few minutes and I carved one for Finney and he hit it home. That's when the old man blew his top. He says, "You were the bloody luckiest team in the world. They were all over you," – and he was right.'

Luck, maybe. But one of the first clichés every athlete learns is that you make your own luck; or, in this case, Walter Winterbottom – in his first game as England's first-ever manager – made his team's luck. His preparations were undoubtedly a factor in the victories. The more astute reporters realized his value. John Macadam, of the *News Chronicle*, wrote:

When you have finished handing bouquets to the classic England side, reach down to the bottom of the basket and grasp one for Walter Winterbottom, team manager, OC tactics, and one of the few intellectuals of the game of association football. And if there is another bunch of flowers there, hand it to the Football Association for having dragged the game out of the public bar. Not only have we a team manager, we have also a physiotherapist, Walter Max, and, between them, they have produced a soccer machine that moves as if it was on ball bearings. Winterbottom's approach to football is, to put it mildly, remarkable. There was a time when handling a football team was a matter of patrolling hotel lobbies with a gun so that the players should not go out after dark, and then wiping them over with a sponge. The day of the sponge is over.

He might use phrases like 'pliability of tactics' and 'variability of approach' and describe his job as moulding 'separate abilities into common understanding', but the prototype gaffer Winterbottom was doing well. Macadam continued:

He is primarily a believer in the team principle in the co-ordination of eleven brilliant individuals into a cohesive machine. Certainly his first effort – the Belfast match – justifies all his theories. The team bristles with individuality and yet remains a team. Lawton, the inveterate scorer, played a beautiful game and scored only one goal. No longer do we believe in one glory-getter standing out there in front to receive all the custom.

An England manager with the press on his side? And a team full of gifted individuals? Surely it couldn't last.

For a former teacher, Sir Walter, as he is now, has a low tolerance of the word blackboard. Mention it in connection with his England job and he gives a polite but firm rebuttal of a supposed slavish reverence for chalk-and-talk tactics sessions.

'I never used a blackboard to show the team how to play,' he says. 'That's a myth. I've heard a few people say it, but it's not true.'

To show up the higher workrate of players from other countries, yes; even to point out opponents' flaws, perhaps; but to show Carter, to name just one arch-sceptic of coaching, and Matthews how to play in a game? No.

'I used to try to gee them up, not scare them witless by telling them the opposition were going to be doing everything. Fill them with hope, not get them thinking, "Oh, we're in trouble today."'

But Sir Walter, now eighty-three, was the first man to try to instil some idea of tactics and organization into the game. Long overdue it may have been, but it was by no means universally popular. For example, Carter, who thought you could play or you couldn't and that was that, was fond of saying: 'Give me a good forward line and to hell with the defence.'

A view after the purist's heart perhaps – and even Kevin Keegan's – but not Winterbottom's. He realized English football would lose its place at the top of the world game unless it learnt from the continentals, with their preparations and calculations for victory. Many of the players, on the other hand, thought they, as internationals, were good enough to get on the park and know how to play. It was not arrogance, but the supreme self-belief of top players whose ability was such that no coach could have instilled it in them.

The players who tended to have more sympathy with Winterbottom's theories and practice were those who had come on through coaching; those whose less natural ability had been turned into international honours through hard work, whose caps were a testament to graft rather than God's gifts. Wilf certainly didn't fall into that category. He still laughs as he remembers a training session before the match against Northern Ireland a year later. Winterbottom had him, Wright and Matthews gathered on the touchline and was telling them how to take a throw-in.

'It was a bitterly cold day and there we were practising a flaming throw-in,' he remembers, 'having to do it the way he wanted. Stan was saying, "Flippin' this and floppin' that. This is stupid. It's absolutely mad." But we had to do it. It was never even thought of until then. You just played. But he [Winterbottom] wanted it to be done. He thought it was all going to be dead smooth, the way we were practising on the training pitch. But in a game it's all about the opposition and where they're going to be situated and what they're doing. That's why you need a footballing brain, to adapt to the situation. What a waste of time that practice was. We're still waiting to use it now!'

Sir Stanley, ever the diplomat, refuses to be drawn too much about the training sessions. But he also laughs out loud remembering the throw-in practice.

'Billy was going to throw the ball to me, I was going to go inside and Wilf would come through. That was the plan,' he says. 'We soon found out the simplest way was if he threw the ball to my feet and I gave it back and he could pass it, which was what we would have done anyway.'

Opposition from the players was the least of Winterbottom's worries, however. No matter how hard he tried, his efforts at modernizing the England set-up were held back by more than grudging players. The FA was as bad. For these were the glory days of 'paid amateurism' – players who were professionals but were expected to behave like gentlemen before all else, even winning, and certainly before financial considerations; managers who had to be called Mr so-and-so or Sir; and the football establishment who disguised their love of power and authority as a desire for order and playing by the rules.

There was no clearer example than the selection process and the logistics of international games. Winterbottom didn't pick the team, but merely took a note of his choices to the selection committee meeting. The chairman would start the proceedings with a call for 'Nominations for goalkeeper'. The committee members, all representing different clubs, would put forward their men – often literally their men, their club's stars. The only time they would be less keen would be if their club had a big match looming and they'd prefer to have the best players at home. In those circumstances the other selectors would realize the scam chairman Jones of Town was trying to pull to make sure his players were picked.

Winterbottom's chances of picking the team he wanted were nil. There would be compromises left, right and centre. Then there was the additional headache of doling out caps as honours. A long-serving professional with a distinguished club career coming to an end might be picked to recognize his contribution.

'In those days it was a selection committee which basically rewarded players who were good professionals,' Sir Walter says. 'It was a question of giving them the honour of playing for England, acknowledging their careers really. They were good players, obviously, who deserved recognition at international level, but not always when they got it. I remember when Leslie Compton, who had never won a cap, partly because of the war, was picked for one game as a mark of respect for him playing so long and so well, generally, for Arsenal. It wasn't on really, but that's the way it was – even though you're not going to build up a World Cup winning squad like that, are you?'

Regional alliances were formed, too – the North versus the South versus the Midlands. The chairmen only saw the players who appeared for or against their side. Only later did Winterbottom manage to convince them of the need to take in a few more matches to assess other players. He also managed to revise the system later, so at least he would nominate a side as the basis of the selection committee's deliberations.

One of the pitifully few mementoes Wilf has of his England career is a small piece of cream cardboard, folded into a small diary-sized booklet. Above where the words The Football Association are solemnly underlined, the name W. Mannion is handwritten in pencil. The front of the card contains all the other important details such as the words 'International match, England v France', and 'To be played at Arsenal Stadium, Highbury, London, N5, on Saturday, 3rd May, 1947'.

Every player received one of these cards before an England game to tell them what was and was not expected of them. They were told where the team's headquarters were and to make their own arrangements to get there in order to arrive at a certain time. Then came the heart of the matter: 'Fees and Expenses. All players will be allowed travelling expenses and professional players a fee of £20. Equipment. Shorts, stockings and numbered shirts will be provided by the Football Association. Players are requested to bring with them soap and towels, gym shoes or plimsolls, shinguards, athletic slips, spikes and football boots, which should be properly studded.'

For the France game, the Grand Hotel in Brighton was the base. On matchday the party left for London on the 10.25 a.m. train. A coach met them at Victoria station and took them to the Great Western Hotel, Paddington, for a forty-five-minute lunch, then on to Highbury at 1.15 p.m. After the match the players were invited as guests of the FA to a dinner at the Café Royal at 6.30 p.m. And: 'bedrooms have been booked at the Great Western Hotel for those players unable to return to their homes.'

The players were warned that none of the above information was to be given to the press. Furthermore they were 'forbidden ... to comment upon the match in press reports after the game. The FA regulations are well known to the players, viz, that the players selected to play in International and other representative matches under the jurisdiction of the Football Association must neither write nor allow to be written under their signature any press article relating to the match or the players taking part.'

Finally there was the typed signature of S. F. Rous, secretary of the FA. To be fair, Rous – who was another later knighted for his football work – was the key figure in dragging the FA into the modern world. He was the man who decided on the need for a soccer supremo and realized Winterbottom was the man for the job.

'Stanley Rous, as he was then,' Sir Walter recalls, 'was insistent on getting a level of education running right through the game, rather than stay as we were and make no improvements. He wanted a director of coaching and it was apparent that the director of coaching would have responsibility for managing all the England teams. I was looking after the full England side, the B team, the amateurs and later youth teams as well as FA XIs for representative games. All that happened pre-war was they took a trainer to games, basically to look after the kit. The captain used to gather the players together and decide on how to play, but there weren't really tactics. They would just go out and play as eleven individuals. You met up with the chaps, said hello and then got on with it, with the captain taking any decisions which might need to be taken on the field.'

But Rous's attempts at revolution were by no means thorough. For example, the first the players would know of their selection would still generally be via the press, or through fans who had read the papers. The late news column of the local evening paper became a budding international's first port of call on the day the selection committee met. So when Billy Wright won the first of his ninety caps as captain, it was a clippie on a bus who told him the good news. The small pieces of confirming cards would follow, accompanied by letters starting Mannion or Matthews, never Dear Wilf or Dear Mr Matthews.

Whatever progress was made was not enough, as Winterbottom knew. He could see foreign sides meeting up earlier than the day before a game, playing together for weeks on end and achieving success that way. Within seven years the gulf which had opened up was exposed by the Hungarians comprehensively beating England 6–3 at Wembley.

'The difference between us and the Hungarians,' Sir Walter says, 'was simple. Their team had been together for years. Each week they used to assemble for three days to practise as an international team and went to play against the top clubs as such and went out on tours together. Not only were the players learning from each other, they were picking up the instinctive teamwork. We just met a couple of days before each game. Basically we didn't meet really other than on the pitch.'

But the humblings, at home and abroad, by the Hungarians and others were still to come. For the moment the sublime skills available in the players Winterbottom could try to choose hid any shortcomings in tactics and preparations, and did so in the most dramatic and swashbuckling style imaginable. Jimmy Greaves later called them the greatest players of all time: Wilf Mannion, Tom Finney, Stanley Matthews, Tommy Lawton and others were about to show why.

First a succession crisis had to be resolved. Raich Carter had kept his place at inside-right from England's match in Northern Ireland, when he had scored. He notched goals in successive games against Holland (an 8–2 win) and Scotland later in the 1946–47 season. Each was a bonus for a player who thought his international career had come to an end once before: after a poor performance for a Combined Services side at the end of the war he had gathered his equally culpable team-mates together to sing 'Auld Lang Syne'. But now, as he listened to news of the team announced for a game being billed as the Match of the Century, Great Britain v the Rest of Europe in May 1947, it was about to reach its very final stages.

A week earlier, Carter had partnered Finney in a scrappy 3–0 win over a shirt-pulling French side, and scored again. But the selectors were known to favour recalling Matthews, and the general view was that Carter, one of the finest England players since his debut in 1934, did not always appreciate Matthews' one-man shows. As this match was a show match, albeit an enormously important one, such wizardry was unquestionably what the crowd would be looking for. More than 500,000 people had applied for tickets, expecting entertainment. Matthews was a guarantee of that; not that Carter wasn't, but some whispered that perhaps his best days were behind him.

The radio revealed that Swift was in goal, no surprise; but then that Hardwick was in, out of position at right-back.

'My heart thumped,' Carter recalled. 'That was one switched out of position. Was it possible they'd switched Wilf to let in Steel? It was.' Billy Steel, of Greenock Moreton, was the Scottish equivalent of the Golden Boy – and was about to secure a transfer to Derby for a then record fee of £15,500, partly thanks to his performance in this Great Britain team made up of players from all four home countries. Carter was not selected to play against Europe's élite, drawn from nine different countries and dubbed Babel United. Technically, the match was a friendly, a celebration to mark the return of the home nations to FIFA's folds. But, unlike some friendlies, its pulling power was not in question: of the 500,000 who applied for tickets, 134,000, some of whom had been queuing for thirty-six hours, eventually crammed into Hampden Park on matchday.

At stake in their eyes, and those of football fans from Stockholm to St Tropez, was nothing more or less than Britain's reputation as the leading power in football. As the *Daily Mirror* put it:

Eleven footballers face the greatest task players from these islands have ever been given. On their shoulders lies the responsibility of proving to the soccer world that the leaders of the game are still better than the pupils.

That one of the masters, Carter, had been expelled from the lesson caused outrage in some sections of the press. While they called for the decision to be reversed, the man himself was more conciliatory.

'To say I'm disappointed is putting it mildly,' Carter said at the time. 'My only hope is that Billy Steel and Wilf Mannion go to Hampden unaffected by all the controversy created by my omission. I envy them. Who wouldn't? But believe me, I bear no malice. May they both strike their best form and justify the confidence Britain's selectors have placed in them.'

He was not to be disappointed. The Golden Boy was about to come of age at international level and dispel any queries over his world-beating talent. Wilf knew he had something to prove.

'Even at home, even in South Bank, there were arguments about my selection,' he said later. 'A bad choice in such high company, lots of them said. So I swore there and then I would play the game of my life. We were to get £20 for playing. But I would have paid that and more besides just for the chance.'

The Boro management made sure he was in top shape with a regime of extra training. The only hiccup came as he packed his kitbag for Glasgow and one of his old boots, from a favourite pair, fell to pieces in his hand. With minutes to go before his train departed, Wilf just had to grab a replacement from trainer Charlie Cole's bootroom store.

When he arrived in Scotland, he found a country in the throes of football fever. In the small village of Aberfoyle he trained with his fellow stars on the village team's pitch. The teachers in the school over the road eventually had to admit defeat and recognize that the famous footballers were of more interest than whatever was written on the blackboard. Lessons were abandoned so the children could watch the team practice, with a lucky few even roped in to retrieve balls which Tommy Lawton was firing past Swift. Of course, it wasn't a case of Tommy not hitting the target. There were no nets, so the shots which beat the keeper were well on their way to the border before they came to a halt.

The Rest of Europe side promised to pose a tough challenge. Among their number was Parola, Italy's supremely skilful centre-half – a stopper, but one who could pass and dribble too – and striker Nordahl, one of three brothers who later in the year would be part of the Swedish team which lost only 4–2 to England at Highbury and the following year returned to London to win the Olympic title. Manchester United's Irish international Johnny Carey was chosen as skipper for his stout leadership and battling football, although his linguistic mastery of French and Italian helped too.

'I learned quite a lot when I was in the Army,' he said at the time, 'enough to talk to my team-mates. The trouble is they all want to know so much about Scotland. That is heavy going for an Irishman.' Never mind that he didn't speak the other seven languages used by players in his team.

Other problems for the Europe team stretched from the sublime, for example how to deploy Parola best in defence, to the ridiculous – how to get the kit washed in time after the muddy trial match in Rotterdam four days earlier. In their practice session at Ayr the players were reduced to playing shirts v skins as the hotel management desperately tried to restore the light kit to something resembling the pale blue shirts and white shorts it once was.

The real debate in the Europe camp was over how the defence should be organized – British-style, with a defensive stopper centre-half and the two full-backs watching the wingers (3-2-2-3), or European-style, with the centre-half as an attacking force in the middle of the park, the half-backs on the wingers and the full-backs marking the centre forward (2-3-2-3). As his team-mates enjoyed a Turkish bath in the run-up to the match, Johnny Carey pondered the question over an ice cream on the wall outside.

Unbeknown to him, Wilf also had his thinking cap on and to greater effect. Billy Steel recalled the plan's genesis: 'At the Aberfoyle Hotel where we had our pre-match training and team-talk, Wilf took Tommy Lawton and me aside and asked what type of tactics we should use. He then stressed a move which he thought would cause havoc in the enemy camp. It was simple and direct and the only point to watch was the timing of it. I had to get the ball in midfield and pass it down between the back and centre-half on the left-hand side of the field. Lawton was to run for it, taking the centre-half with him, and then flick the ball first time back into the centre-forward position. Mannion, by judicious timing, would arrive at the vacant centre-forward position at the same time as the ball, having run from right-half, and with no centre-half there, he was bound to cause trouble.'

When Hardwick – giving Middlesbrough the honour of being the only club with two players in the Great Britain team – led out his four English team-mates, three Scots, two Welshmen and an Ulsterman, the only trouble Wilf was having was with his new boot. As a bagpipe band welcomed the teams, he appeared to be doing a little jig as he tried to loosen the leather. Steel, however, was even worse off as a nail had come through the sole of one of his boots and dug into his flesh for much of the match. But the duo's boot problems didn't stop them giving a definitive display of the inside-forward's arts.

Europe's defence was ripped asunder again and again, by Wilf in particular applying his plan. He scored twice and was only denied a hat-trick by a post, France's keeper Da Rui and the predatory Tommy Lawton. The centre-forward hammered home from less than six feet as a goal-bound effort from Wilf crept towards a gaping net after Da Rui got a hand to it. As Wilf said diplomatically at the time: 'It might have stopped rolling.'

The key moment, both in the match and for Wilf, scorer of the goal which put Britain ahead after latching on to a mis-hit Steel shot, came with the score at 1–1 and thirty-three minutes gone. Matthews beat his full-back, cut in towards goal and squared a pass to Wilf inside Europe's penalty area. Czech left-half Ludl only spoke his mother tongue, so no one could ask why he did what he did next; the thinking behind his full-length dive to palm the pass away remains a mystery. For Wilf it was a question of what was going to happen next.

'Ludl handled the ball in the penalty area and referee Reader pointed to the spot. "Here we go in front," I thought, "if the bloke who takes the kick doesn't get panicky." And then it hit me. I had to take that kick. It was the order given at our training quarters: "Mannion takes the penalties." Every eye in that huge ground watched me as I put the ball on the spot. I walked back, thinking, "I'll kick to the left. No I won't, I'll kick to the right. Or shall I just smack it hard? Take a chance and hope for the best?" I knew that if I scored we'd be back on top, vitally important in a nervy match like this. Miss it and morale would probably sink out of sight. So everything seemed to depend on me – and I was the fellow who shouldn't have been chosen, according to most people. I turned around and picked my target point in the goalmouth and ran up. Smack! ... I knew it immediately. You always do. I'd hit it true and it cracked into the net. There was a long, long second when everything seemed to stop. Then I could have howled with sheer joy. I'd put Great Britain in front. I'd proved, surely, that I was worth my place. And I'd done it with my old and odd, battered and borrowed boots.'

Within two minutes Steel punished a retreating defence by lashing home a thirty-yard drive. Two more minutes and the plan devised at the team hotel worked again as Wilf raced through with only Da Rui to beat. The keeper smothered the shot, but Lawton followed the rolling ball towards the net and finished the job.

In the second half, Europe's defence adapted to counter the threat from the inside-forwards, but still Wilf hit the post and was bundled over for what most observers thought was a penalty before the fifth goal, into his own net by Parola, under pressure from Lawton. With seven minutes left the centre-forward scored his second goal with a header from a precise Matthews cross.

Praise for Wilf's performance came from all sides. On the pitch Da Rui, whose regular shouts of 'Man-e-yan, Man-e-yan' had warned his defenders were the danger lay, produced the most peculiar. He walked out from his goal to Wilf and, with a grin, shook his fist at him. Then he walked back to his goal and slapped his hands on the posts again and again. Alan Hoby of the *People* wrote, slightly sniffily: 'Definitely a character, but not in the same class as Frank Swift.'

Later Steel said of the game: 'I think Wilf had a field day. He certainly caused chaos and it wasn't until the second half that Carlos Parola woke up and refused to "leave his beat". That is typically Mannion, always plotting and scheming to get results the easy way and what is easier than two short passes leaving a player free to shoot at goal. There is not much of Mannion, yet every ounce is worth its weight in soccer gold.'

All this from the player who did not deserve to be picked, according to some. Sir Stanley Matthews remembers: 'It didn't affect his game. He didn't let anyone down. He was different from Carter. Wilf had more ball control. Carter was deadly with his left and right inside the box. He read the game very well and liked long balls. Carter was a great player. But Wilf was too, he was just different. We all have different styles.'

But the greatest accolade for Wilf came at the final whistle.

'I'll never forget those words from a grand sportsman, Raich Carter. He said, "I badly wanted to play. Now I want to congratulate the inside-forwards. They were fine."' Coming from Carter that was praise indeed.

The press acknowledged Wilf's coming of age. The headlines spoke volumes: 'Matthews and Mannion mesmerise Rest of Europe', 'Mannion–Matthews a great right wing' and 'Wilf Mannion was irrepressible'. W. Capel Kirby, of the *Sunday Empire News*, for one, ate humble pie for attacking Wilf and Steel:

> To readers who have accused me of criticizing the omission of Raich Carter to the detriment of these two players I now humbly apologise. Both Steel and Mannion did what the bitterly disappointed maestro had hoped. Carter sat there as one of the substitutes watching his rivals playing the best inside-forward game seen for many a long day.

It wasn't a one-off performance. In the nine representative games – five full England internationals, two inter-league games, one England friendly and the Great Britain game – of the 1946–47 season, Wilf was top scorer. He netted a third of the thirty goals scored – and didn't even play in one of the nine matches. It might not quite have been a case of the king is dead, long live the king, but at least it was clear that Carter had a worthy heir apparent.

If one man managed to sum up England's attitude, in football as in much else, it was Ernest Bevin. The then Minister for Foreign Affairs was guest of honour at an international against France. Captain Billy Wright led him along the line of proud white shirts, introducing stars who needed no introduction. At the end of the line Bevin turned to Wright and gave his approval of the troops.

'They all look fit enough to eat the Froggies,' he announced.

'We didn't eat them but we did beat them,' Wright later said.

But, as Bevin's tone suggested, England were expected to beat every-one, certainly at home anyway. It wasn't until the infamous visit of the Hungarians that England lost at home against overseas opponents. Even defeats against the other home teams were a rarity. Of the twenty-five post-war internationals played in England – at venues ranging from Wembley to Luton Town – before the 6–3 humiliation by Puskas and Co. in 1953, Walter Winterbottom's teams won sixteen, drew seven and lost just two, once to Scotland and once to the Republic of Ireland.

In the first year of full internationals after the war, the record was even better: played six; won five, drew one. After the back-to-back victories against Northern Ireland and the Republic, England beat Wales at Maine Road, Holland at Huddersfield and France at Highbury. Only Scotland managed not to lose, a 1–1 draw secured at Wembley when Carter, clean through with only the goalkeeper to beat, heard what he thought was the final whistle and pulled up. The sound had come from the crowd.

So when the party for the summer tour gathered the week after the Great Britain–Europe game, hopes were high. The itinerary was a full international followed by a B team fixture against the amateurs of Switzerland, before a grand finale against the Portuguese – the first fixture against a team emerging as one of the best sides in Europe, who had just beaten the Republic of Ireland 2–0. It was reckoned to be the toughest game of the three, the one most likely to produce a result to raise eyebrows back in England. It did, but not for the expected reasons, and not before the Swiss had sent brows skyward throughout the football world.

England fielded a strong team in Zürich, including Carter, Lawton, Matthews, Swift, Wright and Mannion, but sensationally lost 1–0. Even Swiss fans were expecting a 6–0 drubbing, according to the incredulous *Daily Express*. England had what appeared to be a good goal disallowed, but then the Swiss had two efforts ruled out too. 'Black Sunday', as the paper dubbed it, showed: 'They have nothing to learn from us, and apparently a great deal to teach.' Reporter John Macadam added:

> Goals or no goals did not matter. What does matter is that we were given a football lesson by a team who were more than footballers. They were athletes, gymnasts, acrobats and all.

Excuses were quick in coming. The pitch, with the crowd only held back by rope, was too small and crammed; the food in neutral Switzerland was too rich for the palates of men still making do under rationing at home. Winterbottom cited probably the most relevant, however, when he mentioned the conditions, particularly the thin air.

'We have only two alternatives,' he said. 'Either to make the tour twice as long and let the boys settle down properly before they play or fly them in immediately before the match and have them playing before the climate has a chance to affect them.'

Stanley Rous admitted the truth when he said, 'The better team won. It was the superior speed, skill and tactics of the Swiss that won the game.' England's acclaimed attack was blunted when it ran into a defence as towering as the Alps. In contrast, England's defenders were bamboozled by centre-forward Bickel, who played neither in the centre nor forward. Lying deep and roaming at will, he allowed the inside-forwards to push up as twin spearheads of the attack. He supplied them, not vice-versa. Equally revolutionary alongside him was the Swiss centre-half, pushed far forward and leaving the full-backs and half-backs to play as a back four. The system amounted to an early version of 4-2-4.

Neil Franklin, England's defensive linchpin, was no mug. A converted inside-forward, he was another ball playing centre-half, unrivalled in England in his position. In one of his first games during the war, Matt Busby had congratulated him on his performance and told him: 'Just remember son, keep playing football at all times and you'll never go far wrong.' The words had been taken to heart. But against the Swiss he was unsure what to do – follow his man deep or hold his position and mark nothing but space?

By the time England sorted themselves out they were 1–0 down. Later, they thought they had managed to score when winger Bobby Langton fired home from point-blank range. Wright reckoned the ball was already over the line when Langton hit it and so disputed the offside decision against the winger, although not to the referee's face, of course. As the soon-to-be captain later wrote:

> In our hearts we felt an injustice had been done but we said nothing. After all, whether you are playing for England or your club, it is pointless and bad manners to criticize a referee's decision and in the long run you invariably lose prestige in the eyes of all associated with the game.

What would he have made of well-mannered players like, to pluck a name from the air at random, Peter Schmeichel?

At least one of the England players enjoyed his afternoon. The initial onslaught over, Frank Swift had the time to wander from his goal and over to the crowd. A quick chat and back he strolled wearing a cap given to him by a spectator and chewing on a couple of toffees. The B match, however, put his rapport with the crowd to a greater test. When Franklin fouled a Swiss forward, the fans showed that neutrality was just another word. Bottles were thrown on the pitch and the rope barriers suddenly looked as flimsy as the Swiss reputation for pacifism. Swift marched upfield, picked up an umbrella which had been thrown at Franklin and continued to the section of crowd from where it had come and which was encroaching on the edge of the pitch.

'Now get back before I have to do something with this,' he ordered, but with a smile.

It was the only victory of the Swiss leg of the tour. The B game ended 0–0. The defence, with Dicky Robinson of Middlesbrough deputising at left-back for his clubmate Hardwick, held firm even if the attack could not score. Lawton had been rested, but more significantly so had Carter. More accurately he had been dropped. As it turned out, he had played his last game for England. In the first match he had come nearest to scoring, but he also got in the way of a goal-bound Lawton effort. It was not a fitting climax to an international career, but the England selectors came to the same conclusion about him as the Great Britain ones had just a couple of weeks earlier. At the age of thirty-three, he had to start thinking about new horizons. A younger man was to take his place. Perhaps it happened too soon.

'Carter was still a great player,' Sir Stanley Matthews says, 'and if Wilf or Stan Mortensen hadn't come along, he would have still been in the England team.'

As it was, with Wilf now established, Mortensen of Blackpool got his chance, grasped it and only finally let it go after the defeat by Hungary. He had never dreamt that he would win an England cap when his club decided he was 'too slow to attend a funeral', and prepared to release him before the war. An international debut looked even less likely when, after signing up as an RAF air gunner, his plane crashed. Two of his crewmates were killed and a third lost his legs. Mortensen, whose Norwegian grandfather provided the unusual surname, was luckier and only suffered cuts and relatively minor injuries. Recovered, he got the chance to hone his football skills in RAF and service sides.

Ever since he had started heading a ball against a school wall in his native Tyneside to practise his aerial control, he had been marked out as a possible star. The school side for which he played reached the last sixteen of a national youth competition and were only put out by a team containing youngsters linked to Aston Villa and Walsall. The run prompted a poem in the *South Shield Gazette*. Young Stan's verse went:

> Stanley Mortensen watches the ball
> As a shepherd watches his sheep
> And should he chance to lose it
> He'd hunt it like Bo Peep.

In the RAF he got a chance to work on the aspect of his game which let him down: speed. He concentrated not on being the fastest over a hundred yards, as he'd never need to run that far that fast in a game, but over a dozen. He honed the skill of the late burst and it was to pay dividends.

Mortensen's mother refused to watch him play football after seeing him knocked out as a schoolboy. Given the poor showings in Switzerland, there were no doubt many reporters and officials looking for a similar excuse to avoid watching Stan and his new colleagues in Portugal. Defeat was a distinct possibility. Instead, it was one of English football's finest ninety minutes.

High above parched Mediterranean plains, history was being made. For the first time English footballers were flying between fixtures – and having treatment en route. Phil Taylor, Liverpool half-back, was having his knee coaxed back to fitness by physio Walter Max. The rest of the party weren't interested. Their eyes were glued to the scene unfolding below them. The Swiss and French Alps had given way to arid flatlands. Rising majestically from them was an architectural vision in white, featuring two horseshoe tiers of terraces in smooth marble and granite. A row of classical columns one hundred feet high stood proud at the top of the bowl, overlooking an oasis of lush green grass in the middle. Beyond the most incredible football arena any of the English group had ever seen was the Atlantic ocean.

Portugal's new national stadium in Lisbon was a dream ground, even by today's standards. When the players got up close it remained as impressive as it was from the air. Its façade was that of a villa, the fittings lived up to the stylish exterior, and the pitch was as good as Wembley's. The grass had been specially imported from Cumberland to create the best possible playing surface. When the players walked back towards the dressing-rooms, through shaded walkways formed by impressive arches, they crossed a small man-made stream. It was there for them to rinse the mud from their boots before going inside. The stream ran around the ground, so that the crowd could wash the dust from their footwear.

'I've often said that's the most picturesque stadium I ever played in.' Tom Finney was impressed. 'It was absolutely fabulous to go down and see it empty. We went down on the Sunday morning, when we were playing in the afternoon, to have a look at it and it was incredible, it really was. All-seated, of course, but that was unheard of in those days, and circular – unlike the grounds at home. There were no stands as we knew them because the weather was always so good over there that you could always sit out in the open. That was the thing you noticed most about the grounds abroad, where, in a lot of cases, there isn't a lot of cover.'

As Finney gazed at the stadium, former Preston North End player Bob Kelly wandered up to him. Kelly was managing a local league side, one which had three or four players in the Portuguese team. Best known as part of Herbert Chapman's Huddersfield side which won three league titles on the trot in the mid-1920s, he was keen to know about things back home. He warned Finney that England had a hell of a match on their hands.

'Portugal are one of the best sides I've ever seen,' he said. 'You'll have to be on your mettle.'

'He was going to great lengths to tell me what a great side they were,' Tom remembers. 'We'd just played Switzerland and lost in the previous game. And Portugal had played the Swiss away and won 2–0, so he was thinking we'd be given a real difficult game. We all did after that.'

Finney was nervous enough as it was. He was being played out of position as Bobby Langton had been injured in the second game against the Swiss and, with no specialist cover, Finney was asked to play on the left flank.

'There were only fourteen or sixteen players and I was the only other known winger, so Walter Winterbottom called me to one side and said, "We've got a bit of a problem. Bobby Langton's injured. Would you play at outside-left?" Of course I said yes. You play anywhere if it's for your country, don't you?'

Fortunately Finney was a natural left-footer. He'd only been switched from inside-left to right-wing at Preston because of an injury to the regular number seven.

'The chairman said, "You can forget about being an inside-forward from now on," and that's how I became an outside-right.' He need not have worried about his international switch; he scored in a 10–0 win which more than made up for the poor performances in Switzerland and was the most remarkable England result for years.

Before kick-off it was unthinkable. The 65,000 home fans were confident of victory and welcomed their side with a roar of expectation. Goalkeeper Azevedo, acclaimed by home supporters as the greatest keeper in the world, took up his position between the posts to a deafening reception. He even took a personal bow to acknowledge it. Seventeen-seconds after the kick-off he was bowing again to retrieve the ball from the back of his net. A quick throw from Billy Wright set up Wilf, who beat a man and slung over a high cross for Lawton to leap and nod home. Wright said Azevedo looked as if he had been smacked.

What had happened was that England had, by accident, chanced upon a way of playing both Finney and Matthews. Each of them had also been linked with an inside man who brought out the best in them and contributed plenty of attacking options themselves. Mortensen could give the simple ball to feet that Matthews thrived on, but could also use his bursts of pace to act like a second, deep-lying centre-forward; Wilf developed an instant understanding with Finney, strong enough for both to know when to use the other as decoys. Lawton, meanwhile, apart from clinical finishing, was creating the spaces for all his fellow attackers by intelligent running off the ball.

It rained goals, but the game was as memorable for the bizarre incidents which punctuated it. The first came as the British size five ball, on its way back to the centre spot from the opening goal, mysteriously disappeared to be replaced by a size four favoured by the Portuguese. There had been a long argument before kick-off between Winterbottom and his opposite number over which size ball would be used. Now there was no choice as the smaller and lighter ball was introduced without warning.

It made no odds. One–nil became two, three and, on twenty-eight minutes, four. Finney picked the ball up just inside his own half and headed for goal. Twice his legs were taken from under him and twice he kept his balance before, as Lawton took other defenders away, the winger nonchalantly skipped past the last man and flicked the ball from one foot to the other over the advancing keeper and into the net.

As Azevedo picked the ball out again, the crowd began a high-pitched hiss at the performance. At the same time Portuguese reserve goalkeeper Capela ambled from the bench around to behind the goal and started to chat to the number one. All eyes moved to the England end where Portugal were attacking and when play came back to the home end Capela was standing in the goal, despite substitutes only being allowed for injuries. Azevedo was trudging around the outside of the pitch in tears, with a few cushions hurled from the crowd to accompany him on the long walk back to the dressing-room. Tom Finney felt sorry for him.

'Being a professional player, you don't feel very happy about losing – and losing heavily in an international match is pretty awful really. There were 65,000 there and I think they had real expectations of giving us a real game or even winning.'

But his sympathy didn't last too long as he was distracted by the case of the mysterious vanishing right-back. The Portuguese had replaced the number two, the captain Cardosa, as well, but no one had noticed.

'The game started off with a fella a similar size to me,' Tom recalls, 'and the next thing I know there was a big six-foot fella playing there. I don't know how that could have possibly happened. To this day I don't know he got on the field.'

Whatever tricks they pulled, however, Portugal couldn't match England's flawless attacking. Mortensen and Lawton both got four, Finney one and even Matthews – whose goals were as scarce as a Portuguese smile in the stadium that day – got on the scoresheet.

'I didn't score,' Wilf says, 'but I was helping to make all the bullets for the others.' Then he jokes: 'I made Stan score and he didn't like that much. They tried to make me score, but I didn't want to know. I wanted to keep an even number. And they weren't going to get eleven back.'

For Finney, who confirmed that Wilf had a hand, or foot, in most of the ten, it was the start of a partnership he still describes as his best ever.

'That game was without doubt one of the greatest achievements of an international side. It was my first game at outside-left – and at international level too. But with Wilf it all seemed to click.'

'Our players started to combine well,' was Sir Walter Winterbottom's view, 'produced one goal and the confidence built. Wilf was typical of this. He was linking up superbly. The Portuguese were playing hard and well, but they weren't scoring and we just kept going back at them and scoring. It was certainly one of our best wins.'

President Carmona and his Cabinet, watching from beneath the huge columns, were no doubt disappointed but, as politicians, they probably managed to paint the day as a great victory for Portuguese net-makers who had shown how resilient their product was. The other 65,000 spectators were as crushed as their team had been on the park. And the players? They were so ashamed that they refused to attend the post-match banquet which was the traditional climax to an international fixture. Not long afterwards, the team were all banned by their football association. Nominally it was for snubbing the meal. Others saw it as a punishment for the defeat.

Either way, England's first airborne overseas tour certainly ended on a high after an unpromising start. Billy Wright wrote in his diary: 'In seven days I have known what it feels like to be humiliated, relieved and proud.' For *The Times* the final result meant Bevin's world view was back. 'England showed that given conditions as they wanted and a perfect surface, they are indeed masters," it said. It was hard to argue, at least for a while longer.

· SIX ·

'You'll never see anything like it again'

Twelve months later England were flying again, literally first and figuratively later. The end-of-season tour a year on from Switzerland and Portugal had been reduced to just one game. A second planned match in Czechoslovakia was called off following the communist coup, while an alternative fixture in Spain also fell through.

So one game it was, but what a game, against Italy, the World Cup holders. Never mind that the title had been won or, more accurately, retained a decade before and that the war had meant it had not yet been defended, Italy remained the main force in football in continental Europe. They had become the first European winners of the World Cup in 1934. Months later they lost to England in the infamous Battle of Highbury, when the visitors produced an X-rated performance of petulance and punches. The brutality of centre-half Monti, who once started a brawl that the police had to quell when playing for Argentina in the 1930 World Cup finals, was at the heart of it and summed up the style of the team.

Four years later, though, manager Vittorio Pozzo had refined that style to retain the Cup with a classy and assured unit. Ten years on, he was still in charge of the national side, still bringing his tactical nous and understanding of the game – learnt from the press benches as a journalist – to bear. The scope of his revolution could be no better illustrated than by the fact that Monti had been succeeded by Parola, whose reputation as Europe's finest centre-half had not been diminished by the Great Britain v Europe game. He remained the complete defender.

The England squad for the Italian match contained familiar faces for Parola. Swift, from the Great Britain team, was in goal, but the forward line was more familiar to him, with Lawton, Matthews and Mannion from the same match. He would have missed the captain, though. George Hardwick had played thirteen successive games as skipper for England, as well as the Britain game, but was missing through injury (and would not play for his country again after regaining his fitness). The immediate problem was who was going to step into his place?

At Geneva airport the question nearly turned into a diplomatic crisis. The team had stopped over to change planes for the journey over the Alps and an unforeseen problem developed which needed skilful handling by a leader. A delegation from the airport headed by a pretty young woman armed with a bunch of flowers, approached the England party. She wanted to honour the visitors during the stop-over. But who would accept the gift? Arthur Drewry, chairman of selectors, stage-whispered: 'Mr Swift, will you please do the honours?' Thus was another England captain appointed, the first goalkeeper to have the honour.

A couple of hours later Swift led the team into what appeared to be the eye of another storm. Milan airport was crammed with 10,000 people waiting to see the English arrive. The press entertained the crowd first as one reporter, whose journey over the Alps had been eased by a bottle of schnapps, fell flat on his face in front of them. The team's progress was almost as slow as they were held up by customs officers less concerned at checking cases than getting autographs. They were surrounded by fans as the impromptu session continued long after all the weary travellers wished they were on their way.

A two-and-a-half hour coach drive to Stresa, on the edge of Lake Maggiore, constituted the last leg of the journey. There to greet the party at the hotel was none other than Pozzo, carrying a small gift, a bag of rice, for each of them, which was invaluable in the days of rationing.

For the next few days Winterbottom worked on their fitness, while a hundred practitioners of Pozzo's former craft filmed and jotted down all they could about the enemy. The real mayhem came when the squad moved to the city hosting the clash, Turin. Everywhere the England party went they were followed by crowds of Italians, with Swift and Lawton in particular mobbed every time they stepped outside the hotel. Sometimes it wasn't too pleasant.

'The war had only just finished and things were still a little bit tricky,' Tommy remembered. 'With some of them, when you walked down the street it was, "Inglese" and they'd spit.'

Most, however, were friendly and only too eager for a glimpse of the men who were heading for a good, sporting beating. For the Italians were absolutely convinced they would not only win but win easily. The 10–0 win in Portugal was written off as luck, and anyway who were Portugal compared to the gods of the *squaddra azzura*? The match would be the football equivalent of a Ferrari pitted against an Austin Seven. The consensus in the papers was 4–0 or so. The fans probably wanted to double that.

'That Italian team was a great, great side,' Sir Walter Winterbottom says. 'They'd played all over Europe and beaten everyone. I saw them play in France and they won 3–0 but they were toying with the French in the second half. They were lobbing the ball to each other, keeping it off the ground all the time and still passing to each other, trapping it on their chests or their knees and then forcing it through to someone else. One clearance went to the centre-half [Parola] and he headed the ball and then followed his own header, trapped it with his head and volleyed a goal from the edge of the penalty area. It was incredible. I told Tommy Lawton and Frank Swift about it and they just said rubbish. Then in the first five minutes of the game against us the same centre-back did exactly the same thing again and Swifty had to make a marvellous save.'

Looking around the away dressing-room on matchday, perhaps the hosts' confidence was justified. A lot of the England players were drained after a long season. Henry Cockburn, of Manchester United, had been at Wembley winning the FA Cup a couple of weeks before and had also helped his team to finish second in the league; Matthews and Mortensen had also been at Wembley, but on the losing side; Jack Howe, of Derby, had been a losing semi-finalist; and Laurie Scott had won a league championship medal with Arsenal.

But the Italians' arrogance had provoked the English into extra training at Stresa and a determination at least to push the Italians in Turin. Mortensen later wrote:

> We trained as never before. I put in two or three days of the hardest work of my football life and when we finally moved off to Turin we were all in the peak of physical condition, more like men in August than in May.

Another source of inspiration barely needed pointing out. Both Wilf and Tom Finney had a special desire to rub the Italians' noses in it. After all, they'd been attacking them rather more literally only a couple of years earlier. The flight into Italy, over Anzio, had only reminded them of that.

It was 10.30 a.m. on a Sunday morning. There were 40,000 people gathered together and it wasn't for an outdoor mass. Even so the crowd, huddled under umbrellas, may have prayed, either in grateful thanks for their ticket – the lucky few, as 400,000 had applied – or to make sure the home team won; or perhaps they sent a plea to the Almighty for the appalling thunderstorm lashing them as they sat in the stadium to stop, which it eventually did.

The fans had begun to arrive early. Kick-off wasn't until 5 p.m. The thunderstorm was uncomfortable, but those already in the ground and another 35,000 who arrived through the day could not have cared less. Nothing short of a natural intervention on the scale of the volcanic shower which hit Pompeii was going to stop them watching this game. They adopted the phlegmatic approach for which their visitors were renowned, shrugging their shoulders and dismissing the weather as only a bit of water. What was that compared to a decisive victory?

When the sun came out, things got worse. The drying rainwater led to humidity so stifling that the ground suddenly became an outdoor sauna. Breathing was hard enough work to start the sweat trickling. Walking, let alone running, put the lungs under severe pressure. Conditions which were not ideal for the home side were almost impossible for the English.

Even so the 40,000 early arrivals were animated. They talked excitedly and cheered, sang and chanted, no one daring to leave their seat just in case someone else somehow stole it. Loudspeakers and bands competed with each other throughout the day, from inside and outside the ground, to add to the noise. Advertising leaflets rained down from above, dropped by aircraft. More fans arrived and found their seats; still more arrived ticketless and milled around outside the ground hoping to find some way in.

By kick-off, the semi-organized chaos was reaching its climax. The cacophony of 75,000 home fans loudly swapping predictions and chanting seemed to build in volume until it could reach no greater level. Then the teams appeared and the noise hit the England players in the pits of their stomachs. Almost a hundred cameramen raced in front of the line-ups, many falling over each other in their eagerness to get the best shot. The pictures showed the contrast between English and Italian football's sartorial development. The famous white tops were literally button-up shirts made of heavy cotton with the FA crest over the heart. The big, baggy, blue shorts, made of the same heavy material, almost reached the knee, and were as cumbersome as the shirts; and the red socks covered shins almost as wide as thighs because of all the cotton-wool padding and guards worn for protection. In contrast, the Italians wore T-shirt style tops and lightweight shorts the English considered almost indecently skimpy. Beneath their blue socks was nothing but shin. It appeared to be a contest of athleticism and agility versus endeavour wrapped up in antique kit.

For the first few minutes the Italians' optimism was justified. They poured forward in flowing waves of attack only stopping at the barrier that was Frank Swift. Sir Stanley Matthews remembers it well

'We went on to the field and it was the most awful hot day. It was steaming hot – steam was rising from the ground. For the first twenty minutes we didn't know what had hit us. It was only Neil Franklin and Frank Swift who kept us in it. The Italians were the best team in the world, a fine team. They were beautiful players.'

Then something happened which suggested England had not read the script. Matthews collected the ball in midfield and jinked past two defenders. But rather than start one of his touchline-hugging runs, he slipped a forty-yard pass into space in the inside-right channel. Mortensen galloped on to it like a thoroughbred, hotly pursued by Parola. They raced on, down the side of the penalty area, but Mortensen was running out of pitch and Parola knew he only had to make a simple tackle. As it came in, the striker produced an instant so skilful – some say so lucky – that it is still etched in the mind of anyone who saw it.

From the tightest of angles and running at full pelt, he hammered a shot towards the near post. The keeper, Bacigalupo, had seen Tommy Lawton coming into the box and had begun to move off his line to intercept a cross, but the tiny gap he had left at the near post was where the swerving shot was heading. He tried to recover, but before he could, the ball had flown in just beneath the angle of post and crossbar. It was probably the only spot it could have gone in.

Mortensen, off-balance and falling out of play after his efforts, watched the net billow from the ground. Parola, whose defending had been flawless, looked over in horror. The crowd was stunned. *Times* correspondent Geoffrey Green later wrote: 'I can still see it, still hear the astonished, painful grunt of the 75,000 crowd, like some huge animal stopped in its tracks by a hunter's bullet.' Not even Pelé, he added, would have thought about a shot from that angle and at that speed.

The suspicion was that Mortensen hadn't intended it either.

'Sizing up the situation instinctively – and before you become a good footballer you must do things instinctively – I shot in the direction of the advancing goalkeeper and into the net,' he later insisted. But Sir Stanley thinks good fortune played a part.

'It was a bit of a lucky goal,' he said. 'I remember I got the ball off Franklin and pushed it through to Mortensen, who ran on to the edge of the box, on the corner of the edge of the area, and he hit this ball. I mean there was no aim for it. He said after the match, "I aimed." But we said, "Don't be crazy." It dipped and he hit it hard. It was so hard the keeper hadn't got a chance. But you don't aim for the top corner when you're in that position outside the penalty box. We were kidding him afterwards, saying, "You didn't aim for that," and he was saying, "Of course I did."'

A ripple of applause spluttered around the ground and quickly stalled. The home fans settled down again; a fine goal perhaps, but like the 10–0, a fluke. Normal service would soon be resumed. Indeed the blue shirts poured forward, passing to each other with such ease and assurance that England and the ball were strangers to each other. Henry Cockburn and Billy Wright, the half-backs at the centre of the midfield battleground, didn't come close to introducing themselves to it for minute after minute. Cockburn even shouted to Matthews, standing on the wing waiting for the ball: 'Get your bloody self in the game, we're chasing shadows.' No one spoke to Stanley like that unless there were special circumstances.

All the time the atmosphere was draining the desire to run around, sapping energy, tightening lungs, exhausting muscles. Yet the Italians couldn't convert their pressure into goals. Frank Swift was playing the game of his life. One save from centre-forward Gabetto's shot prompted the number nine to punch the turf in disbelief; for another, from a free-kick by Carapallese, the ball smashed into Swift's ample chest and away; even when he was beaten, Laurie Scott was on the line to clear. Twice when the score was 1–0 the referee disallowed a goal by right-winger Menti.

Then lightning struck twice. Mortensen was put through again in almost the same position. Surely he couldn't repeat his stupendous opening goal? He didn't need to. For when he saw Bacigalupo nervously clinging to the near post and guarding it as though his life depended upon it, he centred for Lawton to nod home.

It was hard to say who was more surprised by a half-time 0–2 scoreline, Italy or England, or who least wanted to play the second half. Cockburn slumped down in the changing room and said he couldn't play any more. Sir Walter Winterbottom remembers what happened.

'He said, "It's too hot. I can't go on." I said, "Stop it. I've seen the Italian team and they're even worse then you."'

Sure enough not long into the second half Pozzo and his coaches were chasing their players up and down the line spraying water at them to cool them down. Frank Swift was still kept busy. Once his post saved him and, as he fell on the rebound rolling along the goalline, Gabetto buried his face in his hands. Wright said later he thought the Italian was going to cry, but instead he chased after the referee arguing that the ball had crossed the line. Even the photographers mumbled the same claim, so Swift, with the ball safely cleared, invited one of their number on to the pitch and showed him the skid marks he'd made diving for the ball. The Italian took his picture and, not surprisingly, didn't argue with England's captain.

After fifteen minutes of the second half the Italians were all played out. England's fitness regime came into its own and, after an hour on the ropes, they moved forwards. Wilf, referring to the opposing full-back, had promised Tom Finney before kick-off: 'I'm going to have this Italian waiter's feet red hot before I'm finished.' And so he did, twice getting the better of him and providing passes for Finney to fire home – the second a sweeping end-to-end move – to emphasize England's superiority and secure their most famous win until 1966.

At the heart of it was the attacking link between Wilf and Finney. In a book they later co-wrote, Billy Wright and Walter Winterbottom recounted:

> Their skills that day were so sharply defined that, moving often within two or three yards of each other, they could flick that ball continuously with the merest caress, bypassing opponents, pushing it between opposing legs, clipping it away from tackles at the very last moment.

Tom himself remembers: 'That was probably the greatest win an England side had away from home. Italy were then the holders of the World Cup and they had a great side. We were given very little chance, playing them away from home. It was a great result for us and put us on the map really. In those days England were a good force in football and were reckoned to be able to give anybody a run for their money. But that result proved it. We were very fortunate to come in winning 2–0 at half time. Stan Mortensen had scored against the run of the play and then Tommy Lawton made it two. We were winning, but we'd been under a tremendous amount of pressure and Frank Swift in goal was having a tremendous game and brought off three or four magnificent saves.'

Wilf too remembers Swift's heroics: 'In the first quarter of an hour they really pressurized us, but Swifty played out of his skin and made some marvellous saves. If it wasn't for him it could have been seven or eight. After that though we started to run 'em to death. We took complete control by the end.'

In the dressing-room afterwards skipper Swift made a point of shaking each man by the hand and telling them: 'You've made me the proudest man in the world. I'll always remember this victory.'

Walter Winterbottom led his team to the post-match reception with the same pride. But his good mood was shattered when he saw an Italian paper with the headline: 'Pozzo Dead'.

'We were walking up the stairs to this hall and there were people handing out papers,' Sir Walter remembers. 'One of them had a black edge all the way around it and the headline was Pozzo was dead. I thought, "Oh my God." I thought the poor fellow had had a heart attack, but then I saw him. I said, "What's all this about then?" and he said, "My job. That's it. I am finished."'

England managers would soon have similar vagaries of the press to endure, but Winterbottom could savour the result he ranks as probably his best as England boss.

'It was an astonishing result. None of our players thought we could win. I had my doubts.' A few weeks later he received a letter from the British Embassy in Turin. It congratulated him on the team's success. 'It said all the main Turin shops were selling English goods and nobody had done so much for English trade as us.' Ferrari drivers looking for Austin Sevens?

Sadly, the finest hour was also the last stand. After just six games together, the famous five of Matthews, Mortensen, Lawton, Mannion and Finney was broken up. England's best-ever forward line never played together again.

Matters entirely unrelated to how good a player he was put Wilf out of international football before the next fixture four months later. After that game Tommy Lawton joined him on what amounted to a blacklist. Matthews, Mortensen and Finney kept winning caps and eventually Wilf would re-join them, but for Lawton it was the beginning of a very long downward slope, one which would end in court and shame. As he noted in the title of his autobiography, the cheering had stopped.

What could never be taken away from him or any of them – and still can't – are their heroics in the white shirt of England. The Matthews–Mortensen–Lawton–Mannion–Finney forward line's record was phenomenal. In their six games as a unit, England won five and drew one; the quintet scored twenty-six goals between them (and, just in case the defence is overlooked, Swift and his defence only conceded four); they helped trounce the best team in Europe, and another not far behind, each on their own soil.

For Billy Wright, who took over as captain of his country two games after Turin and went on to win 105 caps, the win in Lisbon was the finest he ever played in.

'Our 10–0 victory over Portugal in Lisbon was the nearest thing I've seen to absolute perfection on a football pitch,' he said. 'I doubt if there has ever been a greater performance by an England attack. They were all outstanding individual players but blended together so well as a unit it was a pleasure to play behind them.'

For Matthews, too, the Portugal game was the peak performance.

'In that game, it was the best forward line I played in. They were all so skilful – wonderful players. And these young people today have never seen those skills; they have never seen Wilf play or Tom Finney.'

Tom himself ranks the Italian game as the definitive performance, and a stunning exhibition from the man he first met in Palestine.

'I remember Wilf so well because he was blond-haired, very small – not much more than 5ft 5in or something like that – but such a fantastic player. He had a tremendous amount of skill, he was a great passer of the ball and had a great sense of all that was happening around him. A great player. I've always nominated him as one of my favourite players. Certainly I'd class my greatest partnership as the one with Wilf when he played inside-left and I played outside-left on so many occasions.' It is entirely in Tom's character that he plays down his own role.

Sir Stanley echoes the praise of the Golden Boy.

'Wilf, playing the Italians especially, had scintillating feet. He was so light on his feet you never thought he was touching the ground. Today there just aren't any players like him. Beardsley would be similar perhaps but not the same.'

Tommy Lawton agreed.

'There was no question about it – Wilf was a genius. He had a football player's brain to start with – one which didn't need to be coached. He was quicksilver in his thought. Every time he passed you knew you had bags of time to play the ball. At the height of his career, around the time of the Italy game, he could have played in any present day – or yesteryear – side. The ability was there, the desire was there and the confidence was there. He used to give you the ball at the right time and would always be in the right place to get it back again.'

The greatest England forward line ever? It's hard to argue when there was so much skill, but variety too. Defences could draw a strategy to nullify Matthews or tightly mark Lawton, but that would leave space for Mannion, Mortensen and Finney to exploit, and they needed no second invitation. It meant England had a range of attacking options, including the two most obvious – relying on the best wing duo ever seen to beat the full-backs and deliver crosses so precise that Tommy Lawton said he would laughingly complain if the laces on the ball were facing the wrong way; or using pace and guile, via Mortensen and Mannion respectively, to feed Lawton or each other.

If Walter Winterbottom and England had been dealt a winning hand, there was no question who the ace was. Wilf never really captured the same sublime form again for his country. Equally many say that he never had a bad game in an England shirt. Come the World Cup finals in Sweden, ten years after Italy's home humiliation, Winterbottom, still manager, said: 'I'd give a lot for a Wilf Mannion right now.' But by then English football and one of its all-time greats were going through a messy divorce. He was well on the way to having to sell his caps and the chances of him ever being recalled to replace them were less than zero. There were some more good times, but many more bad.

The first hint of personal happiness, which sadly led in large part to professional discontent, came in what promised to be nothing more than a mediocre game in another mediocre season at Ayresome Park. Blackpool were the visitors, like Boro becalmed mid-table as the hopes of August had given way to grey November days. Their main attraction, Stanley Matthews, was absent injured, although the crowd hoped his England team-mate Mortensen might give them a glimpse of his international skills.

There was, however, another far more important visitor, certainly as far as the other forward on the pitch who was a regular wearer of England white was concerned. She was nineteen-year-old Bernadette Murray who was from Middlesbrough and even lived around the corner from Ayresome, but she'd never been there, let alone to any other ground. Her debut visit was as a VIP, as she and Wilf had just announced their engagement. They met at a dance on Redcar pier. It was also the last time she saw him play. Just like his father, she wasn't that interested in seeing Wilf at work. The one-off visit inspired Wilf, and so 38,936 people got the soccer show of their lifetime, even though it was only intended for one of them.

'I was just showing off for my girl Bernadette really,' he says. 'It was her first game – she went along with her brother – and I thought I'd show her what football was about. I kept hold of the ball and showed what I could do. I thought it was a bad game really, because I wasn't looking out for the team as much as I usually did, but everyone remembers it as a good game.'

That is an understatement. That ninety minutes on 22 November 1947 remains legendary on Teesside; the game is remembered simply as Mannion's Match. It was the day a great player showed how far above his fellows he was, when one man put on a virtuoso show the like of which had never been seen before and would never be seen again at Ayresome; the day Wilf Mannion played for himself – and his wife-to-be – and gave one of the greatest individual displays ever seen in a Middlesbrough shirt. In hindsight, it was also a watershed for his career and possibly the high point of it, coming midway between the heroics of the Mays of 1947 and 1948.

Wilf warmed up the week before by inspiring Boro to a 5–0 win at strugglers Grimsby, setting up four of them. Captain Jack reported:

> He had one of his finest games of the season. He literally dazzled the Grimsby men with his inimitable craft and, having drawn a net of defenders round him, somehow managed to stab the ball to an unmarked colleague. While he does that it is quite unimportant that he has yet to open his own account for Middlesbrough this season. He was, though, very unlucky not to score when, with Tweedy completely at sea, Mannion's crashing drive hit the outstretched leg of a full-back and skidded to safety.

A further spot of practice came at Highbury, playing for England against the amateurs of Sweden. A crowd of 44,282 watched Wilf set up Mortensen for two goals and Lawton bag a penalty before the Swedes tightened up their defence, marshalled by the three Nordahl brothers, and even pulled two goals back. Mortensen completed his hat-trick to make sure of victory. John Graydon, in the *Sports Chronicle*, gave him man of the match in an unconvincing England performance, but added: 'Mannion was the only England player who came near to him in skill, determination and shooting power.'

Perhaps tired by his midweek exertions, Wilf began the Blackpool game quietly enough. The opening exchanges were evenly matched. Mortensen's pace, as always, threatened, while Wilf's probings asked questions of the Blackpool defence to which, for the moment, they were equal. That defence had been miserly in the opening months of the season, with two goals the most they had conceded in any game so far, but they were minutes away from their biggest rout to date.

The first goal game ten minutes before half-time. Inside-right Cecil McCormack claimed it after a fine solo run which took him past two defenders before hitting an unstoppable shot. A couple of minutes later he was upended in the penalty area after Wilf supplied a sublime through ball, but the appeals for a penalty were waved away. The double act was more productive four minutes before the final whistle when Wilf was supplier again and McCormack made it 4–0. In between Micky Fenton and Johnny Spuhler grabbed a goal apiece, with Wilf creating the opening both times.

He didn't score himself thanks to Blackpool keeper Wallace, who made two great saves, but it was his game. He ran the midfield; he passed with aplomb and harried like a terrier; more noticeably, he also showed juggling skills of a standard only usually seen in a circus acrobat. He routinely dribbled, swayed and dummied his way past opponents as if they were no more than tailor's mannequins. He took men with him and then ran over the ball to let it run to team-mates. The *coup de grâce* came when an aerial clearance came his way. He controlled the ball with a header, then played keep-it-up with more headers, all as he ran down the pitch past startled tangerine shirts. Then he allowed the ball to roll down his back and trapped it, in one movement of his heel, as it hit the floor.

Everyone on hand that day will never forget the display. Even today, nearly fifty years on, it is the one game lifelong Boro fans who saw it remember above all others. In the absence of a Cup final – until 1997 – or a game that meant Boro won the league title, Mannion's Match is *the* game which has gone down in folklore. Not so much for what was achieved or what silverware was won, but because of how the game was played – with grace and good humour, skill and sophistication and just a hint of arrogance, in front of 'his' public.

Mike McCullagh, then a boy approaching his teenage years, was among the many who gaped and gasped at Wilf's wonders that day.

'I remember his skill was absolutely fantastic. You wanted to watch the game but you spent most of the time watching Wilf just to see what he was going to do. Every time he got the ball there was a ripple of excitement – that was always true anyway, but that day more so than usual – because there was just that feeling that he would do something exceptional. And that wasn't with the kind of balls they play with now, which are like circus trick balls compared with what they played with then. The nearest I've seen to him in the modern game is Juninho. Wilf was brilliant, he was so skilful and such a brilliant player.'

Stephen Chapman, now seventy-four, is another who rhapsodizes about Mannion's Match.

'He was juggling while the other players were just standing there looking at him. He beat Blackpool on his own. You'll never see anything like it again.' Then in his early twenties, Stephen had been going to see

Boro since before the war. He used to run errands for his mum and the local women to get the price of his admission. After the war he still went, but gradually realized the chances of glory were diminishing. Only one man never disappointed.

'I got my money's worth just watching Wilf – the finest inside-forward who ever kicked a football as far as I'm concerned. He should have all the money in the Lottery. If I won it, I'd give him a million pounds straight-away for all the memories he gave me.'

Stephen's wife Doris, seventy-three, also has memories of when Wilf and the other Middlesbrough players used to visit the confectionery factory where she worked to pick up presents. The boss was a big Boro fan and he let the players have breakages and other rejects for a knock-down price. In the days before BMW 5 series with 'Darren Jones drives a Beamer' scrawled across it, the sweets were the nearest the stars got to a benefit in kind. The gaffer's name was Clough. He had a lad called Brian, twelve at the time of Mannion's Match, who often went to matches with his dad, learnt football the Wilf Mannion way and later practised it, too. By 1951 he had joined Boro as an amateur. He went on to score 204 goals in 222 games for the club, then went on to achieve one or two other things as well.

From her seat in the main stand, Bernadette was impressed. For the press too, the match confirmed their love affair with Wilf. Cliff Mitchell, the inheritor of the *Gazette*'s soccer beat, wrote:

> Behind every Middlesbrough attack – and there were plenty of them – was the guile, the incomparable craft of a brilliant Mannion. Wilf was the consummate football artist. He moved his body a couple of inches and had three defenders running the wrong way; he balanced the ball on his head, let it run slowly down his body to trap it on the move; he drew a net around him to come waltzing out of it, the ball at his feet; he split open one of the most formidable rearguards in the league to flash a goal pass to an unmarked colleague.

T-o'-T in the *North-Eastern Weekly News* confirmed the 'peerless' performance:

> There have been occasions this season when references to Wilf Mannion as the greatest inside-forward in football have made one squirm. Not until last Saturday had we seen – at Ayresome Park – for a long time the real Mannion, the player who is probably the greatest of all. On this occasion he was the inside-left par excellence; his skill was so superb; his judgement so unerring. There can have been few first-class games anywhere at anytime in which a player was dispossessed so rarely.

When he added: 'It was a game which will be discussed with enthusiasm on Teesside for a long time,' he couldn't have imagined for how long.

The players acknowledged the genius among them when they formed a guard of honour to applaud Wilf from the pitch. Among the vanquished was Stan Mortensen, who went up to his England colleague, shook his hand and said: 'A great game, Wilf. We've all had a lesson.'

Blackpool's manager Joe Smith – who must have begun to dread his trips to Teesside, with 1938's 9–2 the previous visit – was equally magnanimous.

'Your boys were brilliant,' he told David Jack. 'And Mannion – what a player. He made that ball do everything but talk.'

Amid the orgy of congratulation, one man's praise really made 'his' match memorable for Wilf – even Tommy Mannion was impressed.

'The only time he gave me a good word was in that match against Blackpool when I put on an exhibition of soccer for my girl,' Wilf says. 'He said, "That's the way you should play – play for yourself." He was so harsh, but to him you had to look after yourself. No one else.'

The tubbing of Blackpool was Boro's third straight win. They had scored eleven goals and conceded only one in picking up the six points. Unsurprisingly, the directors stuck with a winning side – for the sixth successive game – and their faith was handsomely repaid as Blackburn were thrashed 7–1 at Ewood Park in the next game. Boro even had two apparently good goals disallowed. It was Rovers' heaviest home defeat for fifty-seven years. The coachloads of Middlesbrough fans who made the trip – an early away day – were delighted.

The following Monday the Boro players departed on a well-earned break. The five-day trip to Scarborough was partly a reward for their efforts, partly a mid-season break to recharge the batteries. It had the opposite effect, however, and Boro didn't win in their next seven league games.

Wilf had other things on his mind. Three weeks after Boro hit winning ways again, he married. Crowds thronged the pavement outside the grand St Philomena's Catholic Church just a stone's throw from Ayresome Park. They cheered as Bernadette, wearing satin and lace and carrying a bunch of red roses, re-appeared after becoming Mrs Wilf Mannion. Jimmy McCabe, by now a Leeds United player, was best man. Wilf could have joined him at Elland Road, but the Yorkshire club's £15,000 bid immediately after the Blackpool game was turned down. Among the other guests were David Jack and Boro director Tommy Thomas.

It all seemed like happy families, but it was far from it. Wilf wanted to leave Middlesbrough. He had refused to re-sign for the club before the start of the season, but had been persuaded to change his mind. Now, with a new wife to think of and plans for a family, he needed to secure his financial future, while she, a football outsider, couldn't understand why someone so clearly a hero who put thousands on the gate when he played, was on a fixed maximum wage and tied to one club.

The days of playing for fun were over. It was time to put pounds before purism, even cash before England caps. Just three months after the wedding, divorce was in the air – not between Wilf and Bernadette, but between Wilf and his surrogate family, Middlesbrough FC. It might be messy. It might be painful. But Wilf would soon have children to think of, because by May, when it was time to re-sign, Bernadette was pregnant. No one realized how significant that good news would prove to be.

· SEVEN ·

Making a stand for security

Of all the episodes in Wilf's remarkable life one in particular marked him out as different from his footballing colleagues. It did not centre on how much better or worse a player he was than any of them, but on his determination to ensure he received a fair deal however he played. He was not alone in seeking reasonable recompense for footballing skills, but none of his top-flight fellows fought as he did. Some of them were granted their wishes by managements who rode a coach and horses through the strict rules, others were happy enough with some sort of compromise which meant that they did not need to make a stand. Wilf felt he had to.

But his 'strike' against a patently unfair transfer system – which today would keep lawyers in clover, but then ensured players were not – was a story which generated far more heat than light. The very nature of the under-the-counter deals and underhand tactics means that those who know most about them still have the secrets, and as most are either old men or dead, it is hard to pin down exactly what went on.

It is only possible to re-create the story as accurately as possible from failing memories and newspaper cuttings and sometimes the two clash. On occasions, that is because of an innocent lapse in recalling events of fifty years ago, on others because the journalists who wrote the stories were at the time reporting from inside the clubs at the centre of a dispute which was second to none in its shock value and potential for partisan feelings. Somewhere between the extremes of an entirely innocent player and an appallingly heartless club lies the truth; exactly where can only be guessed on the incomplete evidence available.

The saga began shortly after Wilf's wedding when he and Bernadette moved into a new home which, like the man of the house, belonged to Boro. The couple had to pay rent and rates, but even so the home was still a valuable gift as Britain struggled with the post-war housing shortage. Wilf used cash from a recent benefit – all players were entitled to £750 for every five years' service – to furnish the property in Eston, appropriately midway between Middlesbrough and South Bank. Both Wilf and the club were happy, Boro delighted to see their star with a settled home life which might even improve his game if the display for Bernadette against Blackpool was anything to go by. The fans even did their bit by launching a wedding-present fund. The proceeds were used to buy a new bedroom suite.

But such largesse stoked the fires of jealousy among some other players at Ayresome. Behind the scenes, there was an atmosphere you could bounce a ball off, a fact made all too clear when a delegation of Wilf's own team-mates went to the directors and complained at his preferential treatment. In the dressing-room, he was shunned by those of his colleagues who were consumed by envy. On a coach to an away game he tried to pass the time of day with one of the malcontents and was completely ignored.

The petty squabble took its toll on his form and the whole team suffered. After the blistering performance against Blackpool, Wilf scored just one league goal in the rest of the season. It was also half of his total for the season's thirty-eight appearances, his worst return for a full season in his whole Boro career. But don't all players have bad patches? All would come good again, it was assumed, and he would repeat his England form at club level. No one really realized the level of his misery until the end of the season when he made an appointment to see David Jack and handed in a transfer request. He wanted to leave.

He had announced a similar desire the previous summer when he said his wartime experiences had made him want to travel further afield than Teesside.

'I am convinced that I cannot play my best football with Middlesbrough,' he had said then. 'I feel completely unsettled and, even when a game is in progress, I find my mind wandering away from the job in hand. This is not fair to myself or the club and I feel it better we part. Perhaps I have become unsettled after travelling so much in the Army. At any rate I know that I can no longer be happy with my present club.'

He had refused to re-sign for Boro. Stoke City, with £32,000 profits from a bumper season swilling around their bank account, had been circling before the bombshell. An offer also came in from a Dutch club, but Boro refused both the approaches and eventually, Wilf re-signed, albeit somewhat reluctantly.

A year later, the new request was different. For a start it was a formal transfer request rather than just a refusal to re-sign. But Boro were still not going to grant it. Jack, displaying an attitude which did not bode well for the player, said: 'Even if a club came to us with a cheque for £50,000 we would not transfer Mannion. Why should we let the best player in Britain go?' Still Wilf put in his formal request. The dressing-room discontent had fuelled his desire to leave to the point of combustion.

When the *Gazette*'s Cliff Mitchell called at his house, Wilf spoke to him.

'At the beginning of last season there was a grand spirit in the dressing-room and we all got along fine. Then came the wedding-present fund and the provision by the club of this house for my bride and myself. It's been a different story since then. Some of my colleagues have snubbed me and often I've sat alone in a corner of the dressing-room. How could I give my best under conditions like that?'

Boro had sorted out homes for other players, he claimed, so why was he being picked out? Mitchell mentioned that Notts County, of the third division, were already being mentioned as audacious potential employers. He was amazed at Wilf's reply.

'I'd go to any club to get away from Teesside. I wouldn't refuse to go to the third division if the terms were satisfactory.'

It was a stunning statement, like Alan Shearer saying he'd leave Newcastle for Darlington. But it hit upon the central themes – freedom and money – of what was to become a national scandal.

Whatever the discontent, Wilf also wanted to make some money, as he admits now.

'When I got married I thought I had to get away to get some big money, because I knew people were offering it.'

At Boro his wages were fixed, like all the top professionals. He earned £12 per week in the season and £10 per week in the summer. There was also a £2 win and £1 draw bonus, the £750 benefit every five years, and he received £20 for each England appearance.

So in 1947–48 – the season he helped beat Italy 4–0, played for England on four other occasions and put on a virtuoso performance against Blackpool – he earned around £850. The bulk, about £470, was his club wages for the season. Then there was £120 out-of-season club wages, £150 from his average yearly share of his benefit (but which could only be collected at the end of each five-year period) and £100 in England fees. League win and draw bonuses, and Cup ones too, might have just nudged the total past £900. In today's money, that is about £17,000.

A present-day international of the same standing would be looking at a weekly pay packet of at least £17,000. That's not to say that Wilf and other top professional footballers were paupers – their earnings put them among the élite – but the sums were not sufficient to allow them not to worry about the future.

'In comparison with the average working man,' Tommy Lawton said, 'you were doing very well. There was a lot of unemployment and even for those in work the average wage was about £1.50 a week. What we earned was a fortune compared to the man in the street, but you had to live up to it. You had to dress correctly, be seen in the right clothes, and not let the club down like that, which cost money. And you knew you wouldn't be doing it forever.'

Boro, while paying the going rate, paid no more, unlike some other clubs. Some offered cash inducements, others jobs of various descriptions – many of them a mirage to fool the authorities – or backing for private ventures that players set up. It was an open secret but only amongst those in the know in the game. When Sunderland, the famous Bank of England club, were hauled up a couple of years later for practices which made them look like BCCI, fans were shocked at the under-the-counter payments, but few leading players, managers or officials were surprised.

Wilf found out about such scams on his trips with England, learning from other players what their fringe benefits were, how their clubs had 'helped' them to set up businesses or find a part-time, but lucrative, job. It was one of the reasons why clubs were not so keen on international call-ups for players – it gave them too much of an idea of their own worth.

'The chairmen didn't like players coming to play international football,' Sir Walter Winterbottom admits, 'because it meant them getting in touch with other professionals and hearing of what the others' deals were. After playing for England, they often went back and demanded more.'

They might even ask for a transfer if they were really dissatisfied, but that's where the contrast with today's stars was even greater than on wages. Signing for a club could be a life sentence, for once a player put his name on the dotted line he belonged to the club. At the end of each subsequent season all they had to offer was a new one-year contract which, as long as the club offered maximum terms, the player was bound to accept. The only alternative – to reject the contract – would mean he could be kept out of the game. The club was allowed to keep his registration and refuse a transfer.

On the other hand, if clubs wanted to sell, they could so at any time. The only say the players got was in accepting or declining the prospective buyer found by the club. Even if the answer was yes, no matter how big the fee involved, the player's cut was the same: a £10 signing-on fee. Of course, the signing-on fee was only payable to players switching clubs, not those re-signing for their existing teams.

It was slavery. Well-paid slavery perhaps, but slavery nonetheless. Wilf, however, was no revolutionary driven to challenge the status quo because of firmly held personal principles; he challenged it because he was trapped by it. He didn't want to get out of football, but equally he did want security, to provide for the family he and Bernadette were starting. He thought the way to do that, rightly or wrongly, was to get a transfer which would also take him away from the dressing-room bickering. It was not an unreasonable stance, but for eight months it kept him out of football.

Boro would not countenance a transfer. A board meeting was convened to discuss the request. On the eve of it, Cliff Mitchell gave some clear advice via his column:

> My own view – and I think it is shared by many Borough fans – is that the board should give an immediate 'yes' to Mannion's transfer request. I spoke to the player after he had been interviewed by manager Mr David Jack today and he was adamant in his desire – even eager – to move. He has said he has been snubbed by several of his colleagues; that he has often sat alone in the corner of the dressing-room; that he cannot give his best when his pals are 'against' him. Now it may be that one or two other players, annoyed that they did not receive the same treatment, made things a little awkward for him. I do know that the spirit in the dressing-room at Ayresome Park was different towards the end of last season from what it was at the beginning. And so I say to Middlesbrough FC: 'Let Mannion go. He is not happy here and too much has been said to be convincingly retracted. You will miss him, but it will be so much better for everyone if his request for a transfer is granted.'

Mitchell may or may not have spoken for the fans. It didn't matter either way for, no matter if the whole town said Wilf should go, there were only a handful of men whose views mattered, the directors – and they said, 'No. Absolutely not.' It was stalemate: a player, bound to a club, who wouldn't play for it; a club, allowed under football's rules to treat a man as a possession, saying to their player, 'Play for us or no one.' All summer the impasse continued, with neither side giving ground – although either giving any ground would have been a capitulation. The Boro directors were said to be convinced they would win if they held out.

Throughout the time when he should have been preparing for a new season, Wilf was losing his £10 a week wages and living on his savings, although there was a rumour he was being paid by another club to maintain his 'strike'. When the pre-season training started he was missing from Ayresome Park. On weekdays he could still be found training on South Bank FC's pitch. An international genius, wearing an old and slightly threadbare England jersey, juggled and concentrated on his fitness in a deserted non-league ground, his only companions local lads who occasionally turned up to catch a glimpse of their hero, and the amateur players preparing for games in which they aspired to show just a fraction of his ability.

One day he was joined by a familiar face – Alan Hoby of the *People*. He offered to go in goal as he chatted to a star in internal exile. He was soon nursing a wrist nearly snapped by a fierce shot, but he had his story – Wilf was prepared never to play again if Boro refused to let him go. A simple transfer request was turning into something more. Hoby wrote:

> Now personal liberty is a precious thing. It is one of the things we went to war about. David Jack, giving the club's side, told me recently: 'If Mannion won't play for us, he will never play in League football again.' Frankly this seems to me to savour of dictatorship. Security: the roving, restless search for security. That is what the Mannion mess typifies. There is no security in soccer. That is why he is sticking out even though he is leading a life of misery. Saturday afternoons are torture to him. 'I love football,' he says, 'and I feel lost without it.' Security. Liberty. Fraternity. I wonder when the FA and the Football League are going to understand the true meaning of those three words ...

As Boro got off to the obligatory poor start to the new season, a new tone of defiance crept into Wilf's comments, and a new ingredient.

'I will not re-sign. A move would be better for both sides. No man should be denied his liberty of choice, even if he is a professional footballer. Football is my life and the honour of again playing for England is still my greatest ambition. But, as a footballer, this deadlock is getting me nowhere. So, either Middlesbrough must agree to transfer me or I will be obliged to leave the game to take up a job I have been offered.'

A job? Doing what and why? One of England's finest footballers was going to Oldham to sell chicken coops. He needed money, of course, but the new post would also surely force the Boro directors' hand and convince them he was serious about leaving Teesside, not to mention highlighting the absurd system whereby a star could be kept out of the game for no good reason by the men who ran it?

The job came courtesy of businessman Frank Armitage.

'He wanted me to forget entirely about football and look after my family another way,' Wilf says. 'He contacted me just at the beginning after I was out and asked me to move over. He couldn't do enough for me and used to take me all over the place with him. I even used to have all my meals in the Masonic Hall and he wanted me to become a Mason, but I said, "No, you're all right."'

There may have been some conspiracy in keeping with the Masons' reputation afoot, though. Armitage was a dedicated Oldham Athletic supporter and some saw his generosity as having the aim of securing the player's services. Wilf says: 'I think he wanted me to join [Oldham], but he never said anything specific.' Meanwhile, he was overlooked by the England selectors when they announced the squad for the match against Denmark in September because players not signed for a registered club were ineligible.

To fans denied Wilf's skills, the dispute was becoming beyond belief. In the press they vented their feelings. One, William Spellman, wrote:

> Whatever the dispute, it is of public interest that a solution should be found and at once. I hope that he will be given the freedom he asks as soon as possible so that he may give the pleasure of his presence to all lovers of a clean and classic exposition of the game.

Not that that was how the off-pitch game was going to be played during the dispute.

W ilf was not the first to highlight the madness of the transfer system. A year earlier the whole sham was laid bare by Tommy Lawton.

A *Daily Express* cartoon two days before Guy Fawkes' night summed it up best. Two scruffy street urchins were drawn huddled over a rag figure with the traditional sign scrawled on cardboard hung around his neck. Just passing out of the frame was a well-heeled man in a suit, clearly the Chelsea and England centre-forward. One of the youngsters was looking after the disappearing figure and saying to the other: 'Cor! All them thousands for Lawton and not a penny for the guy.'

Lawton was being sold for a world-record fee of £20,000 and his cut? The standard £10 signing-on fee. If he'd been sold for £100 he would still have been entitled to his tenner and nothing more. What was more, he had little say in his transfer. He had wanted a move ever since a rift opened between him and Chelsea when he refused to go on an end-of-season tour. The club wanted to show him off in Sweden and generate some money. They promised their hosts he would play. When he refused, he was dropped for the start of the next season.

He didn't play his first game of the season until more than a month in. Then, the following Monday, he slapped in a transfer request. The club wouldn't grant it; he'd only joined them a season earlier and they weren't going to let him go. He was dropped to the reserves again and left in limbo for weeks. When the directors finally changed their minds it was up to them not the player which clubs were considered.

'I didn't go to the places I wanted to go to,' Tommy said. 'They gave me a list of teams – probably the ones who offered most money. You had to go there, there or there, but nowhere else.'

The fee eventually settled on – £17,000 plus another player valued at £3000 – was a third more than the previous record. Its size staggered football, but the club that paid it was even more shocking – Notts County, fourth from bottom of the third division and in danger of having to seek re-election, were signing England's undisputed top centre-forward. The scorer of twenty goals in his twenty capped appearances was dropping to the bottom of the third division.

County were prepared to spend £100,000 to get back to the first division. So, as the *Daily Express*, put it: 'The greatest manhunt for years ended quietly in a London hotel at 2.33 yesterday when Tommy Lawton signed himself into third division football.' He played for England against Sweden at Highbury in midweek – and scored one in a 4–2 win – and then made his debut for his new club at Northampton on Saturday. It was surreal.

Despite what the system decreed and the cartoonists said, money was a key factor. Lawton's transfer made the front page of the *Daily Express* for that reason. He would be the first footballer to earn so much that he would have to pay surtax because County had arranged a selection of well-paid jobs for him to choose from, each with five-year contracts. Of course, he would have a house too, then there was his equally lucrative newspaper columns. In all his total income was estimated at £3000 – more than Chelsea boss Billy Birrell, a stalwart of Boro's 1927 promotion side – but most of it 'unofficial'.

Even Lawton wasn't the first big-name player to move club in the post-war transfer spiral. After the Great Britain v Rest of Europe game, Billy Steel moved from Greenock Morton to Derby for £15,500. Within hours of the final whistle of that game, Stanley Matthews had signed for Blackpool from Stoke for £11,500. The difference was their clubs were prepared to let them go without a fight.

'They let me go,' Sir Stanley says. 'I think the manager wanted me to leave anyway, so there was no trouble. But in those days you hadn't much choice if the club said no.'

Lawton's significance was as the first star to agitate for a move and show up the pitfalls of the system before signing for a new club under

A schoolboy star, showing off his district and county honours, including a Yorkshire cap from 1931/32.

Wilf (front right) with his older and bigger colleagues in the St Peter's School side. PE teacher Joe McCullagh (far left); head Andrew Skillen (far right); Canon McMullan (centre).

TOP LEFT: A youthful figure (back row, far right) on the fringes of Middlesbrough's side in 1937/8, the season in which he became a first team regular. Captain Bob Baxter (back row, second left), goalie Dave Cumming and Billy Forrest (next to Wilf) were among the senior players.

LEFT: In the thick of the action at Stamford Bridge, January 1938, one of his first matches as a regular. Just behind Wilf, who scored in a 1–0 win, is Micky Fenton.

TOP: Wilf (right) watches as Prime Minister Winston Churchill shakes hands with Stanley Matthews before a wartime international at Wembley in 1941. Note the war kit, without the three lions.

RIGHT: Recovering in the Middle East from injuries sustained fighting in Italy, with his mentor Bertie Mee, later the Arsenal manager.

ABOVE: Goalkeeper Da Rui is beaten as Wilf scores for Great Britain against the Rest of Europe in front of 134,000 at Hampden Park, 1947.

BELOW: Tommy Lawton shows the poacher's instinct to chase Wilf's goalbound effort and finish it off – denying the Golden Boy a hat-trick in the 6–1 win over Europe.

ABOVE: The England team that defeated Portugal 10–0,
May 1947: (back row, left to right) Laurie Scott, Eddie
Lowe, Frank Swift, Neil Franklin, Billy Wright; (front row)
Stanley Matthews, Wilf Mannion, Stan Mortensen, George
Hardwick, Tommy Lawton, Tom Finney.

BELOW: England and Italy,
showing contrasting styles
of kit, line up in the
humidity of Turin, 1948.

TOP LEFT: Wilf wears a threadbare jumper for training during his eight-month strike in 1949.

ABOVE: Back in Middlesbrough colours – and warily watched by three defenders.

LEFT: Wilf back in training with England, watched by Stan Mortensen.

BELOW LEFT: Building up his fitness, Wilf pounds the track at Highbury before the November 1947 international against Sweden, with Stanley Matthews (far left) and Harry Johnston of Blackpool (centre).

ABOVE: Billy Wright leads out an England side which included Tom Finney (fifth from right), Alf Ramsey and Matthews (both following Finney). Wilf, following Matthews, was minutes away from a horrific injury in the game against Scotland at Wembley, 1951.

RIGHT: England trainer Jimmy Trotter accompanies his inside-forward, kit covered in blood, off the pitch after a clash of heads fifteen minutes into the England–Scotland game.

BELOW: Back on Teeside in November 1951, showing local lads the skills which made him famous, on the type of pitch where he learned to play in his youth.

LEFT: Also back at home, with his family: (left to right) his aunt, Katie, his mother, Mary, his brother-in-law, Norman Robinson – another Boro player – and his wife, Wilf's sister, Sally.

BELOW LEFT: Wilf at work, servicing fire extinguishers in a Middlesbrough foundry, 1973.

BELOW: The Golden Boy, aged seventy-seven.

terms which made a mockery of the maximum wage regulations. A couple of days after he signed for County, the 'Football's gone cash crazy' headlines were trotted out again when Southend turned down £20,000 for two young, promising, but unproven, players. The transfer system was becoming a farce. Clubs, awash with cash from the attendance boom – more than 40 million spectators filed through the turnstiles in 1947–48 – were bidding ever-greater amounts for players, some of whom were not even destined to make the grade at the very highest levels. Names like Sutton, Scales, Flitcroft and even Ferdinard come to mind, but today the players share in the bonanza; then it was illegal.

Commentators began to argue for some sort of change. Most only wanted an 'improved' model of the old system. Charles Buchan for one wrote: 'Instead of making it worthwhile for a player to change his club – as the present system does – I suggest it should be made worth his while to stay on.' His ideas included benefits for unbroken service, wage increases in line with the number of years at the club and a maximum transfer fee – which would surely have opened up a new area where an artificial limit would have been flouted by under-the-counter deals.

Some players argued that football shouldn't be concerned with money. Billy Wright said: 'Money is the root of football evil. No footballer is compelled to become a professional. He does so with his eyes wide open and should be fully aware of what he is to receive in return for his services.' Those wages were good compared to the average, but there was no question that the transfer system was blatantly unfair and was coming into disrepute. Frank Butler, in the *Daily Express*, noted:

> ... although the FA and the Football League seem satisfied with it, the transfer system has become a post-war farce. At present a player is allowed to receive a substantial salary outside football, plus a house at nominal rent, but is condemned if he gets half a crown more from his transfer than the rules allow ... If I had my way the old masters like Matthews, Lawton, Docherty and others would receive a percentage of their transfer fees and would be allowed to grow rich directly from football.

That revolutionary idea would not happen for years. Even if it had, Wilf first had actually to get a transfer.

For a few short weeks at least, Oldham, Lancs, seemed like Wilf's nirvana. He had a job he enjoyed and the *Daily Express* had signed him up to write a series of articles on how to play football which also helped his finances. He had a home to his and Bernadette's liking. People living nearby would stop him in the street to offer their support for his stand, and, most importantly, that stand appeared to be close to achieving its aims.

By the end of September, Boro had decided to listen to offers. Their plight without a demon inside-forward highlighted the need for a replacement for Wilf rather than cash, so that's what they asked for. The directors announced they would 'consider parting with Wilf Mannion on an exchange basis for first-class inside-forwards.' Only 'consider' and then for inside-forwards in the plural, but still the queue formed. David Jack said: 'The Mannion rush has started. But money does not interest us. Any Mannion deal must essentially be on an exchange basis and it's inside-forwards we want.'

The move seemed to open the door for his departure to any one of twenty-five clubs soon reported to be ready to buy him, and a possible return to England's colours. As Boro were beginning to invite offers, England beat Northern Ireland 6–2, but the critics were still scathing. Stanley Rous once said: 'No England team should ever take the field without an inside-forward whose brain works as quickly as his feet.' But that's just what was lacking.

John Macadam, of the *Express,* wrote:

All the fatuities about football being a team game and the team being greater than the individual were exploded sky-high by the performance of the England team at Belfast; exploded by the absence of one man – Wilfred Mannion. As the England side floundered shapelessly on the impeccable Windsor Park turf, it was easy to visualize what the Oldham Achilles would have done to it. He would have pulled it together, knitted it and purled and plained it, given coherence to it. As it was the England team was a knotless thread, thanks to a contract system that keeps one of its greatest practitioners out of the game.

Roy Peskett, of the *Daily Mail,* added:

By his temporary departure from football, Wilf Mannion has taken something from the England team that will be difficult to replace – unless he picks up where he left off in Turin or the selectors find a natural successor. The link Mannion provided between forwards and halves is missing – the twinkle-toed genius, also possessed by Carter, Buchan, Jack, James, of being able to alter the course of a match with one quick pass. In the two fixtures this season the England team has not shown the form which took them to the top of the international tree last season.

But, given Boro's statement, he saw some hope: 'I have a sneaking feeling that if Mannion gets back into the game shortly it may be possible for him

118

to re-appear against Wales on 10 November on Villa's ground.' Cliff Mitchell too saw light at the end of the tunnel: 'I do not think it will be long before an agreement is reached ... At any rate soccer enthusiasts in the north east in particular and throughout the country in general will be glad that the Mannion story has reached its last chapter.'

The likely hero appeared to be Celtic manager Jimmy McGrory, who arrived with £30,000 – £10,000 more than the existing record fee – burning a hole in his pocket and the pick of any two of his team, including internationals, for Boro if they allowed him Wilf. But no deal was done. According to the press, the Scottish club was one of five offered to Wilf as possible new homes when David Jack went to see him a fortnight later. It was the first direct contact between club and player for more than two months. Jack was reported to have put offers on the table from all the clubs which had met Boro's requirements: Arsenal, Burnley, Manchester City and Wolves as well as Celtic. But now Wilf says no such choice was ever laid before him.

'They didn't give me that. No way. They refused everything. McGrory offered £30,000 and any two internationals in his team and they turned it down. After that, open cheque books were thrown on the table and clubs were asking them to name the figure, but they [Boro] gave the ultimatum if he doesn't sign here, we'll finish him. I don't know what the press were saying or what Middlesbrough were saying to them. But I knew what they were doing to me.'

What the press were saying was that Wilf told Jack: 'I am quite content to stay where I am for the time being. I am not unduly worried about the football position.' Then he was said to have delivered the *coup de grâce*: 'If I were asked to make a choice of club then I would suggest Oldham Athletic who, as far as I know, have never made any offer for my services.' They hadn't, because they didn't have players of a suitable quality to offer in exchange.

Wilf had been training at Boundary Park with Boro's permission. Some in the Lancashire town had been talking of securing his services from the day he arrived, but he was clearly out of the third division outfit's price range. What his reported comments seemed to indicate was that he was taking his stand against the transfer system a stage further. He'd apparently been given a transfer and a choice of the best clubs in the land, but he wanted the right to choose one of the lowliest. He wanted to decide for himself where he took his services.

'It is not in my power, according to the laws of the game, to go where I will,' he said. 'Middlesbrough must give me permission to do this or do that. The club can put me right out of the game if it wants to. Why, in the name of fairness, must I, or any of my colleagues, be treated like cattle at an auction and be forced to go only where the club desires? I do not hold Middlesbrough entirely responsible. I blame the system which allows such treatment.'

Boro were apparently going to have to consider cash offers if the player would not go to the clubs which had met the exchange criteria. Wilf apparently wanted to stay in Oldham, where he'd settled, but that still meant there were up to a dozen clubs who would be interested. From the big names – Manchester United, Liverpool and Everton, the type of clubs who could meet the estimated £30,000 fee – to Athletic, who frankly couldn't.

Wilf's next bombshell, a fortnight later, appeared to be aimed at allowing Athletic a level playing field. Donald Cameron, of the *Oldham Evening Chronicle,* who had kept tabs on the saga ever since Wilf arrived in town reported: 'Mannion Issues An Ultimatum. "£12,000 Limit For My Transfer."' Cameron quoted Wilf as saying:

> I will not stand for this rocketing of transfer values. I have considered the matter from all angles and with all its implications and I am stating without reserve that I shall absolutely decline to sign for any club that pays, or even offers to pay, Middlesbrough over £12,000 for me. If that is not a generous payment to a club who have had my best services since I was seventeen years of age and who paid only £10 for me in the first instance, then I am indeed a poor judge of values. I admit I have been on top wages all the time, which is now £12 a week in the playing season and £10 in summer, but Middlesbrough would not have paid me that did I not give value in return. Why they should expect to cash in to the extent of the equivalent of forty years of the wages value they have put on me in the past is hard to understand.

Cameron limited himself to commenting: 'If there is money in such abundance in the game, let more be paid to the people who earn it.' But his interview with Wilf was a genuine scoop. The Golden Boy was doing nothing more nor less than trying to blow the lid off the transfer system. If he was allowed to decide which club he wanted to go to and for what price, players everywhere would want the same right. As Cameron noted in an earlier piece: 'If never before, the position is being brought home to clubs now that players are not to be bought and sold willy, nilly. They are determined to have a say in their own destinies, and it is right that should be so.'

But today Wilf denies he issued such a price ultimatum or even wanted to play for Oldham.

120

'I never thought of playing for them – I was holding out for a big club, but Middlesbrough weren't having any of it. I wouldn't have gone there [Oldham] – I'd have been a fool wouldn't I?' Of Cameron, he adds: 'Whatever he did, he did it himself. I think he wanted me in Oldham, but I wasn't interested.'

Even so, the reaction from Boro to the reported comments was stupefaction.

'I am very tired of the Mannion saga,' David Jack said, 'and it would surprise me if people in football generally and on Teesside in particular were not of the same mind. I must confess that I am staggered at the new development. It almost seems as though the tail is trying to wag the dog. If it is true that Mannion has said he will not go to any club that offers to pay more than £12,000 for his transfer I am afraid I cannot admire him much as a businessman. Surely the player does not think I enjoy either paying or receiving these big transfer fees, but it must be obvious to everybody that if this or any other club was prepared to accept a sum of £12,000 for a player of Mannion's ability, they must be in a position to be able to buy a player of comparative skill for a comparative outlay. This means that if we accept £12,000 for Mannion we do not expect to pay more than £10,000 for any other player you could mention.'

He claimed that three of the clubs he had offered Wilf a transfer to were within twenty miles of Oldham, before adding: 'I regret that Mannion, with whom I have always been on the most friendly terms, should have adopted the attitude of a dictator. He has been very ill-advised – if he has been advised, of which I am not convinced – but if it so happens that he is acting entirely on his own initiative, I am afraid I cannot give him many marks for his business acumen or his love of soccer.'

Looking back, perhaps Jack's comments about advisers were the most pertinent of the entire saga. There were no such things as advisers or agents, and it was clear Wilf needed one, as he now admits.

'Boro were so keen to keep me because they were laughing all the way to the bank – they had 45,000 in the ground, 47,000, even 53,000 a couple of times. I was pulling people into the ground and they didn't have to give me a ruddy penny – and they certainly didn't give me a penny. You needed an agent to do your work for you really, you shouldn't be on your own because they would just take advantage.'

Not that the dispute was any easier on some at Boro. Charlie Summerbell, of the *Daily Mirror*, once found Jack in tears over it. Summoned to the manager's office and expecting a ticking off for writing a piece backing Wilf, the reporter instead had to hand Jack his handkerchief.

On the other hand, Boro vice-chairman Harry French showed that such a soft side did not reflect the general opinion: 'Mannion's attitude to his transfer, if he maintains it, will mean that he will be out of football forever. Under such circumstances we will not transfer him.'

Whenever members of the extended football family met, there was only one topic of conversation – the Mannion case. At Villa Park for the England–Wales game in mid-November, which Wilf didn't come close to making despite the press predictions, Fred Howarth, the League Secretary, said: 'All this talk of a slave market is wrong.' Jimmy Guthrie, chairman of the Players' Union, replied: 'The transfer system as it is at present was evolved in the days of Alf Common. It just will not do today. We want a free market and none of this present restriction.' One manager, quoted anonymously, even predicted such a system was not far away.

The reason was that the great and good from outside football were taking up Wilf's case. Labour MP for Stoke, Ellis Smith, raised the matter in the Commons. Guthrie backed the move.

'I think it is against all the principles of our democracy,' he said, 'that human beings should be bought body and soul like these players. What we are trying to break down is illustrated by the case of Mannion. His contract has expired, yet, owing to the system in vogue he can be held by Middlesbrough, who can place a huge sum on his head and in that way stop him playing football. We want to see a contract which gives footballers the same freedom as people in other occupations. While a club can hold a player, perhaps by placing a price of £20,000 on him, they need not offer him a wage.'

He suggested a system whereby a club could buy a player's contract and, if he agreed to be sold while it was still valid, there would be a transfer fee. But when it expired he would become – in a phrase which still strikes fear into clubs – a free agent. David Jack gave Boro's reply: 'We are not in the least bit interested. We intend to let things take their course and we have said our last word on the subject.'

Smith called on the Minister of Labour, George Isaacs, to convene a tribunal into the football transfer system.

'I will try to get the parties together,' he replied and consultations began on the way forward. The union, the FA and League got around to meeting in mid-December and agreed to meet again in January. But by then the affair had moved on again.

Oldham had eventually put in a cash bid of £15,000. They were prepared to mortgage Boundary Park for £10,000 and commit £5000 of unused capital. The answer was simple – no. There wasn't even any point talking about it. Boro's stance was unsurprising given that a potential white knight had appeared in the shape of Everton manager Cliff Britton. Merseyside was near enough, surely, to commute to Oldham? Britton was also a former colleague of Wilf's from during the war when they played together in service teams. What's more, Everton were prepared to pay £27,000.

Britton, trying to make a signing which would lift his team away from the bottom of the first division table, was said to have met Wilf three times. A team which hadn't scored in any of its eight away games needed some forward magic. But, after a couple of days, the man who could provide it said no, without reference to the £12,000 limit he had supposedly put on his own head some weeks before. Wilf didn't comment. It was his boss Mr Armitage who revealed: 'Mannion does not want to be playing away every weekend.' Did that mean he would play for no one but Athletic? Mr Armitage refused to comment.

For the Oldham fans, it did. And if he wanted to play for them, they wanted him. So began one of the most remarkable campaigns seen in post-war football – the public appeal to buy Wilf Mannion. Bakers sold Mannion cakes, collection tins appeared all over town, footballs and scarves autographed by the man himself were raffled and even the money from matchday carparks was donated as were the profits from the refreshment stalls. The British Legion Band chipped in by donating half of the collection from its pre-match playing.

A group going under the name of the Shareholders Association co-ordinated the campaign and called on everyone to do what they could – lend the club money at 2 per cent interest, start subscription lists in workplaces and social clubs or even buy unissued shares to generate extra income. The total swiftly passed £2000 of the £10,000 needed to bridge the gap between what the board was prepared to put up and the £25,000 Boro were said to be ready to accept. The £4000 mark also came and went.

But as November turned to December, problems were beginning to appear with the first hints that the board did not want to co-operate with the association or accept its loans. As the countdown to Christmas began the deal was looking shaky. Finally, two days before Christmas, the news broke that the directors had decided that Oldham did not want Wilf at any price – or specifically £25,000. It prompted one businessman to offer an interest-free loan of £6000 to meet the target. But it was all too late. In a complete about turn, the directors decided they could and would pay no more than £15,000. Cameron reported: 'The Mannion dream is over.'

Wilf headed back to Teesside for Christmas to 'think things over'.

'I am very disappointed Oldham have failed to sign me,' he said. 'I appreciate the difficulties of the position. I would have liked to have played for the club but obviously the cost is too high. I have nothing further to say except that I am happy working as a salesman.'

The Shareholders Association had plenty to say, entirely to the board. A three-hour meeting brought no change of heart from the directors despite the loan offer. Club chairman Percy Skipworth said: 'I don't think my board would be prepared to re-open the matter. Even though the loan might be interest free, it would still be a capital charge on the club. £15,000 was our maximum offer and even that would have required guarantees. I am very sorry that we are unable to sign Mannion. I think he is an artist who ought not to be kept out of the game.'

Shareholders Association secretary Tom Mellor, perhaps wondering why the board had not made that clear before £4000 was raised, could only manage to say: 'The fund is closed. Steps will be taken to return the money after Christmas.' After Christmas, his group launched an attempted boardroom coup against Skipworth's regime. The 150 association members who attended a special meeting called for the heads of nine of the eleven directors to be replaced by five of their own number. What could have been one of Oldham's greatest moments became a civil war, which the board eventually won.

Back on Teesside, Wilf donned his football boots to referee a game at South Bank's ground. The charity match on New Year's morning was between two pubs, the Princess Alice Hotel and the Victoria Hotel. Landlord of the Princess Alice was Tom Curtis, a former Bradford player, and one of his team-mates was another ex-City star, Bob Turnbull; the same Bob Turnbull who had played with Wilf for Smiths Dock all those years before and stood up for him when Micky Ruddy threatened to break his legs. It all seemed such a long time ago.

Birmingham became the next possible destination. Aston Villa were among the first to show in the resumed race for Wilf's signature in the New Year. He took a train to the second city for a meeting with the directors and a very interesting one it was, too.

First up Villa said they would meet Boro's £25,000 asking price. Then they told Wilf they were prepared to slip £3000 his way as well and they would also find him a well-paid job, albeit one which required no more work than sitting at home pretending to be making telephone calls to gee up business. It would be worth £25 per week on top of his wages. Just for his trouble in going to Brum for the meeting and to show the Villans meant business, he'd get £25 for that day too.

'I have told Aston Villa that I am willing to play for them,' Wilf said, 'but they have to get Middlesbrough to agree and then it would depend on the terms offered whether I agree to sign. It is not certain Middlesbrough will agree.' Too true. Now he says: 'The chairman was sitting at this enormous table and he just came out with it and said, "How much do you want?" I said so-and-so and he said, "That's okay. I'll get this sorted out." But it never got sorted out.'

One stumbling block was that Villa were battling with Boro at the bottom of the table to avoid the drop. It would seem unwise to sell to a team who could condemn Boro to an even more desperate plight. Sure enough the deal collapsed within days – but because of Wilf, according to Boro. David Jack said the player was unable to agree terms with Villa. He claimed the Villa secretary had phoned Ayresome Park to say Wilf was stalling, so Boro put out a statement which said: 'Mannion will not sign for Aston Villa.'

Wilf's version was rather different. He angrily dismissed Boro's story.

'I offered to sign for Aston Villa. I was prepared to play for the Villa. The whole affair has been a complete puzzle and a decided worry to me because there was no reason why a story should be spread that negotiations broke down because of any action on my part.' He was no further on. Boro appeared to be still blocking his transfer by any means necessary.

One other potential saviour was Arsenal's manager, Tom Whittaker. He had been determined to get his man from the moment he put in his first bid based on the player exchange then wanted. On New Year's Eve he made it known he was still in the race.

'We are all out to get Mannion. If Wilf Mannion shows the slightest interest in joining Arsenal I shall at once take a train to Oldham to talk it over with him.'

So he did. He cleared it with David Jack, his former player, then sent a telegraph: 'Coming Oldham see you. Please hold yourself available for interview. Whittaker. Arsenal.' Bernadette made a pot of tea as the men talked.

'I understand you'd like a move Wilf,' said the observant Whittaker. 'I've come to see if you'd care to join us at Highbury. I've agreed terms with Middlesbrough. Now it's up to you. Before you decide I must tell you this. You won't get a penny more from us than your legal £10 signing-on fee. The Arsenal don't do business any other way.' Wilf politely turned him down. Whittaker stayed long enough for the tea and to make sure Wilf couldn't be persuaded. It appeared greed had got the better of him.

In fact, Bernadette did not want to move to London. She had a good reason: with her pregnancy getting closer to its conclusion, she didn't want to be so far away from her parents in Middlesbrough.

Huddersfield Town, managed by Peter Docherty, were rumoured to be next in line to try to obtain the most elusive signature in English football, but before they could really try, someone else – and amazingly, Boro – had secured it. Wilf was prepared to keep waiting: 'I definitely wouldn't have gone back to Middlesbrough, even if it meant not playing football again. I was happy to stay out.' But Bernadette's pregnancy forced the decision.

'There were reporters outside throwing little stones at the window at 2 a.m. and saying, "Have you heard the news? Your case is being taken up in Parliament." It was fantastic news. But the next day Bernadette took a turn for the worse. We saw a doctor and he told us that we had to get home immediately and put her into a nursing home. We didn't have any choice.' Mother and son would be fine, but medical advice was to get her into care closer to her family.

Boro director Tommy Thomas made a dash to Oldham after hearing from Wilf that it might not be a wasted journey. The pair immediately thrashed out the differences between club and player, according to the press reports. Just before midnight, Thomas got the signature all football had wanted for eight months. The prodigal was heading home.

A joint statement said: 'Middlesbrough Football Club and Wilf Mannion have agreed to sink their differences. It is agreed that there have been faults on both sides. Middlesbrough are delighted to have the player back and he is delighted to return to the scene of his former triumphs. It would be a pleasure to both club and player if the public would realize that differences in points of view do arise from time to time and that it takes diplomacy to get over these differences.' There was no mention of the reason for the *rapprochement*.

The Boro board's joy knew no bounds. At the very start they had thought Wilf wouldn't hold out and he hadn't. The directors could afford to show some good grace in victory. Chairman Bill Kelly said: 'I am delighted that Mannion is returning. It is one of the finest things that could have happened to the club.' Thomas said: 'I am the happiest man in the world. I have been in football a long time and am proud to think that I am responsible for seeing the end of this dispute and bringing the player home to Middlesbrough.'

Pounds signs lit up in David Jack's eyes as he was equally overcome.

'There is great excitement in the town at Mannion's re-appearance. We expect an increase of 10,000 on our average gate this season.'

Frankly, people wouldn't believe it until they saw Wilf in a red shirt for themselves. Skipper George Hardwick added: 'Glad to see him back? Of course we will be. We can use Wilf. He is a great player and can help us a lot. If there have been hard feelings on either side, these have not lingered and will not crop up again. Mannion at his best, as we know him, can be a big asset to Middlesbrough in their present struggle.'

One man watched sadly as Wilf left Oldham in Thomas's Rolls-Royce. As the *Daily Express* put it: 'Did you ever see a dream walking? Sixty-year-old businessman Frank Armitage did yesterday. It stepped into a Rolls-Royce. The engine purred. And his £25,000 dream left Oldham for Middlesbrough.' Armitage watched Wilf leave the house he had rented for him and tried to put on a brave face. He still wanted the star to be his salesman in the north east, a generous gesture, but one which was declined.

Wilf's comments betrayed his mixed feelings: 'There had to be an end to this state of affairs sometime and I believe the people of Middlesbrough will understand that there no longer is a difference between the club and me.' He was put straight into the team for the match against fellow strugglers Preston and admitted: 'It will feel a bit strange at first and it will probably take me about three or four matches to get back into form.'

When he ran out at Ayresome his face gave away his disappointment. A frown and a furrowed brow replaced the usual smile. He looked down instead of out at the crowd greeting him. The band struck up 'For He's A Jolly Good Fellow' and the Chief Constable broadcast a welcome-home message, which mixed with an overwhelming roar greeting the emergence of a familiar blond figure. His ears might tell him otherwise, but in his heavy heart Wilf knew the rapturous welcome heralded his biggest ever defeat. It had cost him £400 in lost earnings from football, and he was back at Boro on the same wages, as tied to the club as ever.

Despite torrential rain, the crowd was more than 5000 above the average for the season and only just under 5000 behind the bumper 43,455 Sunderland had drawn for the previous home game. In front of them eight press photographers ran on to the pitch to get the picture of the day. A buzz as electric as the camera flashes crackled around the ground.

Wilf wasn't even playing in his preferred inside-left role. Wing-half Jimmy Gordon had been picked to play there – the sixth man to fill the position in Wilf's absence – when the return of its prime practitioner seemed as likely as a killer whale swimming in the Tees, and David Jack stuck with the replacement. Wilf was picked as inside-right and did what was expected of him. In front of a banner declaring simply 'Mannion-borough', he created a goal. He dribbled along the right touchline and cut the ball back for the queuing forwards to try their luck. Fenton and Spuhler had shots blocked before left-winger Geoff Walker smashed home. He made straight for the creator and shook his hand.

Lacking match fitness, Wilf faded. But Boro, fourth from bottom at kick-off, held on for a 1–0 win, their first in six games. At the final whistle, as the crowd cheered itself hoarse one final time, George Hardwick walked up to Wilf and accompanied him off the pitch, arm-in-arm. In the dressing-room Wilf said: 'This is like old times. The first game was tough but I expected that. The boys were fine and, after the most worrying six months of my life, the thrill of having a hand in that winning goal was worth a good deal to me.'

In the boardroom, the thrill was felt even more profoundly. Bill Kelly said: 'There is only one Mannion. Middlesbrough is a team of units and we are hoping to gather those units around Wilf now that he is back.' Tommy Thomas was happier still: 'The relegation threat to Middlesbrough has gone; we are now on the way up the league table. He [Wilf] has brought back unity to the team; he has provided the missing link – that ability to weld the boys into a first-class combination.'

David Jack, perhaps confused by the commotion and emotion of the day, appeared to mistake his number eight for a youth-team player coming back after injury.

'I thought that Mannion had a very good game considering he has been out of it for so very long. He made a very good debut, which promises much from him.'

Wilf delivered, although it was still a close-run thing. Relegation was avoided on the last day of the season by one point. Boro needed to draw at, ironically, Villa. If they lost and Preston won, Boro would go down instead of Finney and Co. Preston won 2–0. Boro drew 1–1.

'It was the longest match I ever played,' Wilf said. 'Villa threw everything at us . . . they were hardly out of our penalty box. And that big clock on the Villa ground seemed to go oh so slowly. How we all breathed with relief when we heard the final whistle.'

Teamed with new signing Andy Donaldson – a £17,000 capture from Newcastle when the Geordies refused to sell their number one striker, Jackie Milburn, and off-loaded his deputy instead – Wilf scored four precious goals in the final thirteen games of the season. Donaldson got six, even though he missed a game, and a promising youngster named Hartnett grabbed four, including a priceless hat-trick in a 3–1 win over fellow relegation candidates Sheffield United.

In that game, the last home fixture of the season, Boro seemed to be slipping away from division one when they fell behind to a Hardwick own goal and then he compounded his error by missing a penalty. But Wilf had other ideas. He dominated midfield, even though he was opposed by Jimmy Hagan, a rival in the North versus South schoolboy trials all those years ago. Mannion was majestic; Boro were saved.

Soon after a sign went up in Ayresome Park. It was a treatise on loyalty, borrowed from Elbert Hubbard: 'If you work for a man, in heaven's name work for him. If he pays wages that supply your bread and butter, work for him; think well of him; stand by him and stand by the institution he represents. If you must vilify, condemn and eternally disparage, resign your position and when you are outside, damn it to your heart's content. But, I pray you, so long as you are part of the institution, do not condemn it . . . not that you will injure the institution – not that – but when you disparage a concern of which you are part, you disparage yourself.'

Such blasé defences of the skewered status quo held sway for another fifteen years before another one-man stand dismissed them. George Eastham used the courts to sue the club which refused to let him go, Newcastle United, for restraint of trade. It was a test case of new rules formulated three years earlier which also registered the demise of the maximum wage.

At Eastham's shoulder throughout was a former Brentford and Fulham half-back who knew the Mannion case and the player all too well. Jimmy Hill, then a young player learning the ropes, had followed Wilf's saga with interest. He tried to follow the player himself in a match at Craven Cottage.

'He was running all over, enjoying himself, and as he was doing it he was taking the mickey out of Walter Winterbottom and me and just making fun of the coaching system, which he clearly didn't have much time for,' Hill says.

Boro won that game 3–2, more than five years after Wilf lost his fight.

Little more than another five years and Hill and Eastham would win theirs. It's hard not to wonder if Wilf could have secured a similar victory if he'd had the backing of Hill's rejuvenated and renamed Professional Footballers' Association. Possibly not – it took times to change before the rules did, but the role Wilf played should not be underestimated, according to Hill.

'George Eastham is the name everyone remembers but he was just the one who got caught in the system and became the test case. Years before, Wilf had been caught just the same and highlighted the problems. Over the years in between, the authorities had relieved the pressure by increasing the maximum wage. It was £8 before the war, £12 when I signed for Brentford in 1949 and then it went up to £14 and then £20. They offered £30 – a 50 per cent rise – and we were tempted to take it just before going to the courts, but it was the principle we wanted to establish.'

By the time the battle was won, Wilf had long finished playing. He even went into print to advise Eastham to back down.

'You're waging a one-man, lonely battle, George. I know ... I tried it once. You can't win. Not unless your club have a change of heart.'

His view was not surprising. He was still paying for his stand. David Jack, who resigned disillusioned with football in February 1952, had revealed after he quit: 'Mannion now knows that he need have no worry when his playing career is over. Wilf will still not be allowed to leave Middlesbrough. The club has already made arrangements to look after him when his playing days are over.' But it didn't happen that way. As Jack noted in his despair with football: 'It's a game without mercy.' Old players who got on the wrong side of the authorities paid with their livelihoods – present and future.

The danger of overstepping the mark in any fight with the authorities was obvious. Wilf later claimed that was another part of the reason why he re-signed. He feared he was about to be painted as a crook himself.

'I only re-signed ... because I was scared into it. Stories were going around – stories that I was holding out my hand whenever I met a Middlesbrough director. They just weren't true. But there was a complication and it frightened all the fight out of me. Frank Armitage ... called me into his hotel room in Oldham one morning and said, "Mr Mannion, I'm making you a little present." He pressed a packet into my hand. It contained £200 in notes! Mr Armitage said it was because he was pleased with the business I was bringing in and, as he repeatedly assured me this was so, I had no scruples about taking the money. But later, remembering it was Mr Armitage's dearest wish that I should stay in the town to play for Oldham Athletic, I realized that my action might be misinterpreted. I immediately had visions of myself on the FA's carpet, facing charges that I was a black marketeer.'

Every time there was a new story of a transfer, there was another bonus.

'Then I heard from a friend in Middlesbrough that there was someone in the town who was going to tell the FA something that would start an inquiry and get me thrown out of the game in disgrace. At that point I decided my stay-away strike had gone too far. I realized that as I had taken the £200 it would be the easiest thing in the world for someone to argue that it was a bribe to stop me playing for Middlesbrough and so that Oldham could get me. And it would be the hardest thing in the world to get the FA to believe my story – the truth. By then I was sick and tired of the rows and those threats were the last straw. I went straight back to Middlesbrough and signed for the club. I swear I never made a penny out of my peace-making with the club. In fact I lost money. "I feel I've let you down," I told Mr Armitage. I told him I was repaying the bonuses. "I don't want the money – you earned it," he insisted with typical generosity. But I was equally insistent that he should have it. And back it went.'

Wilf also admitted he regretted his stand.

'In a way I do because it affected my family. They've all been great, but it put a lot of pressure on them.' He knew what went wrong. 'I can see now that what I needed was a trustworthy adviser. I didn't have much idea of the value of money and was far too free with what I had. I lived for the day and if I saw somebody a bit down I would try to help them.' He was the one in need of help.

And lest anyone thinks Mannion's case was an isolated one, or had more to do with him personally than with football as a whole, bear in mind the stories that two of his playing colleagues tell. Tom Finney remembers being approached by an Italian club and offered £10,000 to sign for them. He informed Preston's chairman that he wanted to leave but was told: 'What's £10,000 to thee, lad?'

'I said, "Well, it's a fortune. I'd have to play here for ten years to earn that sort of money – and there's £120 a week and a villa too." But in those days the onus was on the club and the players were signed to them for life. If I'd said to Preston I'm not going to play for you they would have said, "Okay, that's fair enough but you don't play for anybody else because we'll hold your registration and you'll have no money."'

Then there were the machinations Len Shackleton endured at Sunderland. During his record transfer, for £20,050, just months before Wilf's stand, he was given a 'bung', he recently admitted. When his career was ended prematurely by an injury, he asked for a testimonial and it was slow in coming until he blackmailed the club's chairman, Syd Collings, who later became chairman of the England selectors, into granting one. Around the same time Sunderland's unorthodox financial affairs led to several directors, not including Collings, being fined and suspended, while the club was also fined.

As Shackleton recounted his story for the first time, forty-seven years after Wilf trained at South Bank in an England jersey which provided his only link with a game from which he had exiled himself, another footballer won not just the battle but the war. When Jean-Marc Bosman reached the end of his contract with Belgium's FC Liège he wanted to join Dunkirk in France. Liège would not let him go, demanded a £500,000 fee and cut his salary by 75 per cent. They even played in red, to give the historical parallel an added visual theme.

Five years later he walked from the European Court of Justice a free man and with new freedoms for all footballers metaphorically tucked up in the case notes under his arm. Of the football authorities he beat, he said: 'They are people without scruple. They have no respect for the rights of others and are basically incompetent.' Gordon Taylor, president of the international body of players' associations, added: 'Hopefully, never again will a footballer be denied the right to join the club of his choice when his contract expires.'

Bosman went bankrupt and his marriage broke up during his fight. There were rumours he drank too much. He even lived in a lock-up garage when he found he wasn't eligible for unemployment benefit. When he won, he said: 'The transfer slavery ruined my life and my career, so I have no regrets [about the effects] of my action on everybody else's career.' In a small council house in Redcar there was a old man – also rumoured to have drunk too much when his career was washed up and he had to live through the consequences of it – who wished he could have uttered those words long before Bosman was even born.

· EIGHT ·

'Rio and out'

There are bad losers and bad losers. Everyone who takes to a pitch, from Hackney Marshes to Highbury, dislikes defeat, but to give up your place at the world championship just because one of the other finalists beat you in qualifying takes sports sulking to new heights – or should that be lows? Anyhow, step up Scotland, 1950.

Scotland's clashes with England barely needed extra spice, but the first home international meeting of a new decade was sizzling with added seasoning. At stake was not just the destination of the domestic championship but also for the Scots – because of their own selectors' pig-headedness – a place in the 1950 World Cup finals in Brazil.

All four British teams were eligible for the tournament for the first time. A dispute over payments to amateurs which caused them to resign *en bloc* from FIFA and so miss the first three World Cups from 1930, had been settled. To show there were no hard feelings, FIFA had generously awarded the Brits two places at the first post-war finals, which would go to the top two teams in the home international championship. As England and Scotland had both already beaten Northern Ireland and Wales, that should have been that.

But the Scottish FA made sure it wasn't by deciding that it would only send a team to Rio if it won the championship. So what should have been a warm-up – albeit a fiercely contested one, at Hampden Park – for a possible meeting in Brazil, suddenly became, in effect, a Cup final for the Scots. Thanks to their FA, the team had to win or draw to qualify. As reigning champions, the Scots would retain the home international title if the two countries had the same number of points, but it was unnecessary pressure to get a result nonetheless.

Roy Peskett, in the *Daily Mail*, captured the expectation bearing down on the Scottish players:

Has there ever been a more dramatic meeting in the long series stretching back to 1872, when the gold tasselled caps were worn instead of being tucked away in the glass case of today? Hanging on the match is the biggest-ever 'bonus' any international team has ever been offered. And that goes for Mussolini's Italian team and Hitler's regimented Nazi eleven. The Scots officials have in effect said to their players: 'Win or draw at Hampden and you go to Rio – with an eight-week holiday trip to South America including two fourteen-day boat journeys plus the possibility of six international games at £20 a time in the World Cup play-offs. If you lose, there is nothing.'

There was nothing, except crushing disappointment, as Scotland lost 1–0. Among the Englishmen celebrating was scorer Roy Bentley. The Chelsea centre-forward had been played at inside-left alongside Mortensen in an experiment which created a dual-pronged attack. It worked beautifully as the pair linked up for Bentley to advance on the Scottish goal and beat keeper Cowan. The gasp of anguish as he looked over his shoulder to see the ball hit the back of the net summed up the despair of his countrymen.

But England's formation required the other inside-forward – the only one, in effect – to play for two men, and of course Wilf did. He'd only just made it back into the England team after finding form, fitness and forgiveness after his strike. Back in a white shirt, he also found it was, for the first time, one bearing the number eight, the inside-right's number. The majority of his pre-war Boro appearances had been at inside-right, despite being predominantly left-footed, but switching flanks didn't bother him at any level.

'From my schoolboy days,' he says, 'I always played either inside-left or right. Some players were uncomfortable with their left or with their right, but to me it didn't mean a thing because I could hit with both just as well.'

The Scots knew that all too well. He only finished on the losing side against them once in six international matches and never in four inter-league games, while his Great Britain performance, of course, also took place in Scotland.

Bentley was swift to give credit for the latest win where it was due.

'Wilf really lived up to his reputation. He never stopped running and scheming. What a player! He was small and sturdily built, two-footed and possessed this knack of spraying short passes about with deadly accuracy. He could slow the pace to suit himself. He seemed to have all the time in the world and was always available to take a pass.'

The winner came when he stepped over a ball, allowing it to run to Bobby Langton, then ran to the touchline, taking watchful defenders with him and creating the space for Mortensen and Bentley to exploit. Minutes earlier he had created a goal for Mortensen but it was disallowed for offside. It didn't matter. One was enough.

The victorious England players said their farewells and looked forward to a trip to Rio. Wilf, after his troubles, might have savoured the prospect more than most. But if he was in danger of getting carried away, he was brought back down to earth with a thump within minutes, getting another illustration of his place in the general scheme of things.

At the railway station, as FA officials were counting gate receipts from the game of almost £32,000, he got on the slow train back to Darlington and had to stand in a corridor because no one had thought to spend a shilling on booking him a seat. Carrying a painful knock on his knee from the match, he managed to squat on his suitcase and stayed there for the entire journey. A fellow passenger recognized him and said there was space in first-class, but Wilf's ticket was not valid for it and he couldn't afford to pay the extra himself.

A couple of days later Cliff Mitchell recounted the story to his readers:

> On the field of play Middlesbrough's Wilf Mannion was outstanding. On his way home he was just standing ... It was a sorry lapse on the part of the responsible officials, who should have foreseen that thousands of people would be travelling. Wilf does not complain ... [but] let us hope that the men who pile the money into football's coffers receive slightly better treatment in the future.

They do, as Tom Finney found out when he was recently guest of honour at an England international at Wembley and came out afterwards to meet the chauffeur who had been detailed to take him back to his hotel.

'One of his mates was taking four of the players back up to Middlesbrough and Newcastle – taking them up and then driving back on his own. In our days the game would finish and they'd just say well make your own way back, so you went back by sleeper or whatever. You'd get expenses, but only third class. You wouldn't dream of travelling first class – it was too expensive and you wouldn't have got paid anyway. Changed days now, aren't they?'

Wilf's international comeback trail to make the Rio play-off game had not been smooth, even if it had been relatively short.

He played his last England game before his strike in Italy, then missed four internationals – against Denmark, Northern Ireland, Wales and Switzerland – while out of football. Once he was back in a Boro shirt, the England selectors did not recall him for another two matches, against Scotland and Sweden.

The last of these, a stunning 3–1 defeat against the Scandinavian amateurs, capped a series of poor results, which included a 0–0 draw with Denmark and a 3–1 defeat by Scotland at Wembley. Wilf, back in the squad, was watching the Sweden game from the stands, chewing over the inequities of football, knowing that Juventus scouts were in Stockholm with £15,000 to spend on securing his services, but equally knowing that, even if a formal bid was made, he would not be allowed to leave Boro. Juventus instead bid for Swede Tich Carlson.

Calls for Wilf's England recall had begun almost as soon as he started playing again for Boro. Within two months of his comeback against Preston he appeared for the Football League against the Scottish League and fuelled the debate over his selection. He wasn't the player of old, some said; he'd lost his pace; his passing had gone to pot. But he was still popular. A cartoon at the time showed a politician on the stump pledging: '. . . and I assure you that, if elected, we shall do our utmost to bring back Wilf Mannion and Tommy Lawton.'

Even those less than impressed with his game agreed he was the best man for the England job. Reporter Charles Sampson of the *Empire News* wrote:

> Mannion is not the power he was. Wilf got through a lot of hard work; some of it was brilliant, some of it lamentable. The edge has gone from his speed and there were times when he lost possession of the ball too easily. Yet to offset this, so much of what he did was good and bore the Mannion hallmark. That first goal for instance. It was Mannion who prised open the Scottish defence with a glorious pass out to Finney and the Preston winger completed the move by lobbing the ball inside for Milburn to score. My overall impression is that, despite his weaknesses, Wilf fitted into the scheme of things. The inside-left position has been England's problem ever since Wilf quitted the scene at the end of last season. So far the England selectors have failed to find a successor. Mannion is not what he was, but even so, I can think of no one yet capable of replacing him.

When the recall finally came in May 1949, it was short-lived – a starring role in a 4–1 win over Norway in Oslo (a year and two days after that last cap against Italy) and in a 3–1 win over France in Paris four days later. But England's next match, in September, ended in a 2–0 home defeat to the

Republic of Ireland, the first victory by a visiting foreign side. The Republic's goalkeeper, carpenter Tommy Godwin, was the hero as he played the match of his life on his first trip across the Irish Sea, but the English selectors were looking for villains of the piece. The entire forward line was out of sorts and all but Finney were missing for the next game. Even he was switched back from left to right-wing.

Wilf, replaced by Len Shackleton, missed the 4–1 win over Wales, both countries' first-ever World Cup qualifying match, a 9–2 tubbing of Northern Ireland and a slightly lucky 2–0 win over Italy at White Hart Lane, all in the autumn. But, as the World Cup year dawned, his club form was sparkling once more. On New Year's Day he wooed the press in a 1–1 draw at Portsmouth. Alan Hoby, of the *People,* made a 'personal pilgrimage' and had his prejudices confirmed:

> England must bring back Mannion. Here is a great international footballer. A joy to watch. From his blond hair to his deft, dainty feet, Mannion epitomizes England's greatest need – an inside-forward who can hold the ball and open up a defence. Here is a miniature master of the first-time pass. Mannion broke just about even with Portsmouth's Jim Dickinson, but he still can kill a ball and move it forward more quickly than any other inside-forward I know. Yes, bring back Mannion for Scotland and Rio.

John Macadam, in the *Daily Express*, agreed:

> Now the cry for the return of Wilf Mannion to the England side must be repeated, for undoubtedly he is one of the classiest inside-forwards still in the game. His handling of the ball and his parting with it is absolutely first class.

He was picked to play for the English League to play the League of Ireland in February and scored a hat-trick in a 7–0 win. He was chosen for a B international against Holland a week later and was man of the match.

'Mannion, who played a brilliant, orthodox game, time and again penetrated the Dutch defence,' the *Mail*'s Peskett reported.

But the big test came the following month. Wilf got the final chance to prove he was back to international class before the crunch game with Scotland and of all places at Ayresome Park, in front of 39,352 in a dress rehearsal for the big game to come at Hampden. Bert Williams, Swift's successor in goal, Aston, Wright and Franklin gave the Football League team that met the Scottish League the flavour of the full England team. Mortensen, now at centre-forward, and Mannion, re-united in the forward line to great effect, only added to the impression. Mortensen scored twice in the 3–1 win. Wilf, maker of all three from inside-right, shone as brightly. Albert Booth, of the *Daily Herald*, simply concluded:

> Mortensen and Mannion go to Hampden automatically. A superb Mortensen display of skilful football and electric bursts decided that he is England's centre-forward beyond dispute. Mannion was the real craftsman.

Pat Collins, in the *Daily Mail*, added: 'Wilf Mannion is back and can now start laying up a stock of his special lemonade to take to South America.'

The special lemonade was his after-match tipple, taken in pints from a shop near his home, he told Collins. The reporter took the details down, but noted something far more interesting – the Golden Boy seemed to have grown up.

'We found in talking to him a different Wilf from the one we once knew. The golden-haired glamour picture has faded; today's player is a serious, matured person on and off the field.' Matured or subdued?

Neil Franklin was the finest centre-half England ever produced, according to all who saw him play – subtly skilful, in an era when stoppers were briefed to stop and nothing else, assured and calm. He could do the stopping no problem, but his defensive genius lay in his ability to read the game, intercept the telling attacking pass and then unerringly find a team-mate, with a short or long ball, to start a counterattack. Imagine Paul McGrath without the dodgy knees, or the nights out. For Franklin was a non-smoking teetotaller and a family man too, devoted to his six-year-old son Garry and wife Vera. So much so that when he asked to be excused from England's trip to Rio, few eyebrows were raised.

Of course it would be an inconvenience – after all, this was the player, aged twenty-eight and at the peak of his game, who was the rock of England's defence, the man who had won a record twenty-seven consecutive caps, played in thirty-nine consecutive England games and appeared in every post-war international. But Vera was pregnant and he wanted to stay at home to be with her rather than on the other side of the world playing football. It was quite understandable.

When the truth – that he would be on the other side of the world, as a soccer mercenary – trickled out it was almost incomprehensible. Franklin had defected, not behind the Iron Curtain but to an equally isolated football equivalent – the maverick, newly formed Colombian league. The South American state was outside FIFA. Playing there would mean

138

Franklin was not only ending his club career with Stoke City by breaching his contract but also sacrificing his World Cup chance, and subsequent England career, too.

Of course, there were good reasons to give up what he had. He was unhappy at Stoke, the only club he had played for in peacetime, but one where he disliked the style of play manager Bob McGrory was pushing; and his friend Stanley Matthews had been transferred. But when Franklin's own request was submitted it was inevitably turned down, prompting him to contemplate a one-man strike, à la Wilf.

Instead, a letter which he thought was the making of him, but turned out to be the breaking of him, arrived. It came via City, but the club would never have passed it on had they realized the contents. It asked if he would consider going to Colombia where, it claimed, the weather was spring-like all year around and the conditions were excellent. Then there was the cash. No figures were mentioned, but there was no maximum wage and no limit on signing-on fees.

A difficult decision was eased by the fact that he would have a City team-mate with him. George Mountford cleared his trip to Bogota with the FA, saying it was only a summer job as a coach. Franklin didn't ask; he wouldn't have been allowed to go, given the looming World Cup. A 5–3 win at the Victoria Ground was the pair's last appearance for Stoke. A couple of days later they made their first on the front pages of the papers, pursued like fugitives on the run from British justice. Franklin told the reporters who tracked him to America, en route to Colombia: 'There is no future in Britain. We came because of the money. And we're staying. Here in Bogota we'll live finer than any footballers in the world.'

Soccer fans were agog as Manchester United's Charlie Mitten and Everton's Billy Higgins also headed for South America. Managers and officials were in turmoil but there was nothing they could do. The rules they wrote stopped their footballing serfs moving to any other club – and all the clubs agreed on that – but they applied only in Britain. If the Colombian league took off, more players would go and the whole English league would be under threat. A revolution was in the air.

Wilf received a letter from Colombia too, from Mitten in fact, asking him to coach, just like the initial approach to Franklin had done. It was followed not long afterwards by a stern letter from the FA which warned of the consequences of crossing the Atlantic. Mitten offered £50 a game for between three and six exhibition games, 100 pesos a week spending money, return air fares and hotel expenses. All the security he might have wanted.

But Wilf said no, and says now: 'They asked me to go to help look after them. I wasn't interested though, especially when I got a letter from the FA saying, "Do not go to Bogota." They could put you out of the game, like Neil was. They finished him. When he came back he never got anything. He was never picked for England again, even though he was still good enough and young enough. He was a classy centre-half. Everything he did was polished. But he was finished after Bogota.'

For Franklin's Colombian dream swiftly turned to a nightmare, and a rather violent one both off and on the pitch, where his mostly Argentinian team-mates' dislike of the English stars was only eclipsed by their hatred of the domestic players.

'You hit a man over the head with a bottle,' he said later, 'with the same sort of nonchalance as you would say, "Don't talk rubbish," at home. The players are just as bad. Their tempers are always at exploding point and it only needs a tiny spark to turn a football game into a brawl.'

Then there was the food.

'Maybe it's hard to believe but it took us a couple of weeks to teach them how to cook bacon and eggs ... and every time we asked for soup we were brought porridge.'

And the weather.

'It rained nearly every day.'

When Vera became homesick after finding out their child could be declared Colombian if born there, it was the final straw. She demanded to return home. At the airport Neil joined her after Colombian promises about getting home safely weren't met. He promised to return but, after just six games for Santa Fe, never did.

Some of the other exiles, Mitten in particular, made a better fist of the adventure, but in the end it was a flop. With the most high-profile defector back at home with his tail between his legs, a collective sigh of relief echoed around boardrooms throughout Britain. A humbled Franklin was banned until early 1951, then immediately transferred by Stoke. No first division club would touch him, despite his undoubted class. He moved to ambitious second division Hull City, then managed by Raich Carter, and played out his career in obscurity first with them, then with Crewe Alexandra and Stockport County.

An England comeback was out of the question, even though he remained the country's best centre-half until injury hit him a couple of years later. He was never recognized again by the international selectors, not even when a procession of successors failed. In the end Billy Wright

140

was switched to centre-half to resolve a problem partly of the FA's own making.

There were more of those to come, including one, in Franklin's absence, not entirely or directly the FA's fault, but one for which it had to shoulder a large part of the blame. It was the most spectacular humiliation of English football ever – and still is.

The England players' faces were as white as their shirts. The gaping chasm falling away to the side of the team bus as it climbed an ever steeper mountain road was deeper than the depression which would soon engulf them. One slip by the driver and the only crosses the likes of Jackie Milburn and Roy Bentley would be under would be in a graveyard.

The final stage of the 300 mile journey from Rio de Janeiro to an inland settlement known as Morro Velho was terrifying. More than 150 hairpin bends with sheer drops of up to 1000ft had to be negotiated in the fifteen-mile drive from the airport where an internal flight had dropped the squad. It was enough to make the players insist that they be driven back after their match in a convoy of cars. However, an excursion over the cliff edge might have seemed an attractive option by then.

For England were about to be shamed by losing to a country where soccer was rated as exciting as one-man chess; a country which had long known how to bloody the noses of the Empire's ambitions – America. Even now the 1–0 defeat is remembered as England's nadir. The match, played in the remote mountain town of Belo Horizonte, 5000ft above sea level, produced the lowest low imaginable.

The England team, hotly tipped to win the World Cup on their first appearance, were beaten by a team which even lost their qualifying games to fellow finals makeweights Mexico 6–0 and 6–2; at 500–1, opponents as unfancied as if they were a team of high school cheerleaders flown in by mistake. The fact that they were sporting hangovers as large as their stetsons only added to England's embarrassment.

'It was probably the biggest shock there's ever been in football, from an English point of view,' says Tom Finney. 'They were only really in the tournament to make up the numbers. They were all different nationalities – Poles, Spaniards and others – but they were not rated as a side. It was one of those incidents which happen in football where you can't give any reason why.

'The game was played on a very poor ground considering it was a World Cup. It was one of those games were we didn't play particularly well, but having said that we did enough to have won it comfortably – we just couldn't get the ball in the net. We hit the woodwork on four or five occasions. They had two attacks and scored from one of them. Then they defended, and defended well. We had no excuses. We should have won it and everyone knew we should have won it. It was one of those games where you just wanted to disappear because it was such a disgrace to be beaten by a side like that. But these things do happen in football.'

'Tom went out to look at the ground before the game,' Wilf adds. 'He came back and said, "There's nothing there." They'd just taken us from the ruddy big stadium for our first game against Chile out to Belo Horizonte and it was out in the sticks. We had to go to the hotel or sports club to change and walk back to the ground. Tom said that the ground was like a YMCA ground and it was. You were all hemmed in. The pitch was that small, giving them every chance to play the ball out. That's why you get the shocks in cup ties on small grounds and it was like that. If we'd played at Wembley we'd probably have beat them 11–0.'

But the World Cup wouldn't come to Wembley until 1966 and it wasn't until then that English football could really expunge the horror of Belo Horizonte.

It had all started so differently. Hosts Brazil reckoned England were the favourites to win the title. Manager Flavio Costa watched them beat Scotland to qualify and rushed home to give his charges extra coaching.

'I was so excited and there was so much I wanted to tell my boys about the fine English play that I dashed back to Brazil long before I meant to return,' he said. 'The English play great football. They are formidable rivals.'

The sentiments were echoed throughout the football world and in much of the press. Yet there were hints of what was to come. As the Franklin saga shook English football to its foundations, a series of seismic results which only further undermined the status quo arrived from Europe: Italy B 5, England B (including several World Cup possibles) 0; the amateurs of Holland 3, England B 0; Portugal 3, England 5, this one at least a win, but an exceedingly tortured one, which included two Finney penalties and a man-of-the-match display from keeper Williams; and Belgium, 1–0 up at half-time, only beaten 4–1 after a second-half comeback.

The swashbuckling dominance of the team which swept all before it in Portugal and Italy four years earlier was gone, as was the backbone of the team – Swift retired, Hardwick and Scott never regaining their inter-national class after suffering leg injuries, Franklin the deserter. The outfield defenders picked to fill their boots were raw, with none having more than six caps to his name.

Then there were those simply out of favour – Cockburn but also Lawton, still overlooked despite a scoring record second to none, and Matthews, who hadn't played for England for more than a year. His slow and purposeful style, edging up to a man and drawing a tackle before skipping over or around it and away, was thought to be at odds with the increasing pace of football. The emphasis was on speed not guile, aptitude not ability, workrate not workmanship.

The triumvirate of Finney, Mortensen and Mannion meant the for-ward line had a familiar look to it in the games against Belgium and Portugal. But centre-forward Jackie Milburn was being played at right-wing, replacing Matthews, whose final notices as an international were penned – a mere seven years too soon – when he was omitted from the squad for the Sweden and Norway games of the previous summer. It was a late decision to include him in the World Cup squad and, as he had been sent on a goodwill tour of Canada, partly to prove his fitness, he met his colleagues in Brazil.

There, more than 7000 miles away, the Brazilian squad were locked away – with wives banned – enjoying a settled build-up at a luxury training camp in a millionaire's home hidden away in the hills over-looking Rio. The players enjoyed a swimming pool, a huge veranda overlooking the grounds, chandelier-lit rooms, every boardgame and indoor amusement imaginable – the most obvious excluded, of course – as well as nightly visits by top variety acts, two masseurs, three chefs and two doctors in a pristine medical centre. When they weren't relaxing, they staged practice matches and studied footage of England. Each was so well rewarded with wages and gifts that they were nicknamed the gold-edged team. Each was also told he would be bought an Austin car if chosen by the home fans in a nationwide popularity poll as the best player in their position in the tournament.

Back in the land where the cars came from, the kind of leadership and forward thinking which would later produce the Princess and the Allegro was being applied to England's preparations. The squad met at Dulwich Hamlet's ground for three days light training eleven days before the first game, and didn't even have use of the first-team pitch. Sir Walter Winter-bottom says: 'All the South American teams would give up their best players for six months before the competition, so they could train together and go on days out so they built up an understanding and team spirit. We met in London and had one kickabout at an amateur club's ground because all the league clubs re-seeded their ground in the summer. We played a couple of seven-a-side games and that was it. Off we went.'

The players were sent home for a last weekend with their families, with orders to report back to London again in two days time. One thirty-one-hour flight later, including four stopovers, and the team was in Rio with five days to spare; a working week to get acclimatized, train, assess the opposition, practice and even perhaps look at the stadium where they were to meet Chile. Up to 5000 workmen were crawling all over it, desperately trying, and failing, to finish the £3 million structure in time.

Even in Brazil, the players couldn't escape the pay problem. Aside from the Franklin shock, which was still sinking in, and the contrast between the film-star treatment of the home side and the set-shifters conditions of England, there were lurking agents from cash-rich foreign clubs. George Robledo, the star Newcastle United striker who was leading Chile, was approached with an offer of a £4000 signing-on fee and more than £25 per week wages but turned it down.

Even his possible earning power paled into insignificance compared to the real élite: the referees. 'The Masters' from Britain who were flown in to officiate were paid £70 per week, with free accommodation thrown in. Apologists excused the amount on the grounds that most of the referees had taken unpaid time off work to attend. Meanwhile, the English players, for whom the World Cup *was* their job, were on the standard FA international rate of £20 per game.

At least they got free accommodation and rooms with a view. The ten-storey Luxor Hotel overlooked the golden sands, and dazzling beauties, of Copacabana beach. It was an ideal base for a holiday, but perhaps not for a working football team as the temptations across the way were obvious, while the food was rather less enjoyable. Until Winterbottom sent a delegation to the chef to sort out the meals, the players had to make do with whatever they could find which was edible. For room-mates Wilf, Stanley Matthews, who only arrived the day before the Chile game, and Stan Mortensen that meant fruit.

Sir Stanley says: 'The food was terrible. We were eating bananas, mostly. It's so different today. You just can't imagine that happening.' Sir Walter also remembers the stay vividly: 'It was so hot that the players were exhausted even in the hotel, which had been recommended by Arsenal but couldn't have been worse for us. It was right on the beach, so the players all wanted to go swimming. All the food was being cooked in reams of oil and the smell of it was dreadful and carried all through the hotel. In the end our trainer went to the kitchens to watch over them preparing some other food. When Arsenal were there, it was on an end-of-season jolly, more or less a holiday. Their players, of course, loved it. They went swimming all the time in the waves and thoroughly enjoyed it all.'

Not England, though. Swimming was banned as sharks were known to bask in the water and the type of injuries they inflicted were difficult to shake off. Indeed going to the beach at all was only allowed before 10 a.m. After that it was feared the glare off the sand might affect the players' eyesight. They were even ordered out of the sun completely from 12.30 p.m. to 3 p.m.

Between times they trained on the Botofogo club ground, drawing crowds of several hundred. Wilf soon became the favourite target of the autograph hunters. His team-mates had taken to calling him Vasco de Gama as he was the first to spot land at the end of the long flight from Europe; the fans knew him simply as El Manniano. John Graydon, of the *Sports Chronicle*, reported:

Mannion apparently is one of the best-known of foreign footballers in Brazil. When the England team were at practice the other morning, I noticed a youngster entering Wilf's name down in a nicely-bound book. I asked him what the book was and he passed it over for me to examine. It is on the same lines as those lads who enter up the names of railway engines use in Britain, only Brazilian lads, after entering a footballer's name, then try to secure his autograph by the side of it. This particular lad, who travelled by pushbike something like fifty miles each way specially to get the autograph of Mannion, pedalled his way back home feeling very pleased. Mannion, like all the other England players, has made himself very popular by his willingness to co-operate with pressmen, photographers and even small boys who seek his autograph. Back home in Middlesbrough they should feel proud that he has proved one of the finest sporting ambassadors ever to travel overseas.

On the pitch he proved his worth, too. Chile were dispatched 2–0, with Wilf – who was only cleared to play just before kick-off after suffering a night of 'Rio tummy' – getting the clinching goal. Ominously, the first-half performance was lethargic and only a vast improvement in the second made sure of the win. That prompted Charles Buchan to report:

On their display in the second half at any rate, England can win this trophy. I have no doubt now that they will beat Spain and the US and win the Group Championship. This was as good an England team as I've seen for a very long time.

John Macadam was no less certain: 'The important thing is to win. We shall.' But in hindsight the win against Chile wasn't as significant as two trends highlighted by the match – England's poor shooting, not helped by Jackie Milburn's absence after suffering a bout of nerves, and the anti-English and pro-underdog nature of the crowd. The 45,000 who were in the showpiece stadium, which could seat 130,000 with another 25,000 standing, booed every English back pass and gave vent to the loudest cheers when news of America leading Spain 1–0 came through. The US finally went down 3–1, conceding three goals in the last ten minutes; but their time was coming.

Training began as soon as England reached their base in Morro Velho. Showing no lasting effects of the terror ride through the mountains, Walter Winterbottom sorted out two sides. To start the session, he lobbed the ball to the opening bowler – England's finest footballers started practice for their match against America by playing the press at cricket.

The billiards table was much in demand, too, but not as much as the players themselves, guests of honour in an outpost of South America that was forever England. Morro Velho was the base of a mining company which drew its 200 workers from Manchester, Middlesbrough and Sheffield. Underground, gold was dug at a depth of 8000ft; on the surface, players worth their weight in the precious metal, in the eyes of their hosts, were given free rein of the village. Its impressive facilities were put at their disposal, including a football pitch the equal of any in Brazil – sitting in a forest clearing – and too good to prepare for a game on a pitch as level as a pizza topping.

There was only one question: would Matthews play? Arthur Drewry, in consultation with Winterbottom of course, decided not to change a winning side, so the forward line paired Finney and Wilf on the right wing, Mortensen at inside-left partnered Jim Mullen of Wolves, and Roy Bentley was at centre-forward. Such a line-up should ensure England won by an American football score, it was generally agreed. The players would just enjoy a muscle loosener before the group decider against Spain.

The strength of the American team was summed up by the appearance of one Eddie McIlvenny. He was a Scot who had been given a free transfer by Wrexham eighteen months earlier and emigrated. He was joined by a baseball catcher who played in goal, a collection of students and a Haitian centre-forward called Gaetjens, who had scored against Spain and whose name would soon go down in history for an even more important goal. All of them had enjoyed a big night out on the eve of the match – after all they were there to enjoy themselves. Their hangovers would be bigger still the morning after the game.

Things started to go wrong for England as soon as the team arrived at the compact stadium. Winterbottom was so disgusted by the dressing-rooms that he led his team out of them.

'They were so awful I ordered the team to change at a nearby athletic club. The rest of the ground, you wouldn't really recognize as such. There was also a fourteen-foot high wall around the pitch – it was like playing football in a bull ring – and the grass on the pitch was very rough and lumpy.'

England hadn't practised on the pitch and struggled to come to terms with playing on the matted and bumpy grass. Still they looked the better side, albeit trying to overcome the conditions as well as their opponents. Then, eight minutes before half-time, the unthinkable happened. American right-half Bahr hit a speculative twenty-five-yard shot from the corner of the penalty area. The ball went past centre-half Hughes more like a cross, just over chest high. Lurking behind him, Gaetjens managed to get his head to it and divert it past a mortified Williams. According to American right-back Harry Keough, Gaetjens threw himself at the ball in a superb example of the diving header. According to Sir Walter, the striker knew nothing about his goal.

'The ball struck the fellow in the face and it deflected in.'

The Americans braced themselves for an onslaught and they weren't disappointed. Time and again the woodwork came to their rescue. The man from the *People* counted eleven ricochets from post or crossbar, but the England forwards also cemented the result with a shocking profligacy in front of goal. Sir Stanley Matthews was watching from the sidelines.

'It was disaster,' he says. 'If we'd played for twenty-four hours we wouldn't have scored. It was one of those days. The ground was a bit lumpy and whatever we did, we couldn't score. We hit the bar, post, everything.'

The collective jaw of the press bench was halfway back to Rio as they filed their reports. As the sun set, the gloom which engulfed the unlit stadium matched the mood of the writers. Cigarette lighters were much in demand to illuminate notepads as well as to light up for a hit of soothing nicotine. John Macadam, so confident before, wrote: 'United States footballers – whoever heard of them – beat England 1–0 in the World Cup series today. It marks the lowest ever for British sport.' And that was saying something as the West Indies were winning their first-ever Test in

England, at Lord's, at the same time. *The Times* added: 'Probably never before has an English team played so badly. The chances missed were legion. With the American goal at their mercy, the forwards blasted over the bar or hesitated near the goal to allow [the] defence to rob them of the ball.'

England did manage to score, or so they thought. But the referee said the ball didn't cross the line and ignored the fact that the clearance came from the hand of an American who wasn't in goal. Sir Walter still seethes about the decision to the extent that he makes most uncharacteristically scathing comments about the referee.

'We scored a perfectly good equalizer but it wasn't allowed. The crowd was jeering that decision – the man handled the ball in his own net. But after that the Americans thought they could get away with anything – shirt-tugging, fouls and everything. The refereeing was a farce. If FIFA had wanted to, they could have suspended the referee for a lifetime.'

Another fall guy was needed though and Wilf was it. He didn't play exceptionally well, although who could on the pot-luck pitch? He still created chances, but they were missed by others. He also missed a few of his own. Winger Mullen and centre-forward Bentley were also dropped, but the real criticism was levelled at the playmaker who was accused of not stamping his authority on his third-rate opponents.

Before the tournament, when Wilf was seen as England's match-winner, Pat Collins wrote in the *Daily Mail*: 'I think our Rio hopes hang largely on the output of the wee man from Teesside.' Cliff Mitchell also flagged up the role the local lad would play: 'Wilf is enjoying his soccer. He is back on top, and once again recognized as England's finest inside-forward. It will not be his fault if England fail to win the soccer championship of the world.' Wrong. He was being blamed.

It was unfair. Wilf didn't voice his fury but just to look at his face was to realize how hurt he was. Tom Finney says it was the only time in more than fifty years that he saw Wilf really angry, on the pitch or off it.

'It was sad. I could imagine Wilf's anger at being dropped because you couldn't put the blame on any particular player for that game. We all had to accept as much blame as anybody else, as each other.'

Wilf still bristles at the memory – and offers alternative targets, one in particular.

'Blaming me, honestly. It was shooting practice for all of us. They were getting fed and I was hitting balls too, but it just wouldn't go in. Not for any of us. But Mortensen – I wouldn't have had him in the line then. I'd put him at centre-forward and that's it. I wouldn't play him at inside-forward because you were looking after him. You're making beautiful stuff for him and sometimes he'd lose out and call it a day. That's the time you have to start chasing, but he didn't. That's why you got murdered, like Stan [Matthews] says we did in Italy – because someone's lacking somewhere. Mortensen was in that line. I used to lose my head and I used to get on to Winterbottom and say, "You don't know what you're talking about."'

The new look forward line – including Eddie Bailey of Spurs, Matthews and Milburn – did no better. A rough Spanish side beat England 1–0. Again England did score, through Milburn, but again it was controversially disallowed, this time for offside. For the last twenty minutes the 80,000 crowd in the marvellous Maracana stadium back in Rio waved white handkerchiefs to bid the English bye-bye. To rub salt into the wound, Chile thrashed the Americans 5–2.

England ended up joint second (on goal difference) or joint bottom of the group (on points alone), depending on which way you looked at it. For the only time in World Cup history, there was no final, so no second round for runners-up in the first stage. The four group winners went into a final group to decide who would be crowned world champions. By then, England were heading home.

The *Daily Herald* summed up the despair best in a notice slightly revamped from its original publication in *The Times* years before to mark a cricket humiliation: 'In affectionate remembrance of English Football which died in Rio on July 2, 1950. Duly lamented by a large circle of sorrowing friends and acquaintances. RIP. NB: The body will be cremated and the ashes taken to Spain.'

At Rio's airport, the whole miserable World Cup experience received a fitting finale. The players learnt they would have been in line for £1000 each from the hosts if they had reached the finals. Then their plane was twenty-four hours late.

No sooner had the wheels touched the runway than the post mortems began. The FA's International Selection Committee pulled its head out of the sand for long enough to let its views be known: 'It would be wrong to make excuses for the defeat of England. We were already aware that the players had had a very strenuous season of league football and that they would be faced with unaccustomed conditions of climate, grounds, crowd atmosphere, law interpretation and the like. In most respects these handicaps were less severe than we had imagined they might be . . . but unless an English team is in peak condition and top form and has a reasonable share of fortune, it cannot be expected to win such a tournament.'

There was no mention of the preparations needed to secure peak condition and top form. Reporters who covered the visit to Sweden the previous year had got a glimpse of what the future should have held. There the national side lived and trained at the country's Institute of Sport for a week before each international. Furthermore the manager – an Englishman – spent a fortnight with each first division team in turn to get to know the players and their strengths and weaknesses.

In contrast Winterbottom was lucky to get a couple of days a season – and then often with players he hadn't picked. The skimpy preparations for Rio showed how little the need to do more than just turn up for a game was appreciated. On a good day the skill of the players alone could get England off the hook; but if they dropped below excellent, the short-comings of the system shone through.

Sir Walter says: 'When you look back now, you think we were innocent victims of our own lack of preparation. There was no pre-planning, no going out to look at the facilities. Nothing like that. We just thought we could turn up and play. In some respects we were a good side, but we weren't a good enough side to win regardless on these special occasions and in such circumstances.'

For Finney, Rio was an eye-opener.

'It was new for England. It gave us an insight into how good the South American countries were. They were very skilful players and it was obvious you had little or no chance of playing against those sides in those days. We were by no means the best in the world. That was not true at all. The only reason you were probably thinking that was because you never played these sides, never saw anything about them because they were so far away.'

The $64,000 question, though, is would England have won the World Cup in 1946, when it would have been held but for the war? Sir Walter thinks it is possible.

'I think we would have had a good chance. We had young players such as Finney, Mannion and Wright, who were so good they were keeping the likes of Horatio Carter out, mixed with older ones such as Matthews and Swift.'

Instead English hands had to wait another sixteen years to lift up the Jules Rimet trophy. Harold Shepherdson was there, of course. So was England's right-back throughout the Brazil débâcle, a player who perhaps learnt from the trip not to stick with a rigid system if you didn't have players good enough to fill key positions. His name was Alf Ramsey. And his favourite player of his day? Wilf Mannion: 'The greatest soccer brain in modern football.'

The corner came over and England keeper Williams rose to punch, but only half-cleared it. An England head managed to flick the ball further out, only for a Scot to nod it straight back towards the penalty area.

Wilf was underneath it. He timed his jump to perfection. Anyone who ever saw him play knew of his incredible heading ability given his size. He seemed to continue to float upwards long after other players would be coming back down to earth, hanging like a pint-sized Michael Jordan. This time Scotland's Billy Liddell, a player more than six inches taller, jumped with him to try to get the ball and nearly made it, but instead headed Wilf.

The two heads smashed together with the crack of bone on bone. The two men fell to the ground. Harry Johnston, England and Blackpool centre-half and the nearest player to the scene, immediately knew how serious the accident was. He spread his arms as he ran towards the players, appealing to the referee to stop play. It was the thirteenth minute of a home international clash at Wembley in April 1951, and a crowd of 100,000 seemed to be watching Wilf's career being brought to a premature end.

The débâcle of Belo Horizonte had been quickly forgiven if not forgotten. He missed just the final World Cup game against Spain before being recalled for the start of the home international campaign against Northern Ireland the following October. He retained his place for games against Wales and Yugoslavia – the first continental side to avoid defeat in England. The 2–2 draw gave Wilf his twenty-fourth full international cap. The Scotland fixture brought up his quarter century.

But his England team-mates wondered if there would be any more when they gathered over the fallen player. A grim sight greeted them. A hollow in Wilf's face showed where his cheekbone had been shattered. There was blood everywhere. Liddell was badly dazed, but at least he would be able to play on. Wilf was dipping in and out of consciousness, saying he was okay, wanting to play on: 'I'll be all right. I'll be fine.' Then, as he tried to get up, he collapsed, his legs buckling as his system tried to absorb the pain shooting through his body. And so Wilf made his last exit from the home of English football on a stretcher, tended by a doctor.

Tom Finney described the accident as one of the worst he had ever seen.

'Blood seemed to be spurting everywhere – I remember my shirt was soaked in it – but through it all [his] courage was outstanding,' he wrote in *Finney on Football*. Even today he can vividly recall the scene.

151

'It was frightening looking at him on the ground. His cheek was really dented in. You could see it was a severe fracture. It was a terrible collision. He was carried off and we had to play with ten men.'

'I can remember lying in the dressing-room feeling so awfully cold,' Wilf said later. 'Then I went to hospital with a broken cheekbone and a beautiful black eye that would have won first prize in any show.' Now he recalls: 'I was starting to come down and he was starting to climb. I could sense him coming, but there's no chance to escape when you're in the air. He hit me and I was out cold. I couldn't even remember being carried off.'

His team-mates still managed to more than hold their own. With Walter Winterbottom accompanying his number eight to hospital, skipper Billy Wright switched Finney to inside-right to partner Matthews. The attacking move paid off when debutant Harold Hassall, of Huddersfield, gave England the lead in the twenty-fifth minute. Scotland, with their extra man, soon equalized and pulled away to 3–1. Finney made it 3–2 before the final whistle drew the curtain on a gutsy England performance.

At Wembley Hospital, Wilf was giving one of his own. His cheekbone was fractured, his face deeply gashed and there were fears his eyesight might be affected. Back on Teesside, his family were hysterical. Someone misheard 'facial injury' as 'fatal injury', but like the Dunkirk scare, the fears were soon dispelled.

Bernadette headed for the Queen Victoria Hospital, East Grinstead, where Wilf had been transferred. He was already surrounded by well-known faces. Canon McMullan, from St Peter's, South Bank, had been at the international and went straight to hospital to see the player he'd known for almost twenty-five years. Also at the bedside were two of the Middlesbrough directors.

But the most man important man there was Sir Archibald Hector McIndoe, a surgeon specializing in the pioneering field of plastic surgery. The next day he performed a similar operation to the 600 he had performed on badly burned airmen from the war. By comparison, Wilf's case was straightforward, but it still involved lifting part of the top jaw bone and two weeks in hospital. Photographs of him in bed showed his face puffed up and blackened. An attempted smile looked more like a grimace through the pain. Clearly, he wasn't going to play football again for the rest of the season; some wondered if he would ever play again.

That he was back for the first Boro game of the next season, and even played for England again, was remarkable. But 1951 was a year when personal events off the field were as central to Wilf's life as football. Five days after he made his international comeback from the injury, Wilf's brother Tommy died, aged just forty-four. It was a tragic loss at such a young age, made all the more so as Wilf had already lost a sister, his father and his ten-month-old daughter Kathleen in the space of two years. He claims now that it had little impact on his game, but it is hard to reconcile the turmoil these losses must have caused with his simple statement: 'We had a bad time then. Berney took it badly.' Perhaps one sign of effect was that he missed Boro's game the Saturday after Tommy's death.

For a man who never played football at any serious level, Tommy was handsomely honoured in the *Gazette*, as the greatest player who never was. Cliff Mitchell wrote:

> How many men, I wonder, might have been world beaters in a particular sport if they had decided to make it their living. At benches, in factories, driving buses – in mundane jobs all over the country – are 'ordinary fellows' who, had they wished (or realized) it, could have out-headed Lawton, out-tackled Carey or out-dribbled Mannion. Such a man as this died on Teesside a few days ago. The name? Mannion. Yes, Wilf's elder brother Tommy was recognized as a 'natural' footballer, a player who seemed destined for all the honours the game can offer. Wilf himself it was who told me, years ago, 'If Tommy had stuck to football, he'd have been a far better player than I'll ever be.'
>
> Why didn't Tommy go to the top? Because he just wasn't sufficiently interested in football. He played for South Bank Corinthians and had occasional games for St Peter's, but to suggestions that he should take the game up as a career, he shrugged his shoulders. He enjoyed his game of soccer and that was all there was to it. His potential worth as a top ranker was by no means unnoticed, but he used to grin and pass it off. Not for him the headlines, the glamour, the uncertainties of a professional footballer's life. And who is to say that he did not make a wise choice? By nature Tommy, unassuming and modest, was not, it is certain, fitted for the role of world-famous soccer star. In ability, it is just as certain he was.

So they buried Tommy, the docker, just as they buried his father Thomas, seventy-four, the steel worker, whose death in January 1950, after six months of being bedridden, provided ample illustration of why Tommy held such an embittered view of Middlesbrough FC. The *Gazette* headline read: 'Father had died, but Wilf played'. The story said: 'Shortly before Middlesborough's Cup match at Ayresome Park this afternoon Wilf Mannion, the Borough's international inside-forward, learned that his father had died. Though deeply shocked by the news, Mannion decided to play the match.' Wilf later revealed what really happened. On the morning of the match, as he was preparing at his home, a car drew up outside. George Camsell, by then on the staff at Boro, got out. He said the car was to take Wilf to Ayresome Park, an unheard of luxury.

'What's the matter with this? Why am I honoured?' Wilf asked.

'We're collecting all the players by car today as it's a big match,' came the reply. But when the pair arrived at the hotel where Boro were meeting, manager David Jack sent for Wilf.

'I've bad news for you,' he said. 'Your father died this morning.'

Wilf recalled: 'The private car collection had merely been an excuse. I was so upset that I wanted immediately to go home – who wouldn't have done? I finally agreed to play, but what a way to break the news to anyone.'

Gone were the days when the England team practically picked itself. Goalkeeper Williams was selected for the game against France at Highbury, the first international of the 1951-52 season. He was, however, on the point of being dropped and enduring three years in the international wilderness. Manchester United centre-half Allenby Chilton, who only won his first cap a year earlier at the age of thirty-two, was filling the gap left by Neil Franklin's internal exile. The alternative choice was Fulham's Jim Taylor, thirty-three.

Finney was still there, and Henry Cockburn, not to mention Billy Wright. But there seemed to be few young players good enough to push for places, so Wilf was in with a chance of a recall alongside his former colleagues. It was only six months since the injury at Wembley, but his chances of playing against the French were fair; not that Cliff Mitchell thought so:

> This season Wilf has most certainly been below form. The serious facial injury he received against Scotland last April, followed by a worrying time over his wife's ill-health [a reference to the aftermath of her daughter's death], have had their effect, and we have yet to see, this term, the Mannion of old. For that reason he is virtually certain to be passed over when the England selectors go to work on Monday. If that is the case Wilf cannot – and most assuredly will not – complain, for current form must obviously be the chief factor. He has been having a bad spell and until he plays himself out of it can expect no more caps. But do not be tempted to take a bet that he has played his last game for his country.

Right and wrong. He hadn't played his last game for his country, but he was picked to meet France and that was his last game. Mitchell swiftly repositioned himself:

154

The brilliant little Middlesbrough inside-forward has never let his country down. No wonder the selectors are reluctant to leave him out. Indeed, some of the finest displays Wilf has given in his career have been produced when he has been wearing an England shirt. The bigger the occasion, the better Mannion seems to play.

But the France game wasn't a mammoth occasion, and Wilf didn't turn in a memorable performance in a unimpressive 2–2 draw. France were denied the honour of being the first continental victors in England only by heroics from Williams. Wilf, as well as Chilton, Cockburn and Spurs full-back Arthur Willis, never played for England again. He had won twenty-six caps, scored ten goals as well as creating many more, and played in four wartime internationals.

There is only one footnote. If the war hadn't broken out, how many caps would he have won? He was established as an England player by early 1941. Assuming an average of eight internationals each season, there would have been around forty extra caps, not including those he missed as a result of the strike, making a total in the region of seventy – somewhere between Kevin Keegan (sixty-one) and Gary Lineker (eighty).

Still, there was time for a curtain call. On the eve of the 1954 Cup final, the FA arranged a showpiece friendly at Highbury in which 'England' were to play 'Young England'. Lawton, Matthews and Mannion were reunited (while Finney was to play in the final itself) to oppose Duncan Edwards among others, preparing for the looming World Cup in Switzerland.

It proved to be a triumph of experience over youth: 2–1 to those whose England careers were over or fading out, although it could have been 5–1. The 45,554 crowd were treated to one final exhibition from some of those who tore Portugal asunder and humbled the mighty Italians. Bob Pennington, in the *Daily Express*, reported: 'There were roars of admiration, oohs and aahs of astonishment at the juggling genius of Matthews, Mannion and Shackleton, the deft flicks of Lawton and Langton, the pattern tracing of Cockburn and Johnston.'

Cliff Mitchell added:

England's soccer stars of tomorrow received two lessons from their elders – and betters – in a most entertaining FA trial game. They were bewitched by the dazzling footwork, ball control and anticipation of their opponents; at the same time it must have been impressed upon them that direct methods are still the most dangerous – for they were let off lightly. England beat Young England 2–1, but the not-so-young treated the match as an exhibition in which goals were of academic value and secondary importance. It was like old times seeing Mannion in the white shirt of

England and trotting out those deft moves, flicks, feints and pinpoint passes that have made him one of the greatest inside-forwards football has known.

It was, however, a former opponent, Arsenal and Scotland's Alex Forbes, who paid the greatest tribute. '[Wilf's] dazzling display ... had me jumping off the bench in the players paddock and applauding – something I've never done before. I rated his play even higher than that other ball artist, Len Shackleton. Yet neither could command a place in the World Cup party. I'll gamble they would both waltz into the Hungarian team [of Puskas and 6–3 fame].'

In the nearly three years since his last full England game, there had been other calls for Wilf's recall. After all Matthews and Finney were still regulars and would remain so until 1957 and 1958 respectively. Charles Sampson, of the *Empire News*, wrote before the Scotland game of April 1953, as Wilf was on his way to top-scoring for Boro that season:

> Since Middlesbrough's blond genius, Wilf Mannion, faded from the international scene, the men who dictate England's team-building policy have searched in vain for an inside-forward with his superb holding qualities. So don't be surprised if, out of sheer desperation, the selectors turn to Mannion for the solution of the problem. Some people might call it a retrograde step, but a tried and trusted servant such as Mannion is preferable to a completely unknown stranger.

When England scraped a 2–2 draw, he added:

> Spring is bursting out all over, but I doubt whether it brings much joy to the hearts of our busy little soccer legislators. Even allowing for the changes which can be made [to the England team], there are still too many deficiencies. One of the most glaring is the absence of a holding inside-forward – how England could have used a player with the Mannion touch against Scotland.

But his last match with Scotland had taken its toll, with many swearing Wilf was never the same player after his injury. Tom Finney is one: 'I think it hastened the end of his career, certainly from international soccer.' And sadly perhaps the most lasting legacy of that England career was helping – inadvertently, via his injury – to hasten the introduction of substitutes.

'It did hurry that along,' Tom says. 'People were beginning to say it's not fair to the teams and it's not fair to the public either when they've paid big money to watch these games and it's spoilt by the fact one team only had ten men.'

But life's not fair, and if Wilf didn't know that already, he would be soon finding out.

· NINE ·

Retirement, banishment and the legacy of a legend

Centre-forward Peter McKennan's knee cap was shattered and he was on his way to hospital, ruled out for the rest of the season. Five minutes later George Hardwick was also being stretchered off, another victim of a leg injury and also out for the season. Another ten minutes and Tom Blenkinsopp hobbled off and would have stayed off but for the absence of those already departed. Instead he was put out on the wing and told to do what he could. Then genuine winger Tommy Woodward picked up a knock and gingerly made his way to loiter on the touchline.

Boro were down to seven fit men in the match against Chelsea in the spring of 1950 and Wilf was about to score what he remembers as the best goal of his career. He was dashing around Stamford Bridge, desperately trying to marshal what remained of the side into some sort of defence, while also looking for a way to equalize the home side's opening goal.

The kick-off for the second half seemed as good a time as any. After all, all the the attacking part of the Boro team were automatically almost in their opponents' half. Johnny Spuhler took the kick and knocked it to Wilf.

'I took it a couple of steps, dummied and three of the Chelsea defenders left for Piccadilly,' he later said. 'Johnny had run at an angle. I gave him a short one, doubled around to his left-hand side, got the ball back and hit it from twenty-five yards. It flew home. After that we must have run a thousand miles but right at the death Bentley hit the bar, the ball rebounded to Johnny and, as he tried to pass back, it went in.' Boro lost 2–1.

In the dressing-room, which resembled a hospital casualty unit on a Saturday night, Wilf could reflect on another magic moment. But the goal, and subsequent defeat, summed up his post-war career with Boro. Much of the club's glory was down to him, but it couldn't be matched by team-mates who were not as gifted, and a threadbare squad. There were exceptions: goalkeeper Rolando Ugolini was a fine player, right-back

Dicky Robinson won representative honours and came close to England caps, Tom Blenkinsopp and Johnny Spuhler had their moments and Jamaican winger Lindy Delapenha provided much-needed pace and bite up-front. But the attack was blunt; there was no regular goal-getting centre-forward. The next one along in a red shirt would be Brian Clough, but he was still learning his trade before finally making his league debut in 1955. The defence, too, was shaky, lacking a foundation stone such as Bob Baxter.

Surely the answer was to buy? But the board's ambitions, and willingness to pay for them, did not match the pre-war board's aspirations and easy-going, pipe-smoking manager David Jack was not forceful enough to demand the purchases he wanted. According to Wilf: 'Mr Jack – the man who did so much to build the present team – has admitted that he was "often thwarted in his efforts to strengthen it by the actions of directors who thought they knew better, but didn't." The result was that, over the years, Middlesbrough's efforts at team-building have been hotch-potch, hope-for-the-best affairs. Some players Mr Jack wanted – great footballers like Don Revie (Manchester City), Trevor Ford (Aston Villa, Sunderland and Cardiff) and Billy Steel, the Scottish international – he wasn't allowed to get. And when Middlesbrough did buy a player, sometimes against Mr Jack's advice, they did so often at a ridiculously high transfer fee.'

Revie was a prime example of a player who should have been signed by his home-town club to understudy and succeed Wilf. As a schoolboy he never missed a Boro match and dreamed of pulling on a red shirt and playing alongside his heroes, maybe even Wilf, his ultimate hero. He was due for a trial at Ayresome Park, but it fell through and instead he joined a local club which had links with Leicester City. He signed to play at Filbert Street before moving on to Hull and then Manchester City, where he developed the deep-lying centre-forward role. Copying the Hungarians and Brazilians, he dropped into midfield as a playmaker rather than the leader of the attack. Defenders, non-plussed by his positioning given the number nine on his back, followed him deep, exposing themselves to swift runs into the space by the inside-forwards, playing as the twin spearhead.

The Boro faithful waited in vain for such tactical nous and application at Ayresome. When Revie, then at City, finally got on to the same pitch as Wilf, he was opposing him. His idol didn't let him down, dictating the first half as Boro took a 1–0 lead. In the second half, though, Wilf picked up a knee injury and lost momentum. City scored twice and won, but it didn't make Revie alter his opinion of 'the best player there is'.

Such results only increased Wilf's disenchantment. After more than fifteen years at Boro, he knew the club was going nowhere fast.

'The plain truth is that the club is suffering from years of neglect,' he said once he was free. 'When football restarted after the war, Middlesbrough were reasonably well-off and had good players for the first team and in reserve. But instead of setting out to build sensibly, they sold some of the best men and bought others not so good. That started their downfall. And neglect of the north east as a "nursery" completed it. Some of the finest footballers of all time have come from this district. But the Boro of late years have been content to let other clubs step in and take them away. I've never been able to understand why the club don't send someone like their old star Micky Fenton – who really understands the game – out to watch players instead of leaving the job to directors who know nothing.'

Fenton was still at the club, helping with the coaching. He stayed, looking after the reserves, until the mid sixties, nurturing the likes of Clough and fellow England striker Alan Peacock. He also knew Boro were not the force they were.

'The team was never the same after the war,' he says. 'We had some great players, like Wilf and George, but never a great team. In the period before the war we had class men, all ball players. Later there was no one to match them. Only Wilf. We didn't really have a team under David Jack. I remember Tommy Thomas, the director, once said we didn't have a team without Wilf and he was right. I can't remember anyone who was better in my day.'

A cartoon of the time summed the situation up. A sour-faced Boro fan, scowling beneath a trilby hat, is commenting on a match to a lad with a red-and-white scarf tied round his neck: 'Struth! Them forwards is ruddy murder.' The lad pipes up: 'Except Mannion.' Smiler continues: 'Pitiful. Those half-backs – perishin' pitiful!' The lad replies: 'Except Mannion.' Mouth downturned: 'And the backs ain't filling my 'eart with joy, neither.' Again: 'Except Mannion.' 'Still, ol' Ugo's earned his coppers – nobody could've saved that goal, mate.' The lad admits: 'S right – nobody. Except Mannion.'

Even so, from the earliest days after the war it was clear one man, no matter how good, wasn't enough. In 1946–47 Boro finished eleventh, with Wilf and Fenton joint top scorers. The following year Wilf dried up and only scored two compared to Fenton's twenty-eight as Boro finished sixteenth. But it was in the 1948–49 season, as the centre-forward's career came to an end and Wilf went on strike, that the real struggles began.

159

Fenton only played twenty-five games, but still scored thirteen goals. Wilf played seventeen times, helping to ensure the club's first division survival on his return.

The following season Fenton's replacement, Andy Donaldson, broke his ankle in training. On matchdays things were little better, with Boro losing four out of their five opening home games. By May, manager David Jack, who appeared complacent in the autumn when he said, 'Honours have never been won in September', had managed to raise the team to ninth. Fenton, by then thirty-six years old, played just once, in a 4–0 defeat at Aston Villa, and retired after 162 goals in 269 games for Boro.

Season 1950–51 was the exception that proved the rule. Boro had a good year. They topped the League just before the New Year and even recorded some stylish wins, in keeping with the pre-war demolitions as Everton were beaten 4–0 and Charlton 7–3. But the best was perhaps Wilf's last really great game for Boro when Huddersfield were thumped 8–0, and their goalkeeper still got man of the match for keeping the score down. Wilf scored a first-half hat-trick before turning creator and allowing his colleagues in on the act. His own goals highlighted his all-round ability. The first was a calmly struck penalty; the second, a header; the third, a dazzling dribble topped off with a twenty-five-yard drive. When the Boro tally reached eight a Huddersfield player went over to him and said: 'Come on, that's enough.'

A 1–1 draw at Chelsea took Boro to top spot. Some fools even mentioned the C word, but it was all downhill from then. George Hardwick had departed to take up the player–manager's post at, of all places, Oldham. The defence he left held firm for several games and then suddenly began to leak goals. Five times in eight games their opponents netted three and then Derby managed to bag six without reply. By then the season was going the way of so many before it; Boro picked up just thirteen points from their final nineteen games and finished sixth.

The FA Cup story was no better. In 1950, second division Chesterfield, in a precursor of the 1997 semi-final, met Boro, missing an injured Wilf, in the fourth round and won 3–2. The following season the Teessiders' Cup run ended in even more unlikely circumstances when they went down 1–0 to another second division side, Leeds United. The fog was so bad that no one could see from one side of Elland Road to the other when the referee gave the go-ahead for the third-round clash to start. One home fan was even heard to mutter after the game: 'That's the first home game I've missed all season.' But at least he was happy as Leeds won on a waterlogged pitch which Boro's players were convinced was unfit to step on. Every time the whistle went the players, and fans, hoped it was to abandon the game.

Cliff Mitchell reported:

There is no need for me to draw a veil over Middlesbrough's exit from the FA Cup; the weather did that effectively enough. What is called for from me is an explanation as to why this fantasy of a football match was played. And I can't give it. Three-quarters of an hour before the start referee G. Gibson detected a slight lessening of the density in the fog and declared the game on. Unfortunately, soon after the gates had been opened, most of the playing pitch disappeared from view. In any case conditions under foot should have precluded a start, quite apart from the fog. The ground was hard, with a layer of slush all over it and inches of water forming miniature lakes every few feet.

So little of the play did I – or any other spectator – see that I cannot assess, praise or blame with any degree of fairness. I strained my eyes to little effect. The Aldwych never staged such a farce as this. We expected the whistle to go for 'game abandoned' at any minute.[But] referee Gibson stuck manfully to a task which he should never have undertaken; here was an outstanding example of misapplied zeal.

The result was the catalyst for the slump in form which took Boro from top to sixth in the League. It also marked the end of any hopes Wilf had of winning a medal in his career.

For once the boot was on the other foot. Players were used to finding out about their caps and even their transfer comings and goings in the press; management were used to holding all the cards. Wilf was reversing the roles.

The *Gazette*'s Mandale called on Boro manager Walter Rowley, David Jack's successor, with some bad news. Only three months after an operation for a stomach ulcer, it was not the kind of bulletin designed to aid the former Bolton boss's recovery. Wilf Mannion was refusing to re-sign, not through any dispute like six years earlier, but because he was retiring. At the end of the 1953–54 season, his professional playing days were over. Rowley said: 'This is the first I have heard of it. I was expecting Wilf in my office to re-sign last Friday, but, although he did not arrive, I did not attach any special importance to that.'

Wilf was more forthcoming about leaving football.

'I have had enough of it and have seen enough to make me realize that now is the time to get out and find myself another job. I have not made a sudden decision. I have been turning it over in my mind for a considerable time now, and no one knows better than I do that, if the general standards of present-day football had not been so low, I probably could not have continued as long as I have. I have no quarrel with the club. They have offered me maximum terms for the next season and I am quite happy in Middlesbrough.'

Of course, he would have to move house; the one he lived in was club-owned. But he appealed for an amicable approach from the club.

'I fully realize what this implies. I realize that I am due about £300 in accrued benefit which the club have the power to withhold if I do not re-sign but I am hoping that they will take a different view. I also realize that I am living in a house belonging to the club but the break has got to come some time and that time, I sincerely believe, has arrived.'

The directors and the fans refused to believe it. Rowley, just before heading off to see the player, was determined to persuade him to re-sign.

'I hope Mannion will reconsider his decision. As long as I have a retained list from the directors, it is up to me to try to sign every player on that list. I hope my talk with Wilf will have the desired effect.' Boro chairman Stanley Gibson was clearly stunned.

'We will have to consider this surprising matter in the boardroom. I will be sorry indeed if this is Mannion's last word.'

Fans and management alike thought Wilf had plenty of football left in him. After all, he was just a lad compared to Stanley Matthews, who at thirty-nine was still the best right-winger in the country. Wilf was nearly four years younger and, just like Matthews, his game was based on ball control rather than blistering pace. His perceptive passes, delicate touches and dummies could be executed as well by a thirty-six-year-old as by a man ten years younger. Wilf could even move to the wing, the Boro faithful reasoned.

So why wasn't he interested? By now Wilf and Bernadette had two children, so with a young family to think of and no job to go to, why give up £14 per week, the new maximum wage, plus bonuses? The rumour-mongers went into overdrive. It wasn't surprising that the first story borrowed heavily from the events of the close-season in 1948: Wilf was refusing to re-sign because he was staging another one-man strike against the system. He was after a transfer again, and once Boro relinquished his registration he would move elsewhere.

Then there was the theory that he was angry because he had been overlooked for the job of Boro manager. Rowley was stepping down due to his ill health and Wilf wanted the position, but was passed over. A third rumour had him taking over a pub. But when the letter confirming Wilf's retirement arrived for the directors at Ayresome it stuck to the story he told Mandale.

There was, however, another factor in the equation – division two. Boro had just been relegated after Wilf's more or less one-man battle against the drop failed, as he knew it eventually would. He couldn't keep Boro up on his own, although the *Billingham Press*, commenting the previous season as Wilf topped the club scoring list with eighteen goals, made it clear he tried as he did everything for the forwards 'except run on the field with a sponge. In practically every game this season, Mannion has done the work of two men. Apart from the job of doing practically all the brainwork for which he has had no competitors in the past four or five seasons, Wilf now has to score all the goals too.'

In the penultimate game of that 1952–53 season, he scored twice as Boro beat reigning champions Manchester United 5–0 to banish relegation worries. It was their first win over Matt Busby's side since the war. But 'there was never any doubt about the result,' said reporter Gordon Reay:

> From the moment when Wilf Mannion's scheming golden head popped up from nowhere to nod home the first goal, Middlesbrough were cock-a-hoop and irresistible and Mannion was their ace tactician right through. His second goal, another header just before the interval, was a real gem out of the book. Another of his plots came off within two minutes of resuming and, though it was Walker's centre and Delapenha's head which again did the trick, Mannion marked out the move. The rest was easy. In the last minute there was a final Mannion flourish to grace the afternoon, a clever backheeled pass which put the ball onto Fitzsimon's head for the fifth.

It was the third vital win in four games. Belying any doubts over their first division ability, they had beaten Newcastle 2–1 (Mannion 2) and Blackpool 5–1, a game in which Mannion scored again. Blackpool were about to defeat Bolton in the Matthews FA Cup final. Such a flying close to the season raised hopes for the next. Even Wilf was sucked in by the optimism.

'I think that maybe we have turned the corner. Boro's supporters, I am convinced, will really have something to cheer within the next couple of seasons. It may even be next season.'

He couldn't have been more wrong. Early season form was poor – only one win in the first nine games – and mid-season was even worse with no wins in nine games between January and March. Back-to-back victories at

Wolves and at home against Villa raised hopes but, with five games to go, three of those away, Boro were still struggling. Defeats against relegation certainties Manchester City and Liverpool at home before drawing with Sunderland paved the way for the inevitable exit from the first division, after a twenty-five-year stay. Liverpool beat them again, 4–1 at Anfield, in the penultimate game of the season. The last game, at Arsenal, was doubly significant – Boro's last in the top league for two decades and Wilf's last for the club. He had scored his last goal at Ayresome on 3 April against Villa.

He denied his decision to retire was influenced by the drop.

'I made up my mind long before the relegation threat that 1953–54 would be my last season,' he said. Some remained angry that he wasn't staying on to lead Boro in an instant attempt to regain a first-division place. But how much did an ageing man, who realized he had no other skill to secure another job, want to play against the likes of Doncaster Rovers and Lincoln City? Especially when he could be trying to establish for himself some long-term future away from the pitch.

In an attempt to do just that, he spoke to businessmen he had met via Boro. They promised to help him in three years' time when he would be ready to finish, not now when he wasn't, according to them. But as he told a reporter from the *People*: 'That baby,' pointing to Kathy, 'young Wilf [his five-year-old son] and Berney mean more to me than any club, even Boro.'

There was one last effort to convince Wilf that his future still lay at Middlesbrough. The man appointed to succeed Rowley, Bob Dennison, trod the by now well-worn route to Wilf's door. By his own admission an ordinary player for Newcastle, Dennison tried to soothe an extraordinary talent back to the fold.

'Will you reconsider your decision now if I can produce a signed letter from the directors guaranteeing to find you a pub when the club decide you should finish?' When the *club* decide you finish. Wilf said, 'Thanks. But no thanks.' Promises from football club directors were not what he was after. All those years before, Tommy had been right. Wilf knew that now.

You can almost see the sad shake of the head as Cliff Mitchell wrote what amounted to an obituary. His subject wasn't dead, but might as well have been from a Boro point of view.

An era has ended at Ayresome Park with the resignation of England's greatest post-war inside-forward and, indeed, one of football's all-time star players. The Mannion era saw no soccer honours brought to Teesside – indeed it has closed with relegation – but it saw some brilliant play from 'the little fellow', as football knows him. In any team he would have been outstanding; in some of the sides which have represented Middlesbrough FC since the war, he has been on his own.

That rarity, a 'natural' footballer, Mannion has dominated the Ayresome Park scene since his demobilization. He has been responsible for a large proportion of the entertainment at Borough's HQ, and a large proportion of the goals! His ability to split a defence with one shrewd pass; his mastery of the ball whatever the conditions; his powerful shooting with either foot; his brilliant heading skill – all those attributes have combined to produce a great footballer. That he is a Teessider has helped to endear him to the hearts of Ayresome Park fans, but he would have been a prime favourite there whatever his birthplace, for the folk in this part of the world appreciate real football.

He joins the select few who will always be named when soccer crops up in the conversation of sportsmen in the north east. And that is often enough, in all conscience! Mannion's greatest game? I fancy it was when Middlesbrough beat Blackpool 4–0 on 22 November 1947. He was without parallel that day. He dazzled and bewitched a strong, competent Blackpool defence to such effect that in the end their defenders fought shy even of going in to tackle him, knowing that they would be left flat-footed. Yes, Wilf was dynamic. His was the greatest display of inside-forward play that I have ever seen. Perhaps the greatest I ever will see.

It is a sad thought that we have seen his consummate skill, his twinkling feet, for the last time. The Mannions of this world are, unhappily but inevitably, few and far between. Cheerio, Wilf, and thanks for the memory of football as it should be played . . .

Fellow great players who witnessed Wilf's unique talent at close quarters were also quick to contribute their bouquets. Scottish international Alex Forbes said: 'I never enjoyed a game so much as when I faced up to him. No matter how hard you went in to the tackle, he never complained. Wilf was too good a player for that. He could give and take with the best of them. And even though he was your rival, he always had an encouraging word, or a crack to make, while out on the field.'

Later others added their tributes. Matt Busby, one of the first to experience Wilf's skill, said: 'I played for Middlesbrough during the war. Mannion was hailed as the "wonder boy" then. That was a fitting tag for he became a wonder player. He was one of the greatest in the world. He was the perfect reader of the game.' Raich Carter added: 'What a player!

The ball, when he moved with it, seemed to be part of him. He was so easy to play with ... a natural to end all naturals.'

Yet it was a man who never really made it as a player and who had known him since they were boys whose comments proved most prescient. Harold Shepherdson said first: 'From his schoolboy days to his professional years, soccer came easily to Wilf. It was no strain on him. He was naturally clever and his reflexes were amazingly swift.' Then he added: 'I often wondered if doing what comes easily on the field is good training for the future, which was sure to bring fresh, strange problems. Wilf was a happy-go-lucky lad but I would class him as an introvert. One never really discovered his thoughts.'

On a football pitch, Wilf was the master. What he wanted to do, he did. He was used to working with the very best there was and even when he was in a mediocre team, it was built around him. When he stopped playing he was just another man approaching his forties in search of a job, but with no skills, indeed perhaps less suited to acquiring them than most. After nearly two decades as a star – and being treated as one, even at the worst of times – it would be hard to knuckle down to an office job, to become just another ex-hero.

Carter once said that all former internationals should be shot once they retired. Wilf went further: 'They should shoot old pros when the time comes to hang up their boots.' For, in their day, retirement held nothing that would come remotely close to the glory experienced on a pitch. If a star was lucky, there might be a career as a manager – like Carter, Joe Mercer or Alf Ramsey – or in another business, like Finney. If he was unlucky, there was only a lifetime of people thinking: 'Didn't you used to be ...?' Wilf's unhappy lot was to be among the latter group.

First, there was another attempt to get him back to Boro. Cliff Mitchell was dispatched, a couple of days before the first game of the season in division two, on a secret mission. He knew success was unlikely. Wilf's mind was made up and there was little chance of changing it. He had even lined himself up with a new job as a football reporter and commentator with the 4.5 million selling *Sunday People*.

'Mr Gibson has asked me to see you, Wilf,' the *Gazette* man started. 'He knows you've got yourself a new job with the *People* and he wishes you the best of luck. But, he says, won't you please come back – the Boro really do need you.'

The answer was still no, for reasons given in the new column. First Wilf admitted: 'I'm being branded a deserter. I'm the footballer who doesn't care. They say I am the star who couldn't take it ... the Golden

Boy with feet of brass.' But he quashed rumours that he had walked out in a row over money or not being appointed manager:

I'm thirty-six and I've had eighteen years of it. I figure I've been around long enough. I'd rather finish now, while I'm still somewhere near the top than linger on to fade out gradually. Moreover, to clear the air still further, I must add that I never expected – or wanted – to be made Middlesbrough manager! True, the directors have promised time after time that I'd be 'looked after', as they called it, when I finished playing. One of them, Mr Tommy Thomas, once went so far as to say, 'There'll be a job for you with us as long as you live.' But those, I decided long ago, were just the usual, vague, sweeping promises all directors have a habit of making to players when they're in moods of occasional benevolence. And anyway sweeping dressing-room floors, as I've known some famous old-timers forced to do, isn't my idea of the ideal end to a man's career.

The truth is I'm leaving this club simply because, at the age of thirty-six, I'm reaching an age when I must study the future. Whether Middlesbrough and their fans like it or not, I'm not ashamed to say I put Berney and our two kids in front of any football club. There isn't a club in the league that could offer me the security I seek for them. Because there is no security in football, whether you're a player or a manager. Don't get me wrong. I've had a good time playing soccer and more than an average share of honours have come my way. But the one thing I have never been able to win from football is the thing I want most: a green light for the future.

Seven games into the season – with Boro's form reading: played seven, won none, lost six, drawn one – there was a final approach. Wilf was invited to Ayresome to talk to Gibson and Dennison. The chairman said: 'The door is always open for Mannion and, indeed, we would welcome him.' Even if it was for just a few weeks to steady the ship.

Wilf was again dismissive: 'Not under any consideration would I consent to such an arrangement. It would place me in an impossible position. I appreciate the fact that the club are anxious that I should re-sign for them but I cannot, in fairness to myself, the club, or the players let it be suggested that I consider myself a football superman. Many people seem to forget football is a team game and success comes of each player doing his best. Any suggestion that any player, however good, could simply step in and change the whole picture in the course of a few games puts a player in a ridiculous position.'

The language was again becoming more inflamed. In another piece, that appeared months before his *People* debut, Wilf gave an even better glimpse of what was to come.

Back in 1936 soccer was my life. I ate it, slept it, dreamt it. Middlesbrough signed me at the age of seventeen for less than the price of a second-hand bike. By 1939 I was headlining as 'Golden Boy'. In the same year I signed for the Green Howards – Italy and the rest – and if you think that was a sneeze, try it sometime. The point is that during the whole of my six years' war service I received nothing – not even as a token – from Middlesbrough. But they still claimed me when I returned.

I had the ex-serviceman's itch to move. Middlesbrough said no and that was it. That piece of paper I signed in 1936 really put me in the slave class. And you know the rest. I know another first division player who had given years of good service. Then, because he was due for a benefit, he decide to retire. He said he was washed up. The club's answer? 'You quit and you can forget your benefit.' In the end he got the benefit money – from the club to which he was transferred.

Mr Supporter, you don't know the half of it. Postponed benefits, thumbs down to attempts to better yourself, 'sign-or-else' threats. The TUC can go ahead and investigate. They'll find plenty of material – material that will astonish them and you.

Forget the TUC, all fans would have to do was buy the *People* once Wilf Mannion began an ill-starred stay as columnist, lifting the lid on soccer scandals and embroiling himself in one as a result.

It was a classic illustration of how not to win friends and influence people: choose any number of allegations of bribery and corruption; take aim and fire them at your former employers; add liberal quantities of frank views along the lines of 'They aren't fit to run a hundred yards, let alone the national sport'; leave to simmer and wait for the inevitable inquiry; refuse to co-operate and watch the row boil; contemplate the recipe – for disaster, although you don't know that yet – and wait for it to blow up in your face. You will be banned for life; you will conclude, perhaps, that you should never have entered the kitchen in the first place.

Wilf's career on the *People* was short and sour. The paper signed him up as a football correspondent, but it didn't especially want match reports. It wanted insider tales of bribery and other bungs, with a bit of bitching thrown in. It got it all, no doubt doing circulation no end of good, but it did Wilf no good at all. He told the truth, but the authorities weren't interested if he wouldn't turn over the guilty men to them and put names to the anonymous faces he claimed were corrupting the game.

What could he do? As he said: 'Be a bit smart! Do you suppose an offer like that is made on the back of a picture postcard and sent through the post? These sorts of offers are made by word of mouth. It is strictly between you and the other fellow, and, if it every came to an inquiry, he and every one of his directors would deny it, of course. So I should be made out a liar and scapegoat.' It would be a director's word against a player's, and who was more likely to be believed was obvious. Perhaps Wilf should have thought of that before he began the ghost-written pieces, but there was no one to advise him any better.

Week one of the *People*'s series was: 'I said no to a bribe of £3000' and told of the meeting at Aston Villa but without naming the club.

I would be a wealthy man today if I had listened to even two or three of the black-market propositions put to me during my eighteen years as a player. One offer alone – from a famous first division club – would have put me in clover. It was made to me, unknown to anyone connected with my own club at the time, when I had refused to re-sign for Middlesbrough. And it took my breath away.

Besides paying my club what would have been a record transfer fee – some £25,000 – these money-is-no-object directors were prepared to hand me £3000 in ready cash the moment I signed. On top of that I was to get top wages, then £12 a week, as a player; plus a 'job' – I put it that way because it was a job in name only as a salesman of something or other – which would have brought me another cool £25 a week. And, just as an incidental, I was to be given £25, to be slipped to me on the railway station, merely for making the trip to talk the offer over.

Week two was: 'I walked out – because he paid me too much', the story of why he deserted Oldham, how he found the pressure of the fans there too much to bear, how his wages increased every time there was a new story about a move anywhere other than Athletic and how the fans gathered around his house calling: 'Good old Wilf; stick it out.' It also covered how the original dispute with Boro occurred.

Week three: 'I'm not going back [to Boro]; a pub won't get me either', an instalment which revealed how Boro had begged him to return to the club. It also included some stern words about the mismanagement of the club, which meant he would never return, and the resulting decline.

Week four started with an attack on the England selectors:

The truth about England's failures in the international arena is that Walter Winterbottom – up till now – just hasn't had a chance. He's had to carry the can back for the mistakes of others – the selectors. They, I say, are the villains of the piece in these England defeats.

Then, for good measure, he had a go at Winterbottom as well:

England teams over the past few season have been hamstrung by pre-conceived ideas about how a match should be played. The only possible way – as Mr Winterbottom would probably have realized if he had played longer in top-class football – is to send the men out on to the field free to work out their own tactics as the match develops. It may be that the England team manager has had to follow a line set from higher up. But the fact remains that our best players – men like Lawton, Carter, Matthews, Finney – have been forced to waste hours of special international training rehearsing moves which they knew all about as kids of seven. I've seen Tommy Lawton sent out for heading practice. I've seen Raich Carter being instructed in the art of defence-splitting passes. I've even heard Stanley Matthews himself being told how to tie a defence in knots.

In week five he told of the journey, standing in the corridor, back from the England World Cup showdown game with Scotland in Glasgow. The London-bound players had to share a sleeper, four to a third-class cabin. The officials on the same train got one first-class sleeper each.

Finally, in '£30,000 to desert my country', the paper's readers learnt how foreign clubs were trying to buy up English players.

Every time our international soccer team plays abroad attempts are made to lure Britain's star footballers to continental clubs. Several times while I was abroad I was approached by agents of foreign clubs. They offered me a small fortune if I would desert my country and club. And many other players were approached too. Foreign representatives would make contact with us in hotel lounges or training grounds. And within a few minutes our lads would be listening to the most amazing lures. I was offered £15,000 during one trip if I would agree to join the well-known Italian club Juventus. The agent approached me one morning as I was leaving a hotel to follow four or five of the other England players out for a stroll.

'If you will come to Italy,' he said, 'not only will we pay your club any transfer fee they ask but we'll pay £15,000 into your own banking account besides.' The day after that Italian bid I had a similar offer – only a little below the Italian figure – from the Spanish club, Real Madrid.

Revelation upon revelation upon revelation. Today, in the era of the screaming back-page tabloid headlines, they might not seem like much, but in the 1950s they were explosive. Blaming the England management for defeats, revealing transfer approaches from some of the biggest club sides in the world which would be illegal if attempted by any English team, and alleging bungs from some of the supposedly more upstanding domestic clubs were incredible accusations.

But what could the FA or the Football League do? Wilf Mannion was no longer one of theirs. No club could be lent upon to persuade its player to pipe down. As the initial outcry subsided, he just concentrated on continuing his journalistic career as a columnist, and a pretty good one, rather than an exposé merchant. He often showed a foresight and an understanding of what domestic football needed to catch up other nations in the wake of the double whammy home-and-away thrashings by the Hungarians.

He had some good ideas, some of which were eventually put into practice, while others, some might say, still should be; Sunday football, for example, and no doubt with a fog-bound Elland Road in mind, a mid-winter break 'and not because it means more leisure for players. I'm for an extended season and an end to the screwball soccer that the customers paid to see in February. Comes the character who says: "A good foot-baller can play under any conditions." That wipes me off as a failure, for I've never mastered the intricacies of soccer-on-ice. I'll leave that to the skaters.'

Again he had advice for England, specifically about the still inadequate preparations for fixtures:

Seventeen of England's top footballers report in London tomorrow for two days concentrated training. We're told it's a get-together for the boys – a kind of dummy run before the international match with Wales. It all sounds very jolly indeed. But if any of those seventeen players returns home with more soccer knowledge than when he left, I'm picking Horden Colliery to win the FA Cup. If we must prepare for these big games, let us do it properly. For instance, what's wrong with picking twenty players each season to form the backbone of an English team. Let them play three or four games each month against top league teams. The matches could be played midweek under the lights, leaving the players free for league games on the Saturday.

He also highlighted a young up-and-coming manager: 'Glad to see my old pal is hitting the high spots again at Workington. For [he] is one of those characters with a gift for getting teams out of the doldrums and putting them on the winning trail.' By the end of the decade Liverpool would start to realize that, as Bill Shankly put them on the winning trail.

What I like about Bill is that he never panics. Even when things weren't going so well, he stuck to the same team and gave them a chance to settle down. 'Panic and all is lost,' is one of the Shankly maxims. Everything Bill does is done to plan. Even training is scheduled to a strict timetable. But that doesn't make him a strict disciplinarian. Far from it. He is one of the easiest-going characters I have met. Ask the players. He's always 'Bill' to them. There's no 'Mr' or 'Boss' when he's around. 'Let the players regard you as an equal,' says Bill, 'and you gain just as much respect.' I couldn't agree more.

Everything was going fine until Wilf pulled on a pair of boots again in anger. When he announced his decision to leave Boro several clubs had tried to sign him, but to no avail. It seemed Wilf Mannion, the footballer, would only survive as a memory but then, on Christmas Eve 1954, second division Hull City managed to get him to sign for them, no doubt in large part because his friend and fellow rebel in an England blazer, Neil Franklin, was there.

'I hadn't played football for months,' Wilf says. 'I knew I was gone really. But [Harold] Needler, the chairman of Hull approached me, I think on transfer deadline day. They were in danger of going down and he wanted me to help them. I said to him, "I can barely walk, never mind run." He said, "All I want you to do is hold the rest of them together and be a steadying influence." He wanted me to use my footballing brain. I hadn't done any training or anything, but he said that was okay. I was practically walking around in my first few games.'

For Hull, and for football in general, the Christmas Eve signing for £4500 was staggering, daring and desperate in equal measure. The club had already put down enough markers of its ambition since being reborn after the war. Its new ground, Boothferry Park, which had replaced its bombed-out previous home, had seen a promising centre-forward called Don Revie arrive and make his name before leaving for Manchester City; Franklin, too, had been signed for a club record £22,500 when he was allowed back into football in 1951, and was showing England form still despite a serious knee injury; and the player–manager, albeit recently departed to Leeds, who had led them to promotion into the second division was Raich Carter.

The directors remained ambitious, but with the club's last win more than two months distant, relegation looked more likely than even survival. The board knew what Wilf could do for them. He had amply demonstrated his skills when Boro played at Boothferry Park in an FA Cup tie seven years earlier and scored the opening goal before Hull's biggest crowd for twenty years with a thirty-yard drive. He inspired his side to a 3–1 win despite what one report called 'some of the most savage, all-or-nothing tackles this side of manslaughter'.

When, after 'retirement', he returned to Humberside to play in a floodlit friendly match, the directors made an offer and when he didn't dismiss it out of hand, they approached Middlesbrough for permission to ask him officially to dust down his boots. Boro were so confident he would say no that they said yes and allowed the approach. On Wilf's acceptance, manager Bob Dennison was left to try to wipe the egg off the club's face.

'It's been rather a surprise but we are pleased the Mannion situation has been resolved,' he claimed.

For Wilf the transfer was timely but troublesome. It gave him another chance to show what he could do, even at his advanced age, but it also left him open to charges of hypocrisy and worse. Soon after he left Boro he wrote in his *People* column: 'Take it from me, I am *not* coming back into football. I'm sorry my old club Middlesbrough are in trouble. But after careful thought I've decided that, with the best will in the world, I'm not the man to stage a life-saving act.' But that was exactly what he was being asked to do at Hull.

It seemed that 'finished' meant with Boro, not with all football, and that rankled with certain sections of the game – the Ayresome management for a start; the players union, which had received an application for a payment from its retirement provident fund; and the moral guardians of the game in the press. *Sunday Pictorial* columnist Jack Peart summed up their argument that he was disloyal:

> Mannion refused to resign for Middlesbrough last summer, after eighteen years with the club that helped to make him. The directors and the ever faithful fans begged him to reconsider his decision – even for one season to help the club start the fight back to the first division.

And, moreover, greedy too:

> Mannion was a great player – one of the greatest inside-forwards of our time. But, like a few more I could mention, he never seems to know when he's well off.

Wilf himself said: 'I'm happy to be back in the game again,' and: 'My urge to play again was so great that I happened to be in the mood when approached by Hull.' He even suggested he prepare himself for his comeback by training with his former team-mates at Ayresome, but that obviously wasn't going to happen. Instead he approached Hartlepools United's Fred Westgarth and trained with his side.

'It will be killing him for the next few days,' Westgarth said, 'but I will help him all I can to get fit.'

The transfer had more serious implications, though. It meant that Wilf, bung and black-market exposer, came back under the disciplinary auspices of the Football League. Revenge, the dish best eaten cold, was going to warm up some men at league HQ. A member of the management committee – which, incidentally, included long-standing Boro director

Harry French – told reporters: 'We are constantly receiving sweeping references to a black market in soccer players. These usually come from clubs, not players, but no one has ever come forward with chapter and verse to give us something to work on. This, an allegation by a player, seems to be something different.'

It took until February before he was finally called upon by the committee to explain his allegations. It opened with a mild rebuke, ordering Boro not to pay Wilf's accrued benefit money, then went for the jugular and ordered him to appear before them in May to elaborate on his allegations; to name names or deny his allegations were true. He refused to even attend the hearing, at which he was banned from the League indefinitely. No more playing, which infuriated Hull who were going to lose both money and a fine player. The club's chairman Needler said: 'We are very disappointed. Our advice to him was to obey the League and get matters straightened out.'

Coaching, getting on to the management ladder or even scouting were all out, too, as the ban meant he could have no contact of any sort with a league club. It was a tawdry end to what had been a distinguished professional career. Perhaps Wilf only had himself to blame, but realistic- ally there were others who had blood from the culled career on their hands – Villa's officials for a start, but they were hardly likely to come clean; the authorities who were picking on a small fish when they knew the whole ocean was polluted; perhaps even the staff at the *People* who encouraged him to dig the dirt, but only to cover himself in muck.

The word scapegoat sprang to mind, certainly for J. L. Manning, sports editor of the *Sunday Dispatch*: 'It is the directors of the clubs and not this player who should be called to give information under penalty of suspension,' he thundered. His paper was running a campaign against sleazy dealing in the transfer market. As such, he welcomed the first move to investigate it, while voicing his anxiety

> ... that the net has not been cast more widely to bring in the men of football who have complained that the racket has been going on for years. The *Sunday Dispatch* does not want Mannion alone to bear the burden of proof. That is why we made our offer, and repeat it today, that if the League will grant an amnesty to those concerned we will provide them with far more proof than Mannion can. In this way the League could get evidence of the full extent of the racket instead of merely pursuing a single case.

Wilf told his side of the story in the *People*.

Because I dared to tell the truth about the evils of the football transfer system I am out of the game for good. That is the result of the ultimatum given to me by the Football League. Either I must disclose the name of the club that tried to bribe me to leave Middlesbrough or I must deny that what I wrote was true. I will do neither. They used to call me the Golden Boy of soccer but I reckon the halo is a bit tarnished now. From now on I'll be the Naughty Boy of soccer to the Football League. That's all right by me. At least my case will serve as a warning to other professional players who try to tell the truth. You can whisper these things in the dressing-rooms; talk of them behind closed doors; but for goodness sake don't let the public know.

Wilf's short career at Hull achieved much for the Tigers. Just the word Mannion on the teamsheet generated the season's best attendance of 46,000 at Boothferry Park for his debut, a 4–0 defeat at the hands of Luton Town. The next game was a bit better as Wilf put his side 2–1 up with a glancing header, but then watched as visitors Nottingham Forest scored twice more to condemn Hull to another defeat and their eighth game without a win.

The optimistic line peddled by the club chairman on Wilf's signing was clearly misplaced.

'We think the promotion race is still sufficiently open for us to have a good chance,' he said. In fact the only way Hull looked likely to leave division two was via the trapdoor. They had lost ten out of twenty-five games, six at home. They were the lowest scorers in the division, with just twenty-nine and only nine of them away from home. But by the end of a bizarre season, Wilf had done enough to ensure the club from which he was banned would still be in the second division after he left. He inspired the side back to winning ways often enough to survive; and there's no question which was the sweetest victory for Wilf – the one at Ayresome Park.

When the two sides met, on 5 February 1955, Boro's form was in marked contrast to Hull's. The last nine home matches at Ayresome had been home wins, Boro scoring twenty-eight goals and only conceding six. But the extra 20,000 who headed for the game compared to the last home gate of 12,000, were not drawn by the club's form but by its former star. Wilf's return was simply a must-see.

At the Hall family's rendezvous – mum's terraced house in Ernest Street, close to Ayresome – the clan gathered. One of its younger members, Duncan, aged six, wasn't given the choice of whether he wanted to go to the match or not. His dad and uncles were all Boro fanatics who had mourned the departure of Wilf just nine months earlier and were not going to miss an opportunity to see him at Ayresome again, even if he was in the amber colours of Hull.

'My whole family went to that game,' Duncan remembers now. 'Everybody went. It was, "We are all going." No questions about it. There are only three occasions when that's happened, when I've gone to a match whether I wanted to or not. The first was to see Wilf Mannion; the second was to see Stanley Matthews, so I could say I've seen Stanley Matthews run up and down a football field; and the third was if Middlesbrough ever got to Wembley, so we all trotted off to the Zenith Data Systems Cup when Boro were in that.'

The reception Wilf got would have shamed Wembley. There were none of the boos and shouts of Judas you would hear today, but cheers and applause from fathers and sons like the Halls and from other fans who'd seen him mature from a fledgling genius to the finished article. Even that day's *Gazette*, which ran a rather unnecessary front-page introduction to Hull's inside-forward, was welcoming, with Cliff Mitchell writing:

> It will be good to see the wonderful ball control of Mannion again, but our hopes must be that this week at least he fails to inspire his chums to victory. We wish him and Hull the best of luck, but after today.

His true, mixed, feelings were more accurately reflected later in his piece: 'A sad sight, that of Mannion playing against a team representing Middlesbrough FC, but that's the way it goes in football.' Boro boss Dennison insisted there would be no special plans to quell Wilf.

'Believe me every Middlesbrough player is looking forward to this game because they feel that the run of home successes will be maintained. They are not at all worried at the prospect of playing against Mannion. I know just how good Wilf can be but our defence is in grand form.'

Even so every eye was on one man as the teams ran out and for the next ninety minutes as Wilf showed Ayresome Park what it was missing. Duncan Hall has one incident embedded in his memory.

'The one thing I remember most – and it's going to sound somewhat maudlin, but I can see it as if it was happening in front of me now – was one time when Wilf got the ball right on the centre spot and he just shimmied. No one backed off like they do now, so people were much further up on him. He shimmied and the whole Boro team just shimmied with him. He just stood there and, as God's my witness, put his foot on top of the ball and grinned.'

The crowd roared in appreciation.

'If it was today, the reaction would be the equivalent of Juninho running to take a corner and the whole crowd bowing in reverence to him. That is my undying memory of Wilf Mannion. Just this frail, blond guy stood there. He had such a presence. How does somebody that size have a presence among big, physical fellas? I just think they're born with it. It's just a God-given instinct and you have the privilege – and I use the word deliberately – to see it. When you see it, you know what it is you're looking at: greatness – the attraction of sport of any kind.'

Wilf inspired Hull to a vital 2–1 victory, setting up the winner. True, Boro missed chance after chance, but the Hull players – who all 'pranced for joy' at the final whistle, according to Mitchell – probably needed the points more. Wilf's reaction afterwards was more muted: 'I enjoyed the game all the more because it proved wrong all those folk who imagined I would get "the bird" from Middlesbrough fans.'

His notices were not sparkling. The regional *Sunday Sun* said: 'He showed much of his old accuracy in passing and retains his ball control.' Mitchell wrote: 'Mannion's was a clear, resourceful game. He was scarcely a commanding force but his control and his delightful passes were good to watch.'

Good enough for Duncan Hall's love of football, and Boro, to be confirmed. His father had started a scrapbook of Wilf's cuttings; now Duncan was entrusted with the task of keeping the school exercise book up-to-date and looking after it. Looking over it four decades later, he says: 'If you think of somebody being fanatical about football and a footballer – right down to the fact that if his wife was stood by the front door of their house and a *Gazette* photographer took a photograph of her you stuck it in your book – that was the esteem we had for him.

'In footballing terms, he is quite rightly just a legend. You could talk all day about the greatest footballers past and present and unquestionably – whether people other than me want to put him first or two, three, four or five – he's certainly going to fall into that bracket. I think his skills were self-evident. But what brought it all together was this peculiar mix of things: first and foremost he was a working-class lad in Middlesbrough. Period. If you were a working-class lad, and most people were, you'd have an empathy for him; then there was his tremendous strength, mental more than physical. If you're going to get bashed about, you're going to get bashed about whether you're 6ft 6in or 3ft 6in. But the strength of character of the person, his ability to acknowledge that he wasn't just a serf in a football club is really the ultimate strength. Let's face it, it went from Mannion to George Eastham before anyone else was willing to take that move. At the time he did it, it was an immense thing to do. I think it's very difficult for people to understand today just what he did do. It was extraordinary.

'Combining all of that with the sheer ability of the man, you finished up with somebody who was exceptional – and in a club which never made it. You can wrap it up any way you like, but the bottom line is that Middlesbrough didn't actually win anything. That's quite illuminating to me. You could argue that, other than Mannion, George Best was the greatest footballer born in these isles. So often you will talk about the days of Best, Law and Charlton and Best was a superstar, but there were superstars around him. In a Middlesbrough context you had a super superstar. All that and there was still a bloke who wanted to stand up and be counted and say, "This is an unfair system."'

Duncan Hall has become very familiar with the system in its modern and more equitable equivalent. He still watches Middlesbrough but these days it's from a seat in the new £16 million stadium he helped to create. As chief executive of the Teesside Development Corporation, the body charged with the urban renewal of now-derelict industrial sites, he played a role in the building of the Riverside Stadium probably second only to Boro chairman Steve Gibson. Keen to maximize the publicity for his organization, but minimize his own profile, he is coy about his exact role, but it's impossible to believe that the new stadium – built on development corporation land – would have gone ahead if a chief executive without Boro red pulsing through his veins had been in charge.

Now he sees a new ambition at the club, despite relegation to the first division – the new ground, Bryan Robson, the big-money signings and, crucially, the first signs that the inferiority complex born of more than a hundred years of relative failure may be lifting. Even so, he is still taken back to the days of Wilf Mannion.

'I heard a comment at a game the other week that Juninho is a luxury. It took me all that way back in time. The issue is not about somebody like him – who I think is a supreme footballer, worth paying your money to see walk on the field because he'll do more in the warm-up than the rest can do in a season. No, you suddenly realize a parallel to Mannion – you build a team around players like them. If you can do that, you've got world beaters. The club has got to have the ambition to do that. Perhaps that's what it lacked before.'

178

· TEN ·

The savage injustice of soccer

W ilf was pulling his boots on again sooner than he might have thought possible, certainly sooner than the League had envisaged. The ban it imposed was quickly made to look ludicrous by the FA, which made a mockery of the punishment's supposed all-encompassing severity by deciding that it only applied to league clubs. Wilf was free to join any non-league outfit which would have him and, not surprisingly, there was plenty of interest. He choose Poole Town, managed by former Boro team-mate and England star Stan Rickaby, and moved to the south-coast club on a free transfer in September 1955.

Hull chairman Needler was left fuming. The FA's okay of the transfer was 'farcical' and a decision 'that could only happen in football', he spluttered.

'This is the craziest thing that has happened in football for years. The Football Association have overruled the League. We have been told in a dozen words that Mannion is not our player and that we cannot expect a fee for him.'

Ironically, the FA had finally given Wilf freedom of movement. Meanwhile, Hull were forced into quibbling with Boro over the original £4500 fee. They got no refund, so each of Wilf's appearances for them ended up costing £250.

But Needler was not the last man who lost his temper after dealing with a Golden Boy whose lustre was increasingly tarnished. Next was Poole chairman, Len Matchan, whose relationship with Wilf got off to a bad start when he welcomed his star signing after a 380 mile, through-the-night journey, but found Wilf couldn't return the greetings because his mouth was jammed with a toffee. His initial form, and the fact that he drew a crowd of 5000, five times the average gate, to witness his debut, eased matters.

Then in March 1956, just over halfway through the season, he got back in his car and drove his family back to Teesside. He was unhappy about his accommodation and said playing for Poole was costing him money. The directors hit back by saying a five-year contract was on the table. One board member even offered to move out of his home to allow the Mannions to move in, but all to no avail. Poole even threatened to enforce their right to retain Wilf for another season by offering the minimum terms. For a short while it threatened to be the strike, the sequel. But no one wanted that.

Instead, in June 1956, he joined Cambridge United and managed not to fall out with manager Bert Johnson or anyone else.

'He is to the Cambridge United crowd what he used to be to the Borough crowd in his heyday,' his new boss reported at the end of the year. 'Since mid-October [when he returned from injury] we have only lost one match and Wilf's contribution has been inestimable. Despite the fact that the fans have taken him to their hearts, his fellow players, several with not inconsiderable reputations in league football, are his greatest admirers.'

He was paid £15 per week and the same bonuses as league players to reflect his status, which was reinforced by the crowds who came to see him. Among them was a young lad taken to see one of his heroes by his father. The boy, Bruce Rioch, would himself prove to be no mean player. Later still, as Boro manager in the dark days of the mid-1980s, he would park his car over a manhole cover so that the near-bankrupt club's water supply couldn't be disconnected.

In April 1957, during his stay at Cambridge, Wilf made a successful application for the league ban to be lifted. There was speculation that he would rejoin a league side, perhaps even fulfilling the claim of his ex-manager at Poole, Rickaby, who, fresh from watching an England game, said Wilf should still be playing for his country: 'It was my opinion that Mannion even now could do England a good turn. He is as fit now as at the peak periods of his league career.' It went without saying his skill hadn't left him.

But, as Neil Franklin had discovered, there was no way back from disgrace. Wilf appeared in the pages of the *Gazette,* perhaps as a hint to Boro's management that he was available, under the headline: 'Now my soccer future is brighter.' But it wasn't. 'There is now a much greater chance that I shall be able to extend my career in football in some administrative or advisory capacity after my playing days are over,' he said. 'Even now I have no job outside the game and my hope is, quite naturally, that there will be room for me in soccer, in one capacity or another, for a long time to come.' But there wasn't.

In May 1958, Wilf did leave Cambridge but only for non-league King's Lynn. He spent one season there before taking the perhaps inevitable decision to move out of football and become the landlord of a pub, the Pied Piper, in the new town of Stevenage. The highlight of his stay there was a visit from the Queen – her first formal trip to a boozer – but even that managed to involve a minor scandal when the brewery ordered the removal of two tame pin-ups which adorned the bar. The Royal visit was a success, but the pub tenancy wasn't. Unhappy with the effect the long hours were having on his family life, Wilf quit. Before he left he spoke of his hopes of getting back into football.

'If a really good league club came to me with a businesslike offer to become their manager, I would seriously consider it. I promise you this: if I did manage a league club I would not employ any coaches. Trainers, of course – a footballer's fitness is of paramount importance – but no coaches. No one coached me. No one coached Raich Carter. No one coached Stanley Matthews. If a lad can't play at eighteen or twenty, he'll never play.'

But no offers came. It appeared Wilf Mannion and football were going their separate ways. Staying in the south, he found himself a new job in February 1960, on the production line of the Vauxhall plant in Luton. That was where incredulous reporter Frank McGhee, of the *Daily Mirror* found him later in the year. McGhee had just watched his childhood hero – in his first game for two years – give a reprise of his peak performances in a testimonial match for Tom Finney. One instant brought all the memories flooding back: a high clearance fell towards Wilf facing his own goal, with an opponent closing in behind him. Instead of trapping the ball and waiting for the inevitable tackle from behind, Wilf delicately volleyed it back over his head, flicked it with his left heel as it landed behind him and pushed it back through his legs as he turned. The opponent was still trying to work out what had happened as Wilf moved back up field.

McGhee was enraged that such football genius was clocking on to make cars every day at 7.30 a.m.

> The next eight hours, which could and should be devoted to English international soccer, will be wasted by Wilf Mannion as he screws and humps wood at a car factory ... while the butchers, grocers and businessmen go on choosing bad teams to let England down. If this story sounds bitter that is the way it is supposed to sound. And if it gets a bit incoherent, well sincerity often is and I am desperately sincere about the savage injustice of soccer towards the greatest inside-forward I ever saw. I am no

starry hero-worshipper either – I've met too many of sport's big names and been disillusioned by their pettiness and greed and swollen heads. And don't think that Mannion himself is bitter about his raw deal. It doesn't even seem to occur to him that he has had one.

In Finney's match, he was in the company of, of course, the Preston plumber, but also Stanley Matthews, Stan Mortensen and Bill Shankly. On the pitch, Wilf was first among equals; off it, as McGhee pointed out, the major difference was that Wilf's suit was well kept rather than well cut, and that his wallet was as threadbare.

Yes, Wilf told his disciple, he would love to get back into the game, but no one wanted him. McGhee suggested a solution: scouting for England manager Walter Winterbottom:

> I guarantee his information would be more fruitful for Winterbottom than any he gets from greengrocers, company directors, Old Blues etc who are his present selectors and advisors.

England didn't want him; but another non-league team, Earlestown, of the Lancashire Combination, did. Wilf was appointed player-manager in October 1960, easing his entry back into football. It was to be another short-lived link-up, but it provided one day to remember when, to mark the twenty-first anniversary of a boys' club in Grangetown, near South Bank, Wilf brought his charges to Teesside for a benefit match, and played 'at home' for the first time since his appearance for Hull. South Bank's ground was filled with a crowd of 6000, its biggest for fifteen years. Cliff Mitchell was among them:

> They cheered every time the former Middlesbrough and England star touched the ball; they almost 'willed him' to score, but that final ecstasy was denied them. Mannion didn't score after all. But he showed some of his old deft touches; his ball control was never matched by any other player; he 'made' his team's first goal – and grinned his way through a game he obviously enjoyed. It wasn't Boro v Blackpool (his greatest-ever match, vintage 1947) all over again, but some of Mannion's touches sent the memory tumbling back. For this Teessider is one of the greatest figures football has ever known and his world class kept peeping through.

But in October 1962, Earlestown went bankrupt and Wilf was sacked. He headed back to Teesside and told the *Mirror*: 'Now I'm ready for home.' But was home ready for him? Were there enough people around ready to welcome him back into the fold, or were the sins of the Golden Boy to be taken out on the man? He admitted to the paper: 'Looking back on my career, I realize now that I made many mistakes. There are many things I regret. But it surely wasn't wrong to seek some security when I realized that age was creeping up on me. Soccer is still my life. And I think I have a lot to give if I can find the right place to give it.'

Reporter Charlie Summerbell wrote: 'Easy-going, amiable, with a knack of stepping into puddles as he tries to avoid getting rainsoaked ... that's my summing up of little Wilf Mannion, the man, as he struggles to make a go of it.' There were some sunbeams to come, but after more rain. Indeed, the black clouds were already gathering.

W ilf walked past the noticeboard to the front door, up the two concrete steps and inside the building – the dole office. Hands dug deep in his dark overcoat, he tried not to stand out from his fellow unemployed, but back on Teesside that was impossible. People who had watched his golden years nudged each other and pointed, fathers tried to convince their sons that the slightly sad figure before them was one of the greatest footballers of their – or any – generation. Like South Bank, its most famous son was a shadow of his former glory. In the town there were fewer shipyards and steel foundries, but they still provided the bulk of the jobs, jobs for which Wilf was hopelessly unqualified.

For months Wilf had been on the dole. Eighteen months after returning to Teesside, a short-lived position as steward at a new sports club had been his only job. By April 1964 he was so desperate that, swallowing his pride, he even enrolled on an FA coaching course in Durham. 'Wilf Mannion returns to school – to learn soccer', as the *Northern Echo* put it. Reporter Ray Robertson wrote:

It sounds incredible, but Mannion admits: 'I realize now you are never too old to learn. Football has been my life. It is the only thing I know. I would like to get a coaching job, but everyone demands qualifications these days. I have decided I must move with the times.'

But it was his signing-on, for £7 9s per week, which provoked more interest. When the *Daily Express* tracked him down, he admitted he was desperate.

'Things are looking pretty black,' he said. 'I've just got to find a job soon.' Yes, he admitted, perhaps he'd been his own worst enemy. 'I suppose I've been a fool in some ways, but I don't regret anything I've done. I would like to get back into football and I've even thought about going abroad to get a coaching job.' Great Britain colleague Billy Steel had already set an example by heading to America to coach.

But such talk, and it turned out to be just talk, was a long way from the glorious trips abroad with England, to Lisbon or to Turin. Now it appeared no one in England wanted him. To crown the calamities, his son, Wilfie, had taken up rugby. It was a mournful man who told the *Daily Mirror*:

'I could not care less about my twenty-six international caps. What use are they to me now? I've actually given some of them away. I wish I had never played football. I gave eighteen years service to Middlesbrough but I would have been better off in a trade . . . I will take anything. I still get the glory on Teesside but what good is glory? You can't eat it.'

Frank McGhee, in his column in the same paper, was apoplectic.

Wilf Mannion of Middlesbrough was one of the greatest inside-forwards who ever stamped his feet into studded soccer boots and went out with a ball to put me and you and anyone else who saw him in his debt. But that was ten, fifteen years ago. That was yesterday. Today Wilf Mannion, of Middlesbrough, is broke, out of work with difficult debts to think about – the sort that come through the letterbox to spoil the breakfast of a man whose weekly income is £7 9s unemployment benefit. Anyone who has ever thought present-day players are overpaid, too greedy for cash, thinking more of taking something out of the game than putting something into it, should pause to think about that. Wilf Mannion is broke. He doesn't blame anyone – and perhaps there is no one apart from himself to blame . . .

Except maybe the system that could tie him to one club for his best years – and what memorable years – for the meagre rewards permitted under rigid rules. That club was Middlesbrough FC. And I can't help wondering whether they don't still owe him something. A testimonial game for instance – the chance that only Middlesbrough can give their fans. The chance to say thank you for every time they have been able to start a soccer conversation with: 'I remember when Wilf Mannion . . .' And bring to life again a picture of the fragile, straw blond, arms outstretched to preserve the perfection of balance, pivoting to pass at any point in a circle . . .

But Wilf Mannion doesn't want 'remember whens'. He needs to be remembered *now* . . . As Everton have just remembered Dixie Dean, as Manchester City will next week remember Bert Trautmann, as Preston remembered Tom Finney, as Stoke intend to remember Stanley Matthews. Did they mean any more to their clubs than Wilf Mannion? Don't try to say so at Ayresome Park on a Saturday afternoon. Do they deserve more than Wilf Mannion does from their clubs? Maybe they do. Let's face it, as well as years of pleasure, Wilf Mannion gave Middlesbrough more than their fair share of frustration, aggravation and trouble. He walked out on them once at the start of the 1948 season, fighting for freedoms that only now, sixteen years too late for him, are being conceded . . .

But when Middlesbrough FC directors think about Wilf Mannion is that all they remember – what he did *to* them rather than what he did *for* them in eighteen years' service, studded with twenty-six England caps? I hope not, because Wilf Mannion needs their help now as much as they ever needed his.

As a piece of polemic, it was superb. As a call to arms, it was a flop. The plea went unanswered – at least for another fifteen years, when there were more voices to support it.

Long before then, rumours of Wilf's death swept through South Bank. Years of declining fortunes had taken a toll on his health. He had undergone an operation to cure an ulcer a couple of years earlier. In October 1974, it appeared ill health had finally beaten him. There was much shaking of heads, each member of the community who remembered him recounting their own obituary. St Peter's, by then a social club more than a football team, even held two minutes silence on a busy Saturday night. Such a player; such a local hero; such a crying shame.

Except it wasn't true. Reports of Wilf's death had been greatly exaggerated. He was alive and, if not kicking, at least walking. He certainly wasn't in the best of health, but somehow someone had mistaken his recurring ulcer, and resultant weight loss, for a terminal illness which had reached its inevitable conclusion. Both his son and sister had been told Wilf was critically ill, but, as he and Bernadette could not afford a telephone, they could only call a neighbour who reassured them all was well.

Still the rumours gathered pace. A *Gazette* reporter, sent on the unenviable door-knock at the Mannion's council house, returned with a bit of a scoop. Bernadette told him: 'I am delighted to say that the rumours are nothing more than that. Wilf went out to work today as usual.' Work, with Kenny Beagle among others, was as a labourer and teaboy with a pipe-fitting crew at ICI's enormous Wilton chemical complex. She added: 'We don't know why it all started. But it was very worrying at first. After a bit, Wilf saw the funny side of it.'

It was a rare appearance in the limelight. In his heyday after the war, Wilf would be in the papers all the time. The cuttings began to thin out through the 1950s and sixties until it was only reports of his death which were making news. Any hopes of getting back into football were long gone, even when a generation of his fans made their way into management: Clough, Revie and Bobby Robson to name a few. Any hopes of a reconciliation with Boro were even more remote. Wilf had not stepped inside Ayresome Park for the best part of two decades and had no desire to do so in the next two decades.

But there were fans – or more accurately ex-fans – who rightly thought the impasse was undignified and wrong. They were the small boys who had watched awe-struck from the terraces as Wilf had weaved his spell over the years; boys whose appreciation of football was instilled in them by the magic of a Mannion pass or body-swerve; boys who, as well as going into football themselves, often grew up to be the gentlemen of the press. Frank McGhee was one example, but he was not alone.

For the tabloid sports pages, Wilf's was a great story: the legend down on his luck, the hero working as a labourer and the ex-Golden Boy whose weathered features betrayed nothing of his glorious past. But, despite all the clichés of rags to riches and back again, the best pieces were laced with a genuine melancholy. Peter Thomas, of the *Daily Express* wrote one as a reply to comments made by German team manager Helmut Schön that English football lacked any inspiration:

> To those few who feel superior to me and say they have seen Cassius Clay train, well, I say I saw Wilfred Mannion on the football field and that will do me for a lifetime. Even great players of his day and, young man, let me tell you these were the days of genius at inside-forward, would tell you that no one could make football look so simple and yet breathtaking in one instant.
>
> His living now is not that to which he should have become accustomed. He had somehow, sadly, returned to the darkest roots of his birth; it would have satisfied the moralists who created that dark and fearsome Middlesbrough many years ago; it gives those who saw him in his prime no joy at all, and every reason why things are not getting any better for Wilf Mannion are invalid, answerable and agonising.

Thomas's prose was all the more remarkable because his father was Tommy Thomas, the director who collected Wilf from Oldham at the end of his strike.

Revie also took time away from managing England to pay homage.

'Wilf was responsible for putting me on the football trail. I was taken to Middlesbrough matches by my dad when I was about seven. As soon as the team came out I would fix my eyes on Wilf and hardly ever take them off him. When he approached people with the ball to take them on, he used to remind me of a ballet dancer. He was so neat and tidy in everything he did. That was the outstanding quality, really, his neatness. He would go at somebody at full pace and without even touching the ball he would sell so many dummies that the opposition would go in all directions and he'd run straight on with the ball. He could score goals, beat people, lay the ball off, the lot. Whenever Wilf got the ball there was an expectant roar and he hardly ever let the crowd down.

'I admired Wilf so much that I must have had sixty or seventy pictures of him around my bedroom walls. I would swap four or five of any other player for one of his. On Saturday nights after the match I would go into the cobbled alleyway at the back of our house. There was an eight-foot gap between the brick walls and under the gas lamps I'd dream I was Wilf Mannion. I would dribble round dustbins, lampposts and anything else but I was always Mannion, never anyone else.'

He addressed the question always asked.

'[Would he have] made it [today]? I wish there was a Wilf Mannion around now. He would walk into any team of mine. Of course, the Mannions, the Matthews, the Finneys, the Peter Dochertys would find it more difficult today. If they took the ball out wide today, beat the full-back and went to the dead-ball line, they'd still be confronted with a Norman Hunter or a Tommy Smith covering. But they would overcome it because of their control, balance and speed over the first ten yards. Players are born with qualities like these. Wilf could pick balls out of the air and have them stone dead on the floor in a split second. And he made passes that you didn't have to break your neck getting to. If he'd gone to one of the more fashionable clubs like Arsenal or even Newcastle or Sunderland in the north east, he would have been one of the biggest names in the history of the game. Wilf Mannion would still be out on his own if he was playing today. There was nothing he wasn't capable of doing.'

Revie's eulogy prompted the *Daily Mail* to get Wilf to try his hand as a commentator again, which meant him going to his first football league fixture in fourteen years. Of course it was at Boro – a rejuvenated Boro, topping the League for the first time since the days when Wilf was a youth. But the side didn't impress the frail figure, weighing just over eight stone as he awaited a second ulcer operation. Birmingham City's 3–1 home win in December 1976 confirmed his worst fears for the game he once graced.

'There's so little natural skill and so many manufactured robots out there nowadays,' he said. 'This match was like watching a third division match in the thirties. Why do they keep passing back? They don't seem able to use both feet anymore. Why do they have to stop it every time, instead of keeping the ball running? Why so much bunching? They seem afraid to move into gaps and no one is playing off the ball.

'Football has brought many problems on itself. In my days there was no coaching or even team-talks on the scale of today. My style of play didn't alter one bit from the day I began playing at school to the time I finished. Now they're over-coached. There should be much more free expression. I get the impression that players now are instructed to such an extent that they don't even think of doing anything different, whatever the circumstances.

'If I was twenty again, I'd love to be playing today, but only for the money. I wouldn't enjoy playing the type of football we've just been watching, but they wouldn't be able to make me play that way. I'd still be free.'

His comments provoked a terse reply from Boro's boss, shrinking violet Jackie Charlton.

'I am sure that if Wilf was playing now he would find there isn't space left to use, that runs off the ball are that much more difficult to make in present-day football and that individual skill is, in many cases, looked at and stifled by the opposition,' he told Cliff Mitchell. 'Yes, the explanation is easy. Defenders nowadays can play. In Wilf's day, having looked at television matches and film recordings of that era, defenders could not play.'

One man who disagreed was watching Wilf's re-emergence in the press with interest, professional and personal. John Mapplebeck was a BBC documentary producer, another who learned to love football after seeing Wilf play at Ayresome. He was thinking how he might be able to show his appreciation and affection by making a film.

It was shown as another season of disappointment for Boro came to an end. Charlton had resigned in April 1977 and his successor, John Neal, only managed a mid-table league position in his first full season, and oversaw another good FA Cup run ended, once more, by lowly opposition. Wilf was back at Ayresome – for the first time since appearing for Hull in 1954 – to see Boro play Orient, struggling in the second division, in spring 1978 for that elusive debut place in a semi-final. Fans, many too young to have seen him in his prime, flocked around him demanding autographs, as he was spotted waiting in the queue for the Bob End. One even joked: 'Brought your boots, Wilf?' Perhaps he should have done. Boro only managed a 0–0 draw, then lost the replay 2–1.

Mapplebeck's film, shown a month later, brought back the memories of 'the golden years of the Golden Boy', gilt-edged memories from the likes of George Hardwick and Tom Finney of the Great Britain game and other internationals. But there were also the recollections of ordinary fans and it was one of them who provided the most telling testament to Wilf's lasting status. Tom Kilgour said: 'When Wilf left Middlesbrough and they went down into the second division, I left Ayresome Park as a supporter. Eventually television came on the scene and I used to watch 'Match of the Day' and I saw the likes of George Best and people like that. Shame on me, I began to wonder: "Was Wilfie as good as these people?" I went along Ayresome Park when Manchester United played against Middlesbrough in the FA Cup and for the first time in my life I saw George Best and the rest of them. I was seeing all the mistakes they made that you didn't see on the television. I went home that night and I didn't come out for a pint in the club, I was that disgusted with myself for doubting the talents of Wilfie Mannion.'

Mapplebeck made the film in the hope that it would achieve more than a pleasant trip down memory lane. He wanted some action to help Wilf, specifically, the testimonial he never received despite playing for eighteen years at Boro.

'My first experience of soccer was standing on the Bob End at Ayresome Park with my uncles and watching Wilf. I would have been about eleven or twelve. Because he was a sort of romantic figure, he remained close to my heart. I was aware that he'd had less than just treatment, but in a sense it wasn't just that. Boro were pretty unpleasant to him, but it was also that they could be. It was about the different status of footballers.'

The programme recruited an unlikely convert to Wilf's cause – playwright Dennis Potter. Then television critic for the *Sunday Times*, he led his weekly review with a piece on the Mannion documentary, even though it was only broadcast in a regional slot in the north east. Others also rallied to the rehabilitation. One was George Scott, editor of *The Listener*, a former Liberal parliamentary candidate in Middlesbrough and a schoolboy footballer in the same leagues as Wilf.

> We know for sure that, had Mannion been playing today, he could have been a very rich man, playing for his country and juggling with offers from Europe and America. To see him, one more soccer idol, down if not out is depressing.

Another was John Sadler in the *Sun*:

> They're planning a night of celebration in the north east of England. But as yet they're not sure where or when it will take place. There's only one appropriate venue for staging a testimonial on behalf of Wilf Mannion and George Hardwick and that's Ayresome Park. Sadly, the directors of Middlesbrough FC appear reluctant to be part of this night of fairytale nostalgia.

Reluctant to say the least. One man who watched the documentary and decided to take action was businessman Owen Willoughby. On his beat, selling vending machines in the working men's clubs of Teesside, he heard the reactions and understood how the film had touched a nerve. The general public couldn't believe the treatment meted out to Wilf after playing for Boro 326 times. George Hardwick had also gone without a testimonial for his 166 appearances. Willoughby, a friend of Hardwick's after they had met in the RAF, knew that the great names from Newcastle, Sunderland and even some from Middlesbrough had been honoured with testimonials. Why not Wilf and George? He launched a campaign to stage a match at Ayresome Park.

'I was going into the clubs all over after the documentary was on and the reaction was unbelievable,' he recalls. 'We started staging events to raise money and lobby for a game, but the answer was always no. We even talked about staging it at Wembley and other grounds, but we eventually decided it had to be Ayresome. We did that for two years or more.'

At one of the events, a sportsmen's evening, Brian Clough, then conquering Europe with Nottingham Forest, was guest of honour and added his voice to the testimonial campaign.

'It would cost the club nothing to allow the pitch to be used,' he said. It also cost nothing to get Clough to give his backing; he refused any offer of payment or even expenses to make the trip. Almost as if to illustrate his pressing financial need for a testimonial, Wilf that night sold one of his England caps for £1000.

Middlesbrough Mayor John Stokes was recruited to take the formal testimonial request to the board. But still the answer was no. The *Gazette* reported Willoughby's resulting anger:

> I am shocked, absolutely shocked. How can they do that to us? All we were asking for was the use of the ground. It wasn't going to cost them a penny. Staff at the turnstiles would have been paid by us. We would even have refunded the cost of the electricity used by the floodlights if necessary. The intention was – and still is – to get the game sponsored. We've had tremendous support from so many people on Teesside and now the club turn round and say this. There's bound to be bitterness.

No more than there was already. The eight-man board had 'reluctantly' agreed unanimously to reject the request as they didn't want to set a precedent for any other old player. Chairman Charlie Amer explained why.

'Too many other ex-players who gave first-class service are involved and there are lots of the present staff who deserve consideration as well.

We have a great deal of sympathy for the idea but every member of the board voted against it. We feel it could snowball.'

But sympathy wouldn't pay Wilf's heating bills, nor could it right the wrongs which many agreed he had suffered; and this was another one. Amer prefaced his comments by saying: 'We have nothing against Wilf and George'. But in the opinion of many, then and now, that was not the case. The board would simply not forgive Wilf for his stand against the directors of 1948–49. Shep, by that stage a mainstay of the club's organization, admitted as much just before he died: 'I don't think that was ever forgotten or forgiven by some people.'

Today Amer will not speak about the refusal. He resigned as chairman, but stayed on as a director, halfway through the 1981–82 season as Boro hurtled towards relegation from division one and started on the road to bankruptcy thanks to ill-conceived off-field developments. The best players had been sold to keep the bank manager happy, while the fans, distinctly unhappy, started to stay away. Amer's successor as chairman lasted eight months before giving way to another director, Mike McCullagh, the boy who had seen Mannion's Match and many other of Wilf's performances for Boro, and a fan as well as the chairman.

'My first decision was to grant the testimonial,' he says. 'I knew of the many requests for it and could never understand why it hadn't been the first on the list of games to be held. Wilf and George were two of the most famous players Middlesbrough had ever seen and two of the most loved players. Most players are remembered for a couple of years after they stop but that wasn't the case with them, especially Wilf. Even now people who meet him will tell their friends and say, "I met Wilf Mannion." There was no reason not to have the game, I thought, and once the chairman has the desire it usually happens. It sounds undemocratic, but there are so many things in the life of the football club that need dealing with that whatever the chairman decides is a priority, happens first. But you could feel the will of the whole town.'

At the time McCullagh admitted: 'I am trying to get goodwill at this club and I believe it's vitally important we bring old stars like Wilf and George back into the fold. I want them to feel part of us – for too long Middlesbrough FC has forgotten that it is part of the town.' The reaction was uniformly positive, with a leader writer in the *Gazette* commenting:

For years the club's failure to honour these veterans has rankled with fans. It left a sour taste which doubtless inclined many supporters with long memories to turn their backs on a club which had done the same to the men the fans had worshipped ... This one act alone can do as much for the club's image as a string of successes on the field.

It had taken more than four years from the Mapplebeck film to the granting of the testimonial. It would take the best part of another year for the match to be staged, but it was almost worth the wait. Thousands of fans were happy to get the chance to see Wilf back on the Ayresome pitch, while Mapplebeck, now an independent producer, says he was even more delighted: 'You make a lot of programmes in your life and usually they don't achieve anything. That film is one of the things I'm most pleased about and proud of because it did produce something – even if it was later.'

A couple of months after McCullagh's decision, and before the game, Amer left the board.

One of those ex-fans who returned to Ayresome for the match was George Duffy, known to his mates at Smith's Dock as Judda. He told Mike Amos of the *Northern Echo*: 'Wilf Mannion could miss the ball and still take half a dozen of their men with him. I used to go all over the country with Middlesbrough, but now I wouldn't watch them if they were out our back.'

According to Duffy and his mates in a pub in central Middlesbrough, Amos memorably wrote, Wilf was 'the real idol, as automatically a good bloke because he's from South Bank as a fella from Cardiff is automatically Welsh.' Hardwick, on the other hand, was 'a dapper Dan' and, according to one of the drinkers, 'a bit of a Conservative too' – and that was, and is, not a compliment on Teesside.

Another member of the crowd had flown in from America specially to see the testimonial. Herb Roberts, who had made the 6000 mile journey from Long Beach, California, left Britain the year after Wilf left Boro.

'Before I emigrated I never missed a Boro match, whatever the weather. But a lot went out of the enjoyment when Wilf left Middlesbrough,' he said.

Roberts wouldn't have been one of them, but some in the crowd might have already seen a Wilf Mannion testimonial. An unofficial and low-key affair staged in 1968 on a park pitch drew a crowd of 6000. But at Ayresome, on the evening of 17 May 1983, the day after Wilf's sixty-fifth birthday, a crowd of 13,710 – 3000 more than the average home gate that season – celebrated the formal homecoming of a legend with the help of England manager Bobby Robson, who brought an England XI to play Boro.

Robson, originally from County Durham and once an amateur with Boro, said he felt 'like a minnow in a sea of giants' and would 'feel very low down on the list of people who will be coming'. He added: 'I have a great respect for the old days. It was an age when money was absolutely secondary and even success was secondary to the game.' And the first part of that summary, some might have said, was why there was a need for a testimonial in the first place.

Today, Robson still remembers the few times he saw the 'classical midfield player with supreme talent and vision' play.

'He had a great eye for a pass, could execute it too and was a confident dribbler of the ball – not like Matthews or Finney perhaps, but Wilf could waltz between opponents with such grace and speed. For a little fellow he could also jump well and head a ball.'

Other national figures joined Robson at Ayresome: former Scottish international Billy Liddell, Danny Blanchflower and Jimmy Hill, who compered the pre-match reminiscences. He introduced Wilf on to the pitch – a part of the evening Wilf did not relish. He looked as embarrassed and nervous as he promised he would when he said: 'It didn't bother me playing in front of 134,000, but the thing I won't like will be making a speech at the game. That will be the most frightening thing ever.'

Other footballing celebrities who could not make it to the game passed on their good wishes to Wilf and George in the programme. Brian Clough said:

> I was in short pants when they were in their prime but I can still remember how they were held in so much awe by Middlesbrough supporters. It's not surprising then that it's been regarded as something of an injustice that they have never had a testimonial, particularly when it does not cost football directors a penny to say yes to granting one. I'm delighted that it's been put right and I only wish my father had been alive so that I could have taken him to the game. It's a night he would really have enjoyed.

Raich Carter was quoted, Jackie Milburn, Len Shackleton and Matt Busby too. But perhaps the most comprehensive came from another managerial great, Bob Paisley, who wrote:

> I have not seen Wilf for a good few years, but I ran a few miles in my time trying to keep tabs on him when we played against each other. He was the worst type of inside-forward from the opposition's viewpoint – possessed of devilish cunning and real skill. Wilf covered every inch of the pitch, from a slightly deep position. He would be known [today] as a midfielder – and he would be priceless. A player of genuine class and ability.

On the Ayresome pitch his England successors struggled to overcome Boro, eventually running out 2–1 winners after being 1–0 down. But the result was irrelevant as the ground enjoyed 'one of the most emotion-charged welcomes ever seen', according to the *Gazette*. Testimonial committee vice-chairman Terry Jackson said: 'When Wilf and George finally went out before the match I had tears rolling down my cheeks. The feeling from the crowd came back and hit you where it hurts – and that feeling made it all worthwhile. It was the biggest treat of my life and every member of the committee feels the same way.'

Wilf said: 'I couldn't put into words how I feel. I only wish I was seventeen again and could have performed for the crowd.' Always trying to please. 'It's been a perfect night. I've never had a reception like that before, the crowd were wonderful. I'd like to thank them from the bottom of my heart, not only for myself, but for my family. I'm deeply grateful.'

Self-confessed Boro fanatic *Northern Echo* reporter Brian Page came across a momentarily sadder man outside the room where the post-match presentations were being made and which was full of loud nostalgia:

> Out in the hallway I met a lonely figure. Small, fragile, looking slightly bemused and a little lost. A burly pair of arms suddenly engulfed him. A craggy face planted a kiss on the cheek of the lad from South Bank. 'You're the best bloody footballer I ever saw, the greatest,' shouted a Teesside voice. And Wilf Mannion smiled shyly.

Thirteen years later, there was one last visit to Ayresome. In dazzling spring sunshine, Wilf joined the faithful flocking to the ground as fans had been doing for ninety-two years. This would be the last time for all of them. An era was ending as Boro prepared to move to a state-of-the-art stadium on the edge of the town's long-moribund docks.

The plans, which marked out in steel and concrete the ambitions of a reborn club, had been announced to a somewhat sceptical public only a matter of months before. The skeleton of the new stadium had since started to rise skyward, but there were still doubts among fans that it would be finished in time for the proposed opening – the first day of the next season, 1995–96. More importantly, the question of whether Boro would be playing there in the Premiership was hanging in the air. New manager Bryan Robson had seen his players lead the race for promotion all season, but, with the winning post in sight, they were stalling. Three consecutive draws was not the form with which to canter home, especially with Bolton and Tranmere closing fast on the rails.

Tension would be etched on every face throughout the game against Luton, but beforehand it was a time to celebrate the end of Ayresome and remember its past with a party. Hours before kick-off neighbouring streets were filling up with fans of all ages, many with faces painted red and white and balloons galore, squeezing together in improbable numbers for commemorative photographs. Inside the ground, in the stands from which generations of fans had watched the great Boro names from Common to Clough to Colin Cooper, there were smiles, but also some earnest discussions about the game, and some tears, too, at the thought that the pitch, where George Best had once played for Boro in a testimonial and where Jack Charlton first proved he would be as great a manager as he was a player, would never see competitive action again.

As the clock moved nearer and nearer to 3 p.m., the entertainments organized by the club came to their climax with a parade of former players. Familiar faces from the 1980s – Brian Laws, Tony Mowbray and Bernie Slaven – were cheered as they made their way around the perimeter track, the stars from the sixties and seventies – David Armstrong, Jim Platt and Alan Peacock – likewise. They were followed by the less well-known features, at least to the younger fans, of Hardwick, Shepherdson and Fenton. Even Ralph Birkett travelled up from Cornwall for the day.

But there was only one man who could receive the honour of walking around the ground last, soaking up the appreciation of the fans. At the end of a list of more than sixty names, the last one prompted the loudest cheer: Wilf Mannion. Plenty of people who could remember his heyday joined in, some who could even recall his pre-war emergence. But the remarkable thing was the reception from a new generations of fans, some so young they weren't born when he was working as a labourer let alone a footballer. All eyes turned to glimpse a living legend. Then the chant started and rang around the ground: 'One Wilf Mannion. There's only one Wilf Mannion.'

The object of the adoration, a slight figure in a blue bomber jacket, walking slowly on his slightly bowed legs, waved. His eyes glazed with emotion, he acknowledged the reception and signed a few autographs before posing for the photographers by holding a Boro scarf aloft. The *Northern Echo* reported:

> For one last time possibly the most gifted feet ever to grace Ayresome Park's pitch trod the turf. The hair may no longer be golden and the legs are a little less athletic but there is still no mistaking Wilf Mannion. He came to say farewell to the ground where he made his name; the fans to pay their respects one more time.

That they did. Even the other former players, milling around before they were called on the pitch, had done so. Some who knew him greeted him with a firm handshake and, 'How are you?' while others made a point of going up to him and introducing themselves. There was, after all, only one Wilf Mannion.

Among those watching the emotional reunion between star and fans was Duncan Hall. The new stadium was partly his doing; his love of football was all Wilf's doing. He wasn't surprised by the greeting which a man who hadn't played for Boro for forty-one years and left under a cloud received.

'I think he had that very, very peculiar ability – which perhaps you could see in Bobby Charlton and Gary Lineker – to have an affinity with the crowds,' he says. 'That affinity never went away because it was two-fold: an acknowledgement of supreme skill, together with a level of modesty which I don't think has ever left him, and which I find, with the prima donnas of today, quite staggering. At the same time the man quite clearly had an inner steel, not only as a small man surviving in a hard football world, but also in the ability to look at officialdom and fight it. I think that affection has carried on throughout his whole life. I don't think it ever went away. It transcended Middlesbrough Football Club at that level. He could live with the fact he left the club, he could live with the fact he had the dispute with the club, he could live with the fact that for more than ten years he would not walk into the football ground. So could the fans.'

They adored Wilf as much the club – some might say more as he let them down far less frequently. He was one of them too, more so than Tommy Thomas or any director, David Jack or any manager. He was a South Bank boy who took the skills he learnt there to a world stage; who represented Boro and did the town and the club proud; but who remained at heart an ordinary fella, who you could see in the bus queue. He brought glory and a reputation for beauty to a town not overly imbued with either. But he wasn't afraid to fight if he had to.

In the absence of trophies, Boro fans cherished him like an FA Cup win. Instead of a day at Wembley or a last-game win to clinch the league title, they had memories of games such as Mannion's Match or some other favourite moment. When fathers passed on to their sons and then grandsons football folklore it wasn't about 'where I was when Boro won the Cup' but 'when I saw Mannion beat Blackpool' or 'the best goal I saw him score'. Hall says: 'We've never had the consistency to win. Therefore we're illuminated by great skill and great moments and at the top of the tree, at the very, very pinnacle of that was Wilf Mannion.'

As Boro struggled to overcome Luton in the last game at Ayresome, a lone voice confirmed that. 'Bring on Mannion,' it shouted. Wilf would have shown 'em.

He was never forgotten outside Teesside either. Periodically a piece in the national press would invoke his name, usually alongside those of Matthews and Finney, or in contrast to Vinnie Jones or another tabloid villain.

For example, Joe Haines in the *Daily Mirror* contrasting the veterans with the likes of drug-using Paul Merson and wife-beating Paul Gascoigne; Brian Scovell in the *Daily Mail* wailing: 'Where have all the creative midfield players in English football gone?'; or Gordon Taylor, of the PFA, the exception as he defended a possible players' strike to ensure more money for the union's welfare fund by saying:

'People ask what we do with the money,' Taylor said. 'I'll tell you. Last year we spent £500,000 on a building so we could properly administer a community programme; we paid £250,000 in private medical fees; we paid £250,000 in hardship fund payments to former players like the late Jimmy Mudie and Wilf Mannion.'

Some of the name-dropping came from the most unexpected sources. Barry Fry, then Birmingham City manager, would seem a million miles away from Wilf, but he remembered the maestros when a transfer deal was blocked by his board: 'The board can come up with any names they like – Hidegkuti, Tommy Lawton or Wilf Mannion, but I want my choice in.'

Then there were the equally odd tributes. Top of the list, the guest appearances on the BBC's Fantasy Football in a repeated cameo as strange as it was short. 'Hello, I'm Wilf Mannion,' he said – and that was it. It was as far removed from Wilf's football glories as host Frank Skinner's West Bromwich Albion are from ever matching them.

Of all the appreciation, from the sublime to the ridiculous, one episode stands out. Way before the current rediscovery of football's history, one man remembered Wilf, his skill and his soccer supremacy. He also remembered the horror, for England at least, of Belo Horizonte. He was organizing a youth tournament in 1987, and invited Wilf to attend among the veteran players. It meant that he went back to Belo. It also means there's a snap of Wilf with the tournament organizer, another famous inside-left, signed 'your good friend, Pelé.'

But as the years go by the most common place to find Wilf's name is in the obituary columns as former team-mates' deaths are recorded. Frank

Swift had been the first when, in his job as a football reporter for the *News of the World*, he died in the Munich air crash along with a number of other journalists. Stan Mortensen was the first to die of natural causes, in 1991. Billy Wright and Raich Carter joined him within weeks of each other in 1994. Then, after watching newly promoted Boro play Southampton at the Riverside Stadium, Shep. He could often be seen with Wilf or George Hardwick watching their successors.

'We're all still pals together – me, Wilf and George. We still talk about the old days – the great days,' he said. 'When I look back and remember all those good times, I think I've been very lucky in what I got from football.' The day after the 0–0 draw he died suddenly at his home. He was seventy-seven, five months younger than Wilf.

Just three months later, Bobby Langton, Wilf's wingman on England's left six times before Finney made the position his own, was next; then, the following month, Neil Franklin, the man who but for one decision might have been England's most capped player of all time; and in November 1996 Tommy Lawton, a shadow of his former physical self, but still with his jet black hair slicked back.

The BBC did Lawton a late favour, reuniting him with Hardwick, Finney, Lofthouse (the man who replaced him as England's number nine), Matthews and Wilf for one last time at the Victoria Ground, Stoke, to mark the launch of a new football nostalgia series. Frank Keating, of the *Guardian,* was on hand to witness Sir Stanley egging Lawton on to recreate a Walter Winterbottom team-talk. The piece was also rich in recollections of Wilf.

> 'Tell us, Nat,' said Finney to Lofthouse, 'how Wilf was told to look after you to settle you in on your first trip with England abroad.' Nat had never forgotten.
>
> 'Three nights we were in this foreign hotel. I saw my room-mate and minder just twice, when he was changing to go out on the town and when he played a blinder in the game itself.' Mannion laughs longest at the memory. On these pages long ago Donny Davies wrote that Mannion's football was 'so graceful, so courtly, that he wouldn't be out of place if he played in a lace ruffle and a *perruque.*'

Now, as then, Wilf's reaction is to laugh at such high-faluting praise and tut: 'How soft.'

The group split into two. Matthews, Hardwick, Finney and Lofthouse chatted together – the legend, two company directors and the life president of Bolton Wanderers. Wilf and Tommy, the pair who had hit rock bottom, shared a cigarette or two as they caught up on old times. It was the first time they had met in forty years. Tommy said of the meeting: 'He was still the same Wilf, still with the same dry sense of humour and a joke. I remember when he came into the England team and he took a lot of ribbing because he was just a lad. He soon settled in and he did half the ribbing.'

Keating made the mistake – in the players' eyes – of mentioning Paul Gascoigne, a modern model of the inside-forward, in the same breath as Wilf. But there is one link between them – off-pitch incidents made them all the more newsworthy but added nothing to their, or their public's, happiness. At his testimonial Wilf admitted his shortcomings: 'I was too easy, more or less brainwashed into false security. Money was nothing to me. I didn't know how to handle it, never gave it a thought and always thought I'd end up fixed for life in some capacity. I wasn't ambitious. It was the accepted thing where I was brought up.' And others took advantage of that.

When Keating spoke to Wilf he heard of the days of serfdom.

'In 1938, in my second season with Middlesbrough, we played Arsenal at Highbury in front of 60–70,000. The American baseball star Babe Ruth was over and came to the match. He'd never seen such a big crowd. "Gee, how much are the twenty-two players on?" he asked. All on the maximum wage of £8, he was told. "Jeez, are they bloody idiots or something," he said. We were too, weren't we?'

A couple of weeks earlier, on the first day of the 1995-96 season, Middlesbrough had visited Highbury again and won 1–0. It was the club's first victory at Highbury since 1939, when Wilf was among the scorers. He cost Boro £10 and earned, at that point, £8 a week. The 1995 scorer, Nick Barmby, cost £5.25 million, his wages were in the region of £10,000 a week and, when he became unhappy at the club, he was given a transfer without any quarrel.

Later in the season Boro made an even more impressive purchase: Juninho, a small and skilful sorcerer. For Wilf it must have been like seeing an image of himself back on the pitch. Discussing the South American's arrival, he even used the same metaphor used about himself.

'He will move like a gazelle. He will sense when the rhinos are coming. He may be only 5ft 5ins but size does not count if you have a football brain. Many lightly-built players in my playing years were great foot-ballers because of natural talent and timing. Good players know when to make a move and how to beat an opponent.'

But it was another South American who summed up why players like Wilf, like Juninho, will live forever. Colombian goalkeeper Rene Higuita may not, in theory, have much scope for memorable play, but you can't say he doesn't try. His scorpion kick in an international against England at Wembley will stay in the minds of everyone who saw it. In an interview just before his acrobatics he said: 'When I have finished playing, my name will stay on people's lips and in their minds as a player who brought a bit of magic into the lives of ordinary people.'

And surely that's what football should do.

Stanley Matthews brought that magic, now he has a knighthood. Tom Finney and Nat Lofthouse did too, now they're life presidents of their respective clubs. Harold Shepherdson did so much in the mechanics of preparing the players to perform the tricks that he was awarded an MBE. Wilf has an honorary degree from Teesside University.

Even when that was awarded, he couldn't believe a former shipyard worker deserved to share a stage with the likes of David Jenkins, the former Bishop of Durham. Boro fans were more likely to see it as two-thirds of the Holy Trinity.

For a day his scholar's cap replaced the England ones which are gone, some to family, some to friends; some just gone. His house, where he lives alone since Bernadette died in 1993, is bereft of any sign that it is the home of one of England's greatest footballers. Even the sole trophy which used to adorn the mantlepiece – a cup presented by the Priory Club (Middlesbrough) with the inscription: 'To one of the greatest footballers of all time' – is gone.

Other honours never came. In 1980 councillor Bill Dragg floated one of the oddest.

'I would scrub the name South Bank and call it Mannion's Town,' he said. But it's still South Bank, although there's a Mannion Close as well as a Shepherdson Terrace and Carr Street.

Just along the A66 stands the new stadium. When it was being built there was talk of it carrying Wilf's name: Mannion Park or Stadium. Fans balloted on a shortlist of suggestions settled on the Riverside, but it was not necessarily a popular choice. Duncan Hall for one says: 'I was not terribly happy with Riverside. My view is that they should have gone down one of two routes: linking it with the local identity, Teesside, or a local figure. I would have been perfectly happy with the Mannion Stadium.'

Now what? In the hall at Spurs there is a bust of Bill Nicholson, a player who started the same year as Wilf. At Leeds there is a stand named after Don Revie; at Newcastle one in honour of Jackie Milburn. Hall would like to see the same honour bestowed on Wilf while he's still alive.

'I think Mannion should have the same reverence that Milburn has in Newcastle – the stand named after him. It's immortal. It will always be there. He was a great footballer then; he'd be god-like now; and if he'd been playing today he'd be worth £15 million and be the best in the world. I think there are certain people who deserve immortality and a reverence so far as the football club is concerned. They should never be forgotten because we were blessed – and I use the word deliberately – in a town which produced some of the best in the world. And Wilf was the best.'

For another generation, an official ceremony would be the chance to say they saw Wilf Mannion – not at Ayresome and not in his prime perhaps, but at the opening of a stand named in his honour and on another day when the Boro faithful could chant, 'There's only one Wilf Mannion' and wish for many more.

· APPENDIX ·

WILF MANNION – A CHRONOLOGY

16 MAY 1918	Born in South Bank, Middlesbrough
2 JANUARY 1937	Middlesbrough FC debut in 2–2 home draw with Portsmouth
JANUARY 1940	Enlists with Green Howards and sees action in Italy and the Middle East
28 SEPTEMBER 1946	Hat-trick in England debut in a 7–2 win over Northern Ireland
10 MAY 1947	Scores twice for Great Britain in the 'Match of the Century' against the Rest of Europe
27 MAY 1947	The only non-scorer among England's forwards in a 10–0 rout of Portugal
22 NOVEMBER 1947	Mannion's Match – the individual display which belittled Blackpool at Ayresome Park
16 MAY 1948	A member of England team which recorded an astounding 4–0 win against Italy in Turin
MAY 1948–JANUARY 1949	On strike after a transfer request was refused by Middlesbrough
29 JUNE 1950	The humiliation of losing to the United States in the World Cup finals in Belo Horizonte, Brazil
14 APRIL 1951	Suffers an horrific facial injury in an England-Scotland game at Wembley
3 OCTOBER 1951	Wins last of 26 England caps in a match against France at Highbury, partnering Tom Finney for the last time
MAY 1954	Retires after 368 league and cup games – and 110 goals – for Middlesbrough
DECEMBER 1954	Joins Hull City for £4,500, but only plays until the end of the season, when he is banned following a series of explosive newspaper articles
APRIL 1959	Hangs up his boots after four years of non-league football and becomes the landlord of a pub
OCTOBER 1962	Sacked after two years in his first job as club manager, with non-league Earlestown, and drifts out of football
17 MAY 1983	Testimonial, with George Hardwick, at Ayresome Park after a new board takes power at the club
30 APRIL 1995	Last appearance at Ayresome Park at the final league fixture it hosted, against Luton Town

· BIBLIOGRAPHY ·

Barrett, Norman, *The Daily Telegraph Football Chronicle*, Ebury Press, London, 1996.

Buchan, Charles, *A Lifetime in Football*, Phoenix House, London, 1955.

Ferrier, Bob, Wright, Billy and Winterbottom, Walter, *Soccer Partnership*, Heinemann, London, 1960.

Finney, Tom, *Finney on Football*, Nicholas Kaye, London, 1958.

Finney, Tom, *Football Round the World*, Museum Press, London, 1953.

Franklin, Neil, *Soccer at Home and Abroad*, Stanley Paul, London, 1956.

Glanville, Brian, *Soccer: A Panorama*, Eyre & Spottiswoode, London, 1969.

Glasper, Harry, *Middlesbrough: A Complete Record*, Breedon Books, Derby, 1993.

Greaves, Jimmy and Giller, Norman, *Don't Shoot the Manager*, Boxtree, London, 1990.

Green, Geoffrey, *Great Moments in Sport*, Pelham Books, London, 1972.

Green, Geoffrey, *Soccer: The World Game*, Phoenix House, London, 1953.

Green, Geoffrey, *Soccer in the Fifties*, Ian Allan, Addlestone, England, 1974.

Lawton, Tommy, *Football is my Business*, ed. Roy Peskett, Sporting Handbooks, London, 1946.

Lawton, Tommy, *When the Cheering Stopped*, Golden Eagle, London, 1973.

McCarthy, Tony, *War Games*, Queen Anne Press, Harpenden, England, 1989.

Mannion, Wilf, *Association Football*, Nicholas Kaye, London, 1949.

Miller, David, *Father of Football*, Pavilion Books, London, 1971.

Miller, David, *Stanley Matthews*, Pavilion Books, London, 1990.

Mortensen, Stan, *Football is my Game*, Sampson Low, Marston & Co, London, 1949.

Mortensen, Stan, *Stan Mortensen's International Soccer Book*, Sampson Low, Marston & Co, London, 1949.

Paylor, Eric and Wilson, John, *Ayresome Park Memories*, Breedon Books, Derby, 1995.

Swift, Frank, *Football From the Goalmouth*, ed. Roy Peskett, Sporting Handbooks, London, 1948.

Taylor, Rogan and Ward, Andrew, *Kicking and Screaming*, Robson Books, London, 1995.

Wright, Billy, *Captain of England*, Stanley Paul, London, 1950.

Wright, Billy, *The World's My Football Pitch*, Stanley Paul, London, 1953.

· INDEX ·

210